Monroe County
Tennessee
Records
1820-1870

- Vol. #2 -

By: Reba Bayless Boyer

Please direct all correspondence and orders to:

www.southernhistoricalpress.com
or
SOUTHERN HISTORICAL PRESS, Inc.
PO BOX 1267
375 West Broad Street
Greenville, SC   29601
southernhistoricalpress@gmail.com

ISBN #0-89308-327-5

Printed in the United States of America

FOREWORD

In this Volume II of Monroe County, Tennessee, Records, with Volume I recently published, I have attempted to abstract all Record Books through 1870 now available at the Court House in Madisonville. The majority of these books are not indexed.

Because research is a continuous process, I offer no apology for including in this Volume II some marriage notices which rightfully belong in Volume I.

For help and cooperation in making this study possible and pleasurable I am indebted to the following: to the kind officials and clerks of the various offices of the Monroe County Court House; to the Genealogical Forum of Portland, Oregon, for permission to use Monroe County items from their excellent books, Oregon Donation Land Claims; to Mr. W.G. Lenoir, of Norris, Tennessee, for access to his old papers; and to Mr. and Mrs. Earl Black, Vonore, Tennessee, for giving me the privilege and pleasure of editing their interesting collection of papers and letters of the Thomas White family.

My hope is that these records will be of service to genealogists and historians.

Reba Bayless Boyer

Athens, Tennessee
September, 1970

CONTENTS

EXPLANATORY NOTES

The spelling and wording in the original sources
were copied exactly as written, as far as it was
possible to determine.

Underlining indicates that the original was
illegible.

If the name of a town or county is given without
the name of the state, then it is understood that
the said town or county is in Tennessee.

The notes at the beginning of each section will
supply further explanation.

On the front cover of this half-filled book is written "Will Book 1852". The Wills have apparently been copied from another source. The dates of probate have probably been added at a later date.

(1) JAMES CHAMBERS, exec. 30 Jul 1833. To wife Sarah; schooling children. Execs: friends George Henderson, Elias Hutchison. Wit: Samuel W. Carson, Elias Hutchison. Signed by mark.

(2) HENRY M. BIBLE, exec. 16 Oct 1837. To wife Rachel; raising the family; Execs. to buy land with proceeds from note on William Kerr. Execs: friends Henry Messimer, Jacob Bible. Wit: Nathaniel Magill, Samuel Blackburn.

(3) JOSEPH STRICKLAN, exec. 7 May 1839. To wife Mary; to daughter Abigal Gilbreath, and at her death to grandchildren, viz, William C., John N., Thomas J.C., and Cynthia B. Gilbreath; to two sons James and George; to youngest son Thomas. Execs: sons James and George. Wit: Nath. and Henry G. Hendrix.

(5) RICHARD STEPHENS, exec. 21 Aug 1840. To wife Nancy, land on which I live and another tract on which Thomas Holloway now lives; to two oldest sons Lewis and Daniel L.; to two youngest sons Jasper Newton and William Asbury; to George Irvin Cunningham, heir of daughter Celia Cunningham; to daughters Elizabeth, Faith, and Sarah; to grandson John Worly when he becomes of lawful age. Exec: son Lewis. Wit: Jeremiah Frazer, William and Lewis Stephens. Signed by mark.

(6) WILLIAM RAWLING (RAWLINS), exec. 16 Jan 1833. To wife Agness; to son James and daughter Elizabeth Carter; to sons and daughters. Wit: James A. Hair, Samuel D. Bonham. Signed by mark.

(7) REV. ELIJAH M. EAGLETON, exec. 19 Mar 1838. Noncupative Will. "Be it known that the Rev. Elijah M. Eagleton who departed this life on the eighteenth of this instant died... in presence of Samuel Blackburn and Mary McSpadden make the following request, to wit"; lots in Madisonville to wife for herself and support of the children.

(8) WILLIAM HARRISON, exec. 20 Jan 1830. To wife Nancy; to son James, daughters Jane Humphreys, Winford Harrison, Hannah Harrison, sums which they have already received; to daughters Mary Harrison and Nancy Harrison, sums when they may call for it; to sons Thomas, Calvin, William; to sons Alfred and Michael and daughter Matilda when they reach twenty-one; to "my beloved John" Harrison. Execs: sons Thomas and James. Wit: Henry Stephens, Robert and William Flanigan.

(11) SPENCER COLEMAN, exec. 13 Nov 1834. Far advanced in years; to wife Lucy; to sons William, Jessy, and Absalom, and to daughters Lydia Vinson, Edy Tamnans, Lucy Rains, Polly Mackery. Execs: son William Coleman and George Snider, Sr. Wit: Samuel R. Bell, Isaac Hicks. Signed by mark.

(13) WILLIAM JOHNSTON, exec. 16 May 1837. Advanced age; to wife Levenia; old set of children by first wife; to son John Ruffin

Johnston; to daughter Anna Mariah Hudgeons. Execs: friends Henry
Chesnutt, Esq., and John Pennington. Wit: Jesse F. Jones, Robert
R. Cleaveland, D.P. Walker.

(15) WILLIAM KIMBROUGH, exec. 27 Jan 1836. Children to continue
living together until youngest comes of age; daughter Sarah has
cared for family since her mother's decease; "Inasmuch as it was
my unhappy misfortune in my youth to have a Child laid to me born
out of wedlock by Nancy Barns the child is named Margaret Scregs."
Execs: eldest son John M. and friend Welcom Beard. Wit: D.
Caldwell, John Caldwell.

(17) ALLEN DEARMAN, not dated. 57 years of age the 16th of December
next. /Incomplete/

(18) ADAM SLIGAR, exec. 16 Sep 1834. To daughters Levenia, Sally,
Betsy McCully; children Peggy Wittenbarger, Hetty Byker, John
Sligar; equal division among all children; slaves to be free at
age of 35. Execs: John Ramsey and son Thomas Sligar. Wit: J.W.
Roberts, Daniel Heiskell. Signed by mark.

(19) SAMUEL JAMESON, exec. 20 Aug 1834. To wife Rebecca; having
heretofore given to sons Jehu R., Benjamin C., and David F.; to
three sons Samuel Y., Robert W., and Hiram I.; to three daughters
Jane M. Wilson, Eleanor F. Reynolds, and Rebecca R. Jameson.
Execs: Samuel Y. Jameson, Robert Snead. Wit: Robert Snead,
Leonard Harmon.

(20) JOSEPH CALLAWAY, exec. 20 May 1831. Lands in Western district
of State; mountain lands in Monroe and Blount Counties; all estate
to children, to wit, Thomas Howard, Rebecca Caroline, Nancy Elviry,
and Fanna Lucinda Callaway, as they come of age; Nancy E. and
Fanny L. to have as good schooling as Rebecca C. has got. Execs:
friends John Callaway and Arthur H. Henly and son Thomas H.
Callaway. Wit: Joseph Travis, J.R. Henderson, David Russell,
Justus Stead.

(22) JOHN DYER, exec. 11 Dec 1841. To wife; to children when
youngest comes of age; to each of daughters; to son William; to
John; to Betsey; to Sarah; to Jane. Execs: wife, James A. Coffin,
William M. Stakely, Robert Russell, and John Carson. Wit: Madison
Cliborne, Robartus Love, B.M. Bayless. Signed by mark.

(24) LEROY TAYLOR, exec. 21 Feb 1837. Afflicted with a lingering
disease; to wife Keziah; children until youngest child Leondas
comes of age; to daughter Barsheba; to son Garrett. Execs:
friends Robert Russell, Nathaniel Magill. Wit: Charles Rily,
William Williams.

(26) MATTHEW W. McGHEE, exec. 7 Jan 1832. Of Citico, Monroe
County; to brother-in-law William Lowry and his wife Polly and
their heirs; to nephew and niece William and Jane McDermott; to
niece Margaret W. McGhee; to brothers John and Alexander McGhee;
to brother-in-law Thomas Henderson. Execs: two brothers John
and Alexander. Wit: Justus Steed, Joseph Callaway, Thomas H.
Callaway, John Lowry.

(28) JAMES RICHASON, exec. 9 Jan 1838. To wife Stilly; to sons
Jesse and John; to daughter Ann Christian; to son Samuel, with

what he has formerly received; to lawful heirs of son James, with
what he has formerly received; to children of daughter Dorcas Rhea;
to grandson Pleasant M. Miller, son of daughter Jane; to granddaughter Mahala Alexander, daughter of daughter Polly. Execs:
friends James Witten, Jonathan Pickel. Wit: Lindsey Robertson,
James Cole. Signed by mark.

(30) JOHN SNIDER, exec. 21 Oct 1842. To wife Elizabeth; to William
Snider, land where he now lives; to Margaret Graves; to Washington
Snider, his mother's half of home place at her death; to grandson
George Snider, son of Martin Snider, dec'd; to lawful legatees.
Execs: sons William and Washington. Wit: James W. Taylor,
Pleasant M. Alexander.

(32) ISAAC HIX, exec. 16 Apr 1842. To wife Sarah; $1 each to son
John and daughter Mary, at wife's death; to daughter Sarah; to son
Reuben; to wife's daughter Ann Isbell; to the heirs. Execs: wife
and Martin Isbell. Wit: William Coleman, William E. Hargis.
Signed by mark.

(33) JOHN TORBETT, exec. 16 Nov 1842. All property to daughter
Amanda. Execs: G.C. Torbet, William M. Stakely. Wit: Henry H.
Stephens, William B. Brown, William Henderson, J.A. Coffin.

(34) BURRELL IVY, exec. 22 Oct 1842. To wife Mary; to daughter
Suezen and son John, land at wife's death; $1 each to daughters
Winey McAllister, Mary Ann Bishop, Elizabeth Kenedy, and Miram
Kenedy. Exec: wife Mary. Wit: William Watson, John McClung.
Signed by mark.

(35) THOMAS BUNCH, exec. 19 Jun 1840. To wife Jane; equal division
among three children and grandson Sam Rail, to wit, Sally Bunch wife
of Anderson Bunch, Polly Ritchison wife of Sam Ritchison, Pryor
P. Bunch, and Sam Rail. Exec: Thomas L. Upton. Wit: J.K. Johnston, Daniel Heiskell. Signed by mark.

(36) JAMES M. BROYLES, exec. 15 Jan 1842. Noncupative Will signed
by William M. Stakely and J.W. Roberts with witnesses James
Ghormley and James Smith. James M. Broyles died Monday 10 Jan
1842. To daughter Eliza; to all the children.

(37) WILLIAM C.C.C. GEORGE, exec. 1 Nov 1841. Noncupative Will
signed by Guilford Cannon and Babery Bicknell; made in his last
sickness on 23 Oct 1841; to wife Jane.

(38) SAMUEL SHAW, exec. 6 Jan 1840. To wife Agness; to sons
Samuel, Francis M., William H., John J.; to daughters Ann L.
Wilcox, Louisa G. Tedford, Sarah Shaw, and Hanna Shaw; land in
Roane and Knox counties. Execs: John Duncan, James Montgomery,
Esq. Wit: Thomas S. Kendall, Robert Findly.

(39) SAMUEL DUNCAN, exec. 19 Sep 1839. To sons Andrew J., George
B., Archibald W., William A., John C., James K.; to daughters
Sarah Duncan and Issabella Johnston formerly Issabella Duncan.
Execs: friends John Duncan, Sr., Robert Russell, Andrew J. Duncan.
Wit: Josiah Rowan, John E. Grigsby.

(41) JOHN SHARP, exec. 1 Mar 1840. "Principal part of property now
in my possession was purchased by my wife's father & by him given

to my wife for the use & benefit of her and her children"; to wife
Polly; to two sons James A. and Joseph; "to other children, namely,
Jane B. Lettitia Mary H Samuel T and John C (Robert having received
his full part)". Execx: wife. Wit: Jeremiah Frazier, Joseph
Smith, Preston G.B. Melton.

(42) JACOB SECREST, exec. 21 Dec 1835. To wife Nancy; equal
division between son Michael, daughter Ginsey Helm, and heirs of
daughter Melinda Osborne, dec'd; to son Thomas; to daughter Rachel
Harris; $5 each to son Evan, son Wiley, and daughter Patsey Hollo-
way. Execs: son Thomas, son-in-law Goodwin Harris. Wit: Samuel
Low, James H. Duff, Hilliard J. Harris.

(43) THOMAS GLEN, JR., exec. 4 Apr 1838. To wife Harriet R.; child
Sarah Ann to be educated; mercantile business of Spillman & Glen to
be wound up; wife to move to Cannon house. Execs: Squire S. Glen,
Newton J. Spillman. Wit: John S. James, Drury Miller.

(45) JAMES WALLIS, exec. 2 Apr 1841. Noncupative Will signed by
William Wallis, Temperance Wallis; made 27 Mar 1841 in his last
sickness; to wife Biddy; to the children.

(46) ALLEN DEARMON, not dated. Being fifty seven years of age the
16th day of December next; to wife Polly; $1 to son James; balance
to be divided amongst balance of children including "Thompson A.
Dearmon & Allen J. Twomey J E Catherine Elizabeth, Saml Allen,
Jackson, Sarah, William, Richard"; between "Catharine Elizabeth
Allen J. William R. Sarah and Thompson A. Dearmon and Allen J.
Twomey"; the eight children aforenamed. Execs: wife, Allen J.
Dearman, Peter Twomey. Wit: J.H. Holloway.

(47) JACOB HACKER, exec. 29 Apr 1844. To wife Martha for support
of her and my son Register; to four sons Isaac, James, Jacob, and
Francis; to daughter Elizabeth Cole; to daughter Margaret as long
as she remains single, the cabin where Washington Cole formerly
resided; $1 to daughter Debora Rian. Execx: wife. Wit: William
Upton, Samuel Lusk. Signed by mark.

(48) DICY TUCKER, exec. 9 Jul 1844. To niece Dicy Clark and to
Matthew, Derius, and Edward Hudgins, money in hands of Carter
Hudgins after the death of said Carter and Rachel Hudgins. Execs:
Matthew and Derius Hudgins. Wit: James Montgomery, Lawrence
Forkner. Signed by mark.

(49) JANE CARTER, exec. 12 (18) Oct 1844. To daughter Margaret
Carter; to two granddaughters Louisiana and Mary K. Sawyers; to
sister Katharine Sawyers; to grandson Robert Carter, "one half of
a note of hand I hold on him and M.C. Dibbrell if he will carry
Louisiana and Mary K. Sawyers and Katherine Sawyers to them and
the other half of the note I give to M.C. Dibrell". Exec: grandson
Robert Carter. Wit: John Duncan, Gabriel Ragsdale. Signed by mark.

(50) WILLIAM LILLARD, exec. 16 Dec 1844. To wife Nancy; to
children. Wit: E.H. White, F.K. Berry.

(51) JOSEPH SCOTT, exec. 23 Apr 1845. To wife Sarah Ann and
family; to son T. Ellison; when children come of age. Execs:
friends Samuel P. Hall, G.W. Carmichael. Wit: James W. Kelso, R.
Hunhirn.

(52) JOHN LOTSPEICH, exec. 16 Apr 1845. To wife; farm in Rhea
County to be sold; all children to be made equal taking in view the
sums already received by some of them; sons Ralph, Henry, Samuel
T., Felix, Christopher M., John W., daughters Mary A. now Robinson,
Emeline now Pickle, Elizabeth J. now Browder all having received.
Exec: son Samuel T. Wit: John Ramsey, William Neil.

(54) JESSE MILSAPS, exec. 8 May 1845. To wife Polly; to youngest
son John E. and youngest daughter Ludesa; to daughters Elizabeth,
Trifina, Jemima, Polly, Jane, and Rebecca. Execs: wife, John E.
Milsaps. Wit: J.S. Milligan, Benjamin Johnson. Signed by mark.

(55) HANNAH CLAYTON, exec. 10 Apr 1845. "in case my claim against
the Government of the United States for a pension shall be obtained";
to daughter Lucinda Webb, for the care she has taken of me, and to
each of remainder of children, to wit, Elijah Clayton, Malinda
Partin, Robert Clayton, Hannah Boyd, Patsy Dunn, Frances Sutton,
and Betsy Collins; to sister Lucinda Avans. Execs: son-in-law
Martin Webb, son Robert. Wit: Elizabeth Givens, Montgomery McTeer,
Anne Dill. Signed by mark.

(56) JONATHAN WRIGHT, exec. 14 Jan 1844. To wife Sarah; daughter
Malisa Louisa to be schooled; to daughter Artiless; 25¢ each to
sons William, James, and daughters Mahala Davis, Angeline Marr,
Polly Ann, Elizabeth Whitlock. Exec: wife. Wit: John Wilson,
John Cox. Signed by mark. Codicil, 17 Apr 1846. Wit: John Wilson,
David W. Kennedy.

(58) ROBERT FERGUSON, exec. 8 Mar 1844. Body to be interred at
Fork Creek Brick church yard; to wife Ruth; to sons John and
Robert, land; to daughter Polly Ann; $1 each to son Moses, daugh-
ters Hannah Dickson, Jane Haune, and heirs of son James, dec'd,
also "my daughter Margaret husband James McCully one dollar also
one horse". Execs: son Moses and neighbor Jesse Cunningham.
"In witness whereof I John Ferguson the said testator". Wit:
Samuel M. Johnston, Samuel McAmish. Signed Robert Ferguson. /Date
1844 is written over 1835._7

(59) GINCY DOUTHET, not dated. Noncupative Will signed by Mary
McClure and Elizabeth McClure; special request made to Mary Ann
Douthet: "give Sophia my blue calico dress, give Betsy Howard my
best caps"; Mary Ann to have rest of things when her papa is done
with them; statement made a few days before death and written down
two or three days after.

(60) GEORGE SNIDER, exec. 27 Aug 1846. Land to grandson George D.
Snider son of son George, but son George and family to have
possession until death; to son George; to grandchildren Isaac W.,
Mary E., James M., John H., Samuel V., and Alexander B. Snider;
balance to be divided among heirs. Exec: son George. Wit:
Robert B. Billue, Samuel Lusk.

(61) FRANCIS A. PATTON, exec. 16 Dec 1846. To wife Amanda Ann; to
oldest daughter Mary Adaline, when she comes of age; to oldest son
Harris Flavins; to daughter Mary A. and son Harris F., money from
estate of their grandfather Samuel Bell; to other three children,
Francis Taylor, Ann Elizabeth, and James; wife to educate all
children; my five children. Exec: John Ramsey. Wit: James H.
Reagan, William Patton.

(63) MATHEW McSPADDEN, not dated. To wife Margaret and children James F. and Mary I., both minors; to son Samuel A. and daughter-in-law Lucinda McSpadden; note for land surveyed 14 Sep 1847; to daughter Martha P. and son-in-law A.G. Taylor; to daughter Easter E. and son-in-law Hugh M. Magill. Execs: Samuel McSpadden, Nathaniel Ewing. Wit: N. Magill, I. Magill.

(64) ISAAC BURLISON, exec. 1 Aug 1846. To wife Polly; to sons Isaac M.H., William, John R.D., and Vanburen; to daughters Octavy D. and Charlotte Burlison. Exec: Holloway Giles. Wit: Arch McCrary, Hugh P. Holland. Signed by mark.

(66) JAMES REVELEY, exec. 21 Nov 1847. To daughters Malinda Teressa, Cornelia Ann, and Elenor Caroline; my mule and a few small articles I have at the widow Brights and my carreall, to Samuel Glass for taking care of me in this my last illness. Exec: Samuel Glass. Wit: A.R. Cheyne, Rufus M. James.

(66) JOHN R. ROBERTS, exec. 5 Apr 1847. To father Philip and brothers Philip, Jr. and Jackson, the land "I am to receive from the Government of the U.S. for services in War against Mexico in Capt. P.B. Anderson's Company". Exec: Philip Roberts. Wit: H.H. Stephens, B.B. Land.

(67) WILLIAM GADD, exec. 9 Apr 1848. To wife Sarah; to children, viz, Nancy McDaniel, Polly Brannon, Ansel Gadd, Ellender Brannon, Talitha, William, Daniel, Amos, Betsy Ann, Sarah Jane, and Martha Gadd. Execs: sons Ansel and Amos. Wit: Mathew M. Young, Daniel Layman. Signed by mark.

(68) SAMUEL LUSK, exec. 1 Apr 1848. To wife Betsy; to son Elijah Patton Lusk; to grandson William Vance Lusk when he comes of age. Exec: son Elijah P. Wit: Armstrong Morrow, William Upton.

(69) SAMUEL McCROSKY, exec. 9 Aug 1848. To two sons Solon and Samuel; tombstones for graves of late wife and myself; balance divided among all children, to wit, Hetty Ann Hammontree, Emily Renshaw, Solon, Elizabeth, Loona, Sophrona, Samuel, and Sarah Josephine. Execs: brother John of Monroe Co., William Meston of Blount Co., son Solon of Monroe Co. Wit: William Heiskell, Charles Kelso, and William M. Heiskell.

(71) ISAAC HAGLER, exec. 27 Jul 1840. To wife Susannah; to son Benjamin Burton Hagler, to care for parents during remainder of lives; "whereas Elizabeth Stepp, Nancy Curtis, David H. Hagler, Matilda Howard, William L. Hagler, and Edah Snider have each received a bed and furniture I desire that my remaining children receive the same amount namely John, (Wilson having received a bed &c) Benjamin B., Cyntha, Elvira, & Ralph". Execs: sons Wilson and Benjamin B. Wit: Jeremiah Frazier, Charles Bogart, Armstrong Morrow.

(72) MARK McKENZIE, exec. 30 Sep 1848. To Kinneth McKenzie. Execs: James Ray, John Clayton. Wit: James Clayton, Martin Dotson.

(73) ARTHUR H. HENLY, exec. 10 Feb 1849. Being age 67 and subject of a lingering disorder; all children to share equally and landed property to remain undivided until youngest surviving child shall

become of age; by surviving family I mean my wife and my younger
children; wife Ann Evelina; six elder children, Sarah, David,
Elizabeth, Mary, Alexander, and William; given to elder daughter
Sarah H. when she was married to John R. Williamson; given to
elder daughters Elizabeth M. McGhee and Mary K. McGhee (their
expenses for schooling in Tuscomba, Ala.); remaining younger
children Ann Evelina, Arthur H., Thomas, Samuel, Lavinia W.,
and Charles F. Henly to be provided for as elder children have
been until twenty five being average age at which they drew their
amounts; on 30 Oct 1847 I put my son David in possession of one
of my farms in Blount Co.; three half acre lots in Knoxville,
Tenn. and one small tract of 200 acres in Monroe Co. on Notchey
Creek now occupied by Claibourne Reamy. Execs: wife and sons
David and Alexander S. Wit: E. Johnson, A.B. Howard, Jeremier
Skidmore.

(78) GEORGE SELVIDGE, exec. 7 May 1849. To wife Nancy; given to
all children their marriage portion; to Joseph his marriage portion and rifle gun if he stays at home and conducts himself well
until after my death; to Melisa Caroline and to son James, as their
marriage portion; to minor children Joseph, Caroline, and James;
Polly Ann Duggan, offspring of daughter Elizabeth now dead, to
receive her mother's share; son Green K. to receive less because
he left home when he was eighteen; son Irby M. left when he was
seventeen and has acted ungrateful; to four oldest children,
namely, Unice, Nancy, George W., and John. Execs: William
Stakely, John Ricket. Wit: Robert Wright, John Vance.

(81) EBENEZER JOHNSON, exec. 26 Nov 1839. Of Buffalo, Erie Co.,
N.Y.; to wife Lucy E., each child I now have or may have to be
educated; to son Herbert L., gold watch, seal, chain, and pencil;
daughter Mary E. Lord and son William H. have already received
money. Execs: friends Joseph Clary, Albert M. Tracy, and Charles
Townsend. Wit: N. Laroon and C.B. Lord both of Buffalo. State
of New York, Erie County, Surrogate Office, 15 Nov 1849. Will of
Ebenezer Johnson late of Telico, Monroe Co., Tenn., of which foregoing is a copy, proven before Peter W. Vosburgh, Surrogate, and
administration granted to Smith Inglehart. Albert H. Tracy, the
surviving Executor, having renounced.

(84) WILLIAM TAYLOR, exec. 12 Jan 1850. To wife Mary Ann; all due
from estate and by Will of father Leroy Taylor to mother Keziah
Taylor, sister Bersheba, and brothers Garret R., James, Isaac if
alive, John Douthet, and Leroy. Wit: James A. Coffin, Wilson
Weathers. Signed by mark.

(85) JOHN H. BRIGHT, exec. 10 Apr 1850. To wife Sarah F.; to
lawful heirs if wife marries. Exec: Harvy S. Bright. Wit:
William M. Morrow, James W. Taylor.

(86) JOHN McGHEE, exec. 20 May 1849. Land, 2755 acres, and 27
slaves both valued at $40,500, to daughter Margaret W. Humes; to
son Barclay McGhee, 24 slaves, land assigned by Chancery Court,
19 Sep 1842, to Thomas L., John Jr., and Mary Jones McGhee,
children and heirs of brother Dr. Alexander McGhee, dec'd, land in
Blount and Hamilton Counties, and land assigned by said decree to
Barclay McGhee one of sons of said Alexander McGhee, all valued at

$41,800; to son Charles McGhee, 29 slaves and land granted to my
father Barclay McGhee, all worth $40,500; to negro man James and
to his wife Sally, their freedom, $1000 as they need it, and per-
sonal property; also $7000 each to children named; balance of
property to be divided among said three children. Execs: sons
Barclay and Charles M. Wit: John M. Coffin, Edmond Wayman.

(93) WILLIAM WALLACE, SR., exec. 25 June 1851. To wife Tempy;
to all children. Exec: son William Wallis, Jr. Wit: J.K.
Fitzgerald, N.C. Hood, James H. Patton.

(94) PARKER HOOD, exec. 10 Jul 1851. To wife; three children to
be educated. Exec: Joseph Johnson. Wit: James A. Haire, Syney
A. Clark.

(95) ASA MULLINS, exec. 9 Oct 1851. To wife Margaret; all children.
Wit: Charles Bogart, John McLemore.

(95) ISAAC WEAVER, exec. 2 Nov 1851. To wife Harriet; to all lawful heirs at her death or marriage. Execs: wife and William
Denton. Wit: John H. King, Robert Sharp.

(96) JOSEPH SMITH, exec. 17 Nov 1851. To wife Margaret; to children, viz, Lucinda, Phebe, Eliza Jane, Nancy Lavinia, Margaret
Eveline, Flora Isabella, Martha Ellen, four last named being minors
and Martha Ellen the youngest. Exec: friend John A. Wright. Wit:
William L. Caldwell, Nathl. Ewing.

(97) JAMES SMITH, exec. 22 Dec 1851. Of Madisonville, Monroe Co.;
lot in Madisonville to S. McSpadden, W.G. Bogle, James A. Coffin,
Amos Carson, and others, Trustees of Chestua Presbyterian Church
in Madisonville, for use of said church whenever they may have
obtained an amount of subscriptions sufficient to build a handsome
church edifice such as will add to the appearance of the town, the
said building to be of tasteful modern style; lands owned by late
firm of Stakely and Smith to be disposed of by William Stakely;
daughter Martha Adaline to remain under parental care of George
Montgomery and his wife Alpha; all estate to said daughter. Execs:
William M. Stakely, James A. Coffin. Wit: Guilford Cannon, N.W.
Haun. Codicil, 4 Feb 1852. When Will was made my sister Sarah
Stakely was very low but she is now convalescent; daughter Martha
Adaline to be under her care.

(100) ABRAHAM BUCK, exec. 16 Aug 1836. To son Mathias and he is
to pay to each of lawful heirs. Exec: son Mathias. Wit: Samuel
Patterson, William Heiskell, John Mosier, M. Screvener.

(101) ANDREW THOMPSON McKINNEY, exec. 31 Mar 1852. To wife
Elizabeth; $1 each to daughters Aseneth Gunn, Nisomey Roberts,
Elvira Hawkins, and to son David; balance to four youngest chil-
dren, Andrew Thompson, Jane, Margaret, and Josephine McKinney.
Exec: friend James A. Coffin. Wit: J.B. Gilbreath, John R.
Williams.

(102) FREDERICK SNIDER, exec. 30 Apr 1852. To daughters Mary Best
and Susannah Wilson; to heirs of daughter Elizabeth Best, dec'd;
to son of daughter Lucinda Snodgrass, dec'd; to sons John H.,
Samuel, Elisha, and Daniel. Execs: Elisha Snider, David Lowry,
Sr. Wit: William M. Lowry, Daniel T. Shaffer.

(103) JESSE FORSHEE, exec. 30 Feb 1853. To wife Mary for herself
and family; four sons J.W., Francis A., James A., and William
M.K.; five daughters Lucindy L., Nancy E., Tabitha J., Sarah E.,
and Lucretia A. Forshee. Exec: David Lowry, Sr. Wit: John F.
Gilbreath, Robert L. Cochran. Signed by mark.

(104) MATHEW NELSON, exec. 3 May 1852. To wife Martha; to three
sons Mathew, John, and William; to all living children and grandson
John O. Cannon. Execs: wife and son Mathew, Jr. Wit: James and
H.D. Chesnutt.

(105) ANDREW VAUGHT, exec. 21 Jan 1853. To daughter Tildy Courtrell,
bed that is at Richard Cottrell's for her trouble in waiting on
her mother during her sickness and "her trouble with me, the
allowance to be made to Richard Cottrell and family for keeping
me"; division among children, David, John, Tildy Cottrell, Betsy
Belt, Margaret Best's children (to get a child's part), Andrew,
and Washington. Execs: Samuel Thompson, Samuel Tullock. Wit:
Anderson Rowan, John Caldwell. Signed by mark.

(107) GEORGE LONG, exec. 10 Mar 1853. To wife Bethany and the two
daughters living with her, Rebecca and Margaret; to five children
William, Rebecca, Squire, Alexander, and Margaret; tract in Harden
Co., Ky. to grown children, namely, George Long, Mary Blanton,
Catherine Carter, Roda Howard, Anne Taylor, Betsy No, and Jackson
Long, land to be sold by son-in-law George Howard. Wit: I.D.
McReynolds, James Hickman. Signed by mark.

(108) JACOB SHEETS, exec. 3 Dec 1849. Land to son John; $10 each
to daughters Polly Gaston, Katy Bogart, Malty Mosier, Peggy Shields,
and to son Henry. Exec: son John. Wit: David Lowry, William
Lowry. Signed by mark.

(109) MARY ANN BROWN (BROWNE), exec. 2 June 1853. To four children,
Leonora, Lucinda, Gordon K., and Martha M. Brown. Wit: Mary J.
Montgomery, Sarah L. McReynolds, J.H. Montgomery, T. Nixon Van-
dyke.

(110) MARK MORGAN, exec. 7 Aug 1852. To wife Mary and stepsons and
daughters; to stepdaughter Mary Jane Tipton; to stepsons and
daughters, to wit, I.G. Tipton, Jacob J. Tipton, Abram H. Tipton,
Catharine B. January, Leonia Lunard; if Mary Jane Tipton stays
single and desires to live with her Grandmother then she be allowed
to do so. Wit: S.W. Haun, G.W. Givens, John Warden.

(112) CHARLES KELSO, exec. 22 Oct 1853. To wife Elizabeth; to all
children; school and support daughter Mary Josephine Kelso and
land to my wife her mother; all children to be charged with amounts
which they have received. Execs: Findly Wadkins of Hamilton Co.,
Tenn. and neighbor Lorenzo Tipton. Wit: Solon McCrosky, William
Kile.

(114) JOHN LOVE, exec. 6 Feb 1851. To son Robartus; to grandson
William D. Snodgrass and sons Byler and David, land in Cherokee
Co., Ala. where sons Byler and David now live. Execs: Robartus
Love and William M. Stakely. Wit: H.H. Stephens, William Dyer.

(116) DANIEL H. JONES, exec. 23 Dec 1853. To wife Hannah, town
property in Philadelphia /Monroe Co.7; to daughters Mary, Caroline,

Hester, and youngest, Susan, and to sons Hardy and Thomas, all under twenty-one; to brother John L. Jones, saddler's tools. Exec: friend Hugh E. Martin. Wit: G.A. Long, A. Allen, J.D. Jones.

(118) JONATHAN DAVIS, exec. 16 Mar 1854. To daughters Sally Wittenburg, Nancy and Margaret Davis; to sons Thomas C. and Charles T.P.; to Eliza Jane Watts a girl I have raised. Execs: son Charles T.P. and daughters Nancy and Margaret. Wit: Thomas Robison, Crockett Godby. Codicil, 16 Apr 1854 at night about three days before said Jonathan died; said Jonathan called all children to his bedside and all were there except Sally; said Jonathan wanted Sally to have $400 to make her equal with others; Signed by George Bowman, James E. Bright, John B. Simpson on 23 Apr 1854.

(121) MARGARET S. WEAR, not dated. $1 each to all children, to wit, Matilda Garner, Nancy Jenkins, James M. Wear, Joseph Wear, Thomas Wear, Margaret Stapp, and Samuel Wear; balance to son John M. Exec: son Joseph. Wit: Henry Donohoo, Thomas J. Burris. Signed by mark.

(122) ADALINE HUMPHREYS, exec. 25 Mar 1854. To brother Van Buren Humphreys; to sister Sophronia Beard; to nephew James Anderson Humphreys infant son of William C. Humphreys, dec'd; to mother Nancy Humphreys; right as heir of father James Humphreys, dec'd to slaves. Exec: brother-in-law Ignatius W. Beard. Wit: E.E. Griffith, Harriet C. Humphreys.

(123) WILLIAM DICKSON, exec. 27 Jul 1824. To wife Sarah; slaves to be freed at wife's death. Exec: wife. Wit: Athiel McAlister, John Lickens, Jones Griffin. Signed by mark. Certification 18 Jul 1825 by William S. Blair, Clerk of Court of Pleas and Quarter Sessions of Monroe Co. that foregoing is true copy of Original filed. Certification by John B. Tipton Clk. & M. by John O. Cannon DC & M that the above is true copy of Will and exhibit filed in office.

(125) SARAH BAYLESS, exec. 17 May 1853. All property except slaves to Thomas Dixon Belott; slaves to be freed; to John L. Hopkins, a reasonable sum for superintending affairs and drawing Will. Execs: Robert F. Cooke. John L. Hopkins. Wit: John M. Haire, A.T. Hicks, H.H. Stephens. Signed by mark.

(126) HENRY CHESNUTT, exec. 20 Oct 1849. Wife Tabitha and three daughters now living with me and sons George, Hugh, and R.D. all to remain on farm; to daughter Mary Reynolds; to granddaughter Mary Love; children to wit James, George, Hugh, Richard D. and daughters Altmira, Elizabeth, and Tabitha, equal division and they are to give A.G. Love and Mary Love $100 each; to son John. Wit: James and Hugh Chesnutt.

(128) JOSEPH FORSHEE, exec. 2 Apr 1855. To wife Elenor; to son Avan; until youngest child Ann Rebecca shall arrive at age of twenty-one; single daughters, married daughters, other sons. Wit: Phillip Keller, William Brakebill, Jacob H. Bruner.

(130) JOHN CALDWELL, exec. Dec 1854. To wife; to two sons John E. and Thomas L., to support their mother and my daughter Elizabeth M. as long as she remains single; to all children except John E.

and Thomas L. Execs: James H. Johnston, son John E. Wit: E.
Kimbrough, E.E. Griffith.

(131) SAMUEL MAGILL, exec. 7 Aug 1855. To wife Margaret; to son
James and daughter Matilda when they become twenty-one; to step-
daughters Sarah Magill and Mary Shadden; J.H. Magill and A.N.
Magill to refund cash advanced to firm of J.H. Magill & Co. and
upon such refund they are to have interest in land bought from
L.R. Hurst. Execx: wife. Wit: James A. Coffin, N. Magill, Nat
Ewing. Signed by mark.

(133) ROBERT HUTCHESON, exec. 30 Mar 1855. To wife; all children
to be educated. Exec: E. Kimbrough. Wit: D.W. Latimore, James
Steed.

(134) LEONARD CARDEN, exec. 6 Dec 1854. Being old; to wife Sintha
and her children as they leave her; first wife's children, namely,
"John Carden, Paly Reuben Adaline, Larkin, & Malinda Case & Alfred
Carden & Andrew Carden, & James Carden" have already received
their share; to Catherine Clawers; land to sons Leonard and Joseph
Calloway Carden when they come of age and their mother to remain
on land. Execs: wife and son Larkin. Wit: Larkin Carden, Jr.,
Leonidas Taylor, Jacob F. Peck. Signed by mark.

(135) ROBERT W. HICKS, exec. 17 Jan 1856. To wife Mary Ann; to
family; bought one interest in mother's land from brother John W.
Hicks and one interest in same from Isaac Hicks. Wit: W.N.
Bicknell, Thomas L.D. Trotter.

(136) WILLIAM GRAY, exec. 12 Mar 1855. To wife Francis; to sons
and daughters, Warren Gray, William Gray, Jr., Anna Arpe, Thomas
Gray, Nancy Brown, Miria Jones, Fanny L. Howard, Wilson Gray,
Amanda Anderson, and Polly A. Triplet. Execs: Francis Gray, B.L.
White. Wit: R.B. Billue, B.L. White. Signed by mark.

(137) ROBERT R. YOUNG, exec. 13 May 1855. To be buried in a
suitable suit of clothes "as though I was visiting my patients";
to wife Polly; to two daughters Mary Jane and Celina Young; to son
J.A. Young; to son T.J. Young; to W.D. Young, all medical books
hoping that they may remain in the family; to son D.C. Young, my
historical and other books and the leather trunk left me by my son
R.W. Young, dec'd; to son W.D. Young; to grandson Robert R. Young;
other children already provided for. Execs: sons J.A. and T.J.
Wit: John Prock, Hezekiah Witt.

(138) JOHN WOLF, exec. 21 Feb 1856. To wife Jane B., all the
property she brought with her after our marriage and has purchased
with her own money since that time; three youngest children,
James Monroe, Sarah Catharine, and John Peeler Wolf to be educated;
to two daughters Flora and Nancy Jane; to son Joseph; to all the
children; wife Jane B. and William Dyer to be guardians of three
youngest. Execs: William M. Stakely, Robert Russell. Wit: W.L.
Eakin, Daniel Bruner. Signed by mark. Codicil, 18 Aug 1856; "if
I survive said son Joseph", his children to receive his share.

(141) JOHN HANKINS, exec. 3 Sep 1856. To wife Susan and to sons
Bird P. and Newton Cannon Hankins; to children Edward, Jonathan M.,
Anne Stephens, and Melissa Broome; other children already provided
for. Execs: Joseph Divine of this County, Bird P. Hankins. Wit:

John Wilkins, Joseph Divine, William K. Morgan, M. Raper. Signed
by mark.

(143) JEREMIAH H. DUNCAN, exec. 3 Sep 1856. To wife Mary; the
family to wit, Samuel, Josephus, and Mary L. Duncan, minor heirs;
three oldest sons William, James, and John; three married daughters,
Catharine Singleton, Maryanall Taylor, and Margaret Roddy; the
house and lot in Ringold, Ga. to daughter Margaret. Wit: Robert
Carter, J.H. Montgomery, Benjamin Franklin.

(144) B. McGHEE, no date. To wife Mary K. Henly; children to be
educated. /Will seems to be incomplete, no signature./

(145) HENRY CLICK, exec. 9 Jun 1849. Cocke Co., Tenn. To wife
Ruth; to daughter Hepsaba Click; to Eliza Jane Lewis formerly
Eliza Jane Click daughter of James Click, dec'd; heirs, to wit,
Lewis A. Click, William Click, Jeremiah Murr and his wife Rachel,
Charles Hartsell and his wife Amanda, Alfred Denton and his wife
Dorcas, have made agreement with heir Andrew H. Click that he have
land which gives him all land except interest of heirs Henry J.
and Hepsaba Click. Execs: son Lewis A. and Charles Hartsell.
Wit: William McSwain, William P. Carnes. Codicil, 23 Oct 1849.
Mary Jane and Martha, heirs of Henry J. Click to have equal
interest as one of my heirs; son Andrew to pay them. Wit: William
and James McSwain.

(148) J.T. ROWLAND, not dated. To wife Louisa; educate children.
Wit: David Caldwell.

(149) HUGH E. MARTIN, exec. 10 Jan 1857. To wife Nancy Ann and
children until youngest comes of age; two oldest sons William E.
and James G. and daughter Margaret Ann when they come of age; five
youngest children. Exec: John Ramsey. Wit: James M. Blair,
John Stanfield, Josiah McGuire. Signed by mark.

(151) JOHN FINE, exec. 22 May 1855. To wife Nancy; to daughters
Polly, Nancy, and Martha; to all heirs except Isaac and Elizabeth
Hill, who are to get $5 for the reason they and their family have
removed on other side of the rocky mountains and it being so far
off I fear Elizabeth and her family would never get a dime of the
money as it would all be spent in coming after it. Exec: son
Peter L. Wit: N.W. Haun, Joseph Walker.

(153) MARY M. BLACKSTON, exec. 6 Sep 1856. To mother. Exec:
Archibald Bacome. Wit: A.O. Howard, James West.

(154) HUBBORD HUDSON, exec. 15 Jul 1850. To wife Temperance; son
Payton to support his brother Peter Ellick Hudson during his
natural life; to Richard Thomas Larrison Hudson. Exec: son Payton.
Wit: George C. Harris, John Wilson. Signed by mark.

(155) JOHN DAUGHERTY, exec. 2 May 1857. Two eldest sons, Alexander
and Brazzeal, to run farm and pay to their mother and brothers and
sisters; until all heirs come of age; four sons, Alexander, Brazzeal, Jason, and William and four daughters, Sarah Catharine, Eliza
Jane, Melinda, and Nancy Ann; brother William Daugherty; Joseph
Daugherty /no relationship given/; son Alexander to be Gdn. in my
stead for minor heirs of Eliza Jane Daugherty living now in Mo.,
their property being in Monroe Co. Execs: Miram Calfee, Alexander

and Brazzeal Daugherty. Wit: John Thomas, John Morgan. Signed by mark.

(158) JESSE CUNNINGHAM, exec. 21 May 1855. Son James R.R. to have farm and support me and my wife Mary during our lives and to give to each of his sisters, viz, Caroline E.W. Cravens, Charlotte E.M. Marshall, Margaret J.G., Sarah N.F., and Harriet M.J.W. Cunningham; son W.G.E. Cunningham who is a missionary in China; daughter M.G.E.; to James H. Marshall son of William N. Marshall; buggy to be sold and money given to M.E. Church South for China missions. Exec: son James R.R. Wit: R.E. Doak, John H. Bruner. Signed Jesse Cunnyingham.

(161) ELIZABETH ALLEN, exec. 23 Mar 1834. All estate to grandson James Allen, youngest son of William Allen; son William and his family to have benefits until James comes of age. Execs: friends William Allen, James Bacomb. Wit: Josiah Rowan, J.G. Hankins. Signed by mark.

(162) SAMUEL SMALLING (SMALLEN), SR., exec. 6 Sep 1857. To wife Betsy; to son Jefferson and he is to furnish horses to Betsy Ann and Margaret Jane Smalling; to Kings Berry McSpadden who married daughter Nancy; to all heirs; to Cynthia Smalling and same to Polly. Execs: wife and son Jefferson. Wit: Howard F. Hunt, Mathew M. Smallin. Signed, Samuel Smalling.

(163) SUSAN MEICE, exec. 22 Jul 1856. Dying request that John Moser and Maglin Moser shall take two little girls, Catharine and Mary Meice. Wit: J.P., John, and A.J. Moser. Signed by mark.

(164) ROBERT McREYNOLDS, exec. 31 Jan 1858. To wife Mary in her old age; already given to children. Exec: Nathaniel Magill. Wit: William L. Eakin, Samuel McCaulie. Signed by mark.

(165) WASHINGTON BREEDWELL, exec. 8 Apr 1858. "I, George Breed-well"; to wife Uphemia; to two children Elizabeth and Henry; has paid debts for son John; William Dyer to be Gdn. for two children Elizabeth and Henry. Exec: Robert Russell. Wit: William Dyer, R. Love. Signed Washington Breedwell, by mark.

(166) JACOB WARREN, exec. 29 Sep 1853. To wife Sarah. Execx: wife. Wit: S.T. Brown, Daniel Heiskell. Signed by mark.

(167) PLEASANT KITTRELL, exec. 9 Feb 1854. Already given to sons William and Solomon and daughter Betsy Ann Rosin; at death of me and wife, two sons John and James to have all estate and they are to raise William, son of son Solomon. Wit: Samuel Edington, David Lowry.

(168) PAULINA TAYLOR, exec. 3 Jul 1858. Tombstones to be placed at grave similar to those at graves of mother and husband; remainder to John Stanfield, Sr., for attention paid during widowhood and afflictions. Exec: friend John Stanfield. Wit: J.D. Jones, James West. Probated Dec Term 1859, Record Book P 154.

(169) SARAH HART, exec. 7 Sep 1857. Stones to be placed at graves of husband and daughter Melissa Louisa Wright; to stepson John Hart; to sister's daughters and Mary Ann Woods, daughter of Robert Woods; to M.E. Church South; to sisters. Exec: Bronlow Swisher now of Knox Co. Wit: Allen C. Broome, George Brown. Signed by mark.

(171) JANE GRIFFITH, exec. 13 May 1858. To brothers Edward and John Griffith and sister Delilah Griffith; to sister Rebecca Marshall and her five children, William N., Henry S., Robert G., Joseph E., and Martha Jane Dyer. Exec: brother John. Wit: Nathl. Ewing, Amos Carson. Signed by mark.

(172) JOSEPH ROY, exec. 21 Oct 1858. Has given farm to wife and daughter; to two sons John and Harrison. Execs: wife, eldest son John O., and John A. Rowan. Wit: R.H.G. McCarroll, H.H. Morris. Probated Dec Term 1858 Record Bk p 9.

(172) JONATHAN TIPTON, exec. 23 Sep 1843. To wife Margaret, the property that I got with her in marriage and half of land; balance to children with advancements deducted, Mary An Wear, John B. Tipton, Edmond W. Tipton, Willie B. Tipton, Lucretia Bradford, Tryphena Wear, Sarah Wilkerson, Lorenzo D. Tipton, Pleasant M. Tipton, Eldridge G. Tipton, Johnathan C. Tipton, Quincy A. Tipton, Lavina and Calvin Hall. Execs: William Heiskell, John B. Tipton. Wit: John McClain, John Rider. Codicil, 28 Nov 1855. "Altho George P. Tipton one of my grandchildren is made equal by law with one of my own children Yet I think proper to make George P. Tipton equal with each one of my Grand children to wit the children of John Wilkinson and his wife Sarah Wilkinson". Wit: John Rider, John McClain. Probated Dec Term 1858 Record Bk p 9.

(175) LARKIN CARDEN, exec. 17 Mar 1866. "being old and my wife dead and having eleven children"; children: James, Patsy Erwin, Robert, Jones, Leonard, Caroline Evans, Jourdin, Nancy Morelock, Sophia Erwin, Sarah Edaline Ellis, Hetty Heflin; to James Cardin, Abner Erwin, Robert Cardin, Jonas Cardin, Leonard Cardin, Careline Evans, Jourdin Cardin, Nancy Morelock, Washington Erwin, B.D. Ellis, and Leander Heflin. Execs: sons James, Leonard, and Jordan. Wit: Larkin F. Cardin, F.M. Bradford, Francis M. Satterwhite. Codicil, 16 Nov 1866. Wit: W.J. and L.F. Cardin. Codicil, not dated. Wit: Benedict Ellis, David Baker. Probated Dec Session 1866 Ledger P. 269.

(180) A.L. WILSON, exec. 8 Oct 1866. Religious library to William Porter; books and bound volumes of Presbyterian Tracts to N. Magill; Smith's Dictionary Three volumes and eleven copies of Marriage Certificates to W.B. Rankin; to A. Vance; to A.W. Wilson; to W.R. Magill; to friends who have waited on me at night in my last illness; to Wallace Shadden; to Harrett Magill. Exec: William Porter. Wit: David H. Lowry, W.R. Magill. Probated Dec Session 1866 Ledger p 269.

(181) SAMUEL HENDERSON, exec. 11 May 1861. To wife Nancy; to children, namely, Martha E. Henderson, Elizabeth McEnolly wife of James McEnolly, Rebeca Morris, Mahala Beard, John C., Samuel P., Rufus M., George L., Oliver C., and Hugh; to Amanda Henderson, widow of dec'd son William, and her children; Samuel, Henry, Cardin, John, Mariah, William, and Catharine. Exec: son George L. Wit: George Brown, Guilford Cannon. Codicil, 4 Dec 1866. Son Samuel P. now dead. Wit: I.B. Kimbrough, H. Hix. Signed Codicil by mark.

(187) JOHN McCROSKEY, exec. 31 Aug 1866. To wife Priscilla; land to son Henry M. but he is to pay rest of children, to wit, Malinda

A. McCray, Francis L. Golliher, Thomas E.H., Robert C., Benjamin
B., and Edgar J. McCroskey; claims against U.S. government; said
son Henry M. to care for son Edgar J. until he reaches age of
twenty-one and sons Robert C. and Benjamin B. for two years, and
to provide for his sister Penelopy A. McCroskey while she is
single; to son Thomas E.H. in consequence of his being disabled;
half acre set apart for graveyard. Execs: sons J.P.T. and Henry
M. McCroskey. Wit: Thomas G. Boyd, John J. Grubb. Probated Mar
Term 1867 Ledger p 302.

(190) (194) JOHN PENNINGTON, exec. 27 Aug 1867. To wife Alpha;
daughter Polly Ann and Robert S. may live with wife while they
remain single; has given to sons H.B., J.C., F.M., Robert S. and
daughters Emaline Cleveland and L.C. Bryant. Execs: J. C.
Pennington, L.F. Bryant. Wit: Robert Snead, Peter Morris. Probated Jan Term 1868 Ledger p 424.

(191) JOHN COLTHARP, exec. 17 Nov 1856. To sons Andrew Jackson,
James, Eli S., John H., George H. and to daughters Lavicie
Stephens, Sarah wife of Christopher Gast, Susannah wife of Thomas
Henderson; to son-in-law Mastin Henderson; to children of daughter
Mary Upton, dec'd. Execs: sons Andrew J. and John H. Wit:
George Brown, proven by Brown, Sarah S. Jordan, John Scruggs, Aug
1, 1867, Joseph Upton Apr 8, 1867, proven. Adm. Bond Jun 1868
Ledger p 520.

(195) JAMES CURTIS, exec. 29 Jul 1867. To son S.C., his portion
and portion of son H.W.; son S.C. to pay to heirs of son W.R. out
of portion of son I.A.; to son I.A.; to daughter S.A. Pealor; to
James and J.R., sons of son W.R.; to William and I.B., sons of son
D.B. Exec: son S.C. Wit: Thomas J. Russell, J.A. Carter.
Signed by mark. Probated Feb Term 1867 Ledger p 429.

(197) ALEXANDER A. HENDERSON, not dated. "All estate to -" /sic7;
they are to pay to sister Ester Johnston, brothers William and
John, $5 each; to wife Matilda; tombstones to be placed at graves
of father, mother, and brother Josiah P. Henderson; to brother
Samuel and sister Rosannah Land. Execs: said Trustees. Wit:
J.M. Barton, Fork Creek Monroe Co Tenn, Joshua P.T. McCrosky,
Monroe Co Tenn, and R.W. Hudson, Monroe Co Tenn.

(199) JAMES W. KELSO, exec. 8 Jun 1868. Land deeded to me by
father Charles Kelso; to youngest sister Mary Josephine, wife of
William J. Fowler; to sisters Caroline L., wife of Doctor Milten
Y. Heiskell, now of Abingdon, Va., Margaret Elizabeth, widow of
Garland Smith, Terreesa M. widow of Findly P. Watkins, dec'd, of
Hamilton Co., Tenn.; to children of dec'd sister Martha M.
Carter, who are now in Texas with their father; to children of
sister Mira S. Carmichael, dec'd, former wife of George W.
Carmichael, now of Madison Co., Ala.; children of brother David
Kelso to have nothing. Exec: brother-in-law William J. Fowler.
William J. and Josephine Fowler to take good care of mother in
her old age. Probated Oct Term 1869 Record B p 120.

(203) ELIZABETH M. and FANNY L. LOWRY, exec. 16 Oct 1869. Property to go to remaining sister. Exec: brother David H. Lowry.
Wit: N. Magill, Martha I. Wright.

(204) PHILLIP KELLER, exec. 15 Nov 1869. To wife Catherine; to

four unmarried children, Mary M., Henry M., Franklin L., and Hughy
J.D. Keller to be equal at age of twenty-one with two married
children, G.W. Keller and Martha Jane /no last name/. Execs:
wife, son George W., son-in-law J.H. Forshee. Wit: W.N. Bicknell,
William Dyre. Signed Phillip Keller by J.A. Coffin by request.

(206) JOHN RIDER, SR., exec. 22 Nov 1869. Already given to sons
William and Clinton B. and to daughter Laursana Hall and husband
Joseph Hall; to daughter Amanda M. Tipton and husband Malcom M.
Tipton; to son David W. and John M.C., land I formerly lived on
in Blount County on Baker's Creek. Exec: son-in-law Malcom M.
Tipton. Wit: John B. Tipton, W.C. Conner. Probated Feb Term
1870 Ledger 185.

(208) FRANCES L. LOWRY, exec. 18 Dec 1869. To Mrs. Josephine
Lowry; to brother David H. Lowry. Exec: David H. Lowry. Wit:
W.W. Porter. J.J. Crippen. Probated Mar Term 1870 Record B P 192.

(209) MARY DYER, exec. 4 Oct 1860. To four children, William,
Elizabeth D. wife of Lewis Stephens, Sarah H. wife of James
Cliborne, and Mary Jane wife of William L. Eakin. Wit: R. Love,
John F. Gilbreath. Signed by mark. Probated Aug Term 1870
Record B P 303.

(211) WILLIAM WATSON, exec. 25 Nov 1858. To wife Rebecca; to
children, Nancy, James M., George W., Robert D., Mary Malone,
William P., Rebecca J. McDaniel, Henry T., and Betsy M. Atkinson.
Wit: S.M. Haun, John McConkey, Allen C. Broome. Probated Jan
Term 1859 Record Book p 19.

(213) WILSON WEATHERS, exec. 9 Apr 1859. To wife Sarah; to youngest
son James; to three daughters; oldest son Henry J. has received
his share. Execs: friends John A. Rowan, John Hightower. Wit:
John Hightower, George Stephens. Probated Jul Term 1859 Record
Bk p 94.

(214) JESSEE RHEA, exec. 20 Oct 1858. To present wife; equal
division among lawful heirs with exception of James Rhea's heirs,
$5 to them. Execs: William Rhea, Elisha Griffith. Wit: David
Stephens, William Richy. Probated Aug Term 1859 Record Bk p 106.

(215) JAMES EWING, exec. 25 Dec 1854. To son Nathaniel; to daughter
Margaret McSpadden; rest of children, namely, Alexander, Samuel,
George, and James, have already received their portion. Exec:
son Nathaniel. Wit: N. Magill, Amos Carson. Probated Aug Term
1859 Record Bk p 107.

(216) STERLING RAGSDALE, exec. 6 Aug 1859. To wife Sarah Ann;
"heretofore Daniel Hicks my wife's brother bought of me all my
wife's undivided interest in lands willed by her Father to her and
her two brothers lying in McMinn County". Exec: Henry Kile or
Abijah Fowler. Wit: Elijah Wiggins, George W. Wiggins. Probated
Oct Term 1859 Record Book P 132.

(218) WILLIAM HENDERSON, 7 Aug 1859. Noncupative Will, signed by
R.F. Cook, J.C. Henderson, H. Hix; to wife to raise the children.
Probated Sep Term 1859 Record Bk P 114.

(218) VALENTINE MAYO, SR., exec. 2 Jul 1859. To daughter Martha
Washington Mayo; to other five /sic/ children, to wit, Blackmore

Mayo, Hughes Mayo, Nancy P. Woods, George W. Mayo, Valentine Mayo,
and James Mayo. Exec: son George W. Wit: James T. Blair, Isaac
W. Brown. Probated Sep Term 1859 Record Bk P 114.

(220) ELI CLEVELAND, exec. 26 Jan 1856. To daughter Malinda Chestnutt; to all children, to wit, Robert R., Jessee F., Eli M., David
H., Joseph D. Jones in behalf of Alcy M. Jones' children to wit
Lodusky Caroline, Mary L., Alcy M., Eli C., James C., Joseph M.,
Robert A., and Jesse F. and Clarissa Jane; given heretofore to
daughter Alcy M. Jones now dec'd and to Joseph D. Jones to be vested
in land in western Country for her five sons; given heretofore to
daughter Clerily Jones; land already given to United Baptist Church
of Christ where meeting house now is; to wife Polly; wife to keep
with her Roxanna and Calvin Martin her niece and nephew as long as
she may wish; to Lodusky Walker. Execs: sons Robert R. and
Jessee F. Cleveland and Joseph D. Jones. Wit: Robert Snead, E.H.
White, John H. Johnston. Signed Eli Cleveland by Robert Snead.
Probated Dec Term 1859 p 153.

(225) MARY BELL, exec. 30 Oct 1859. All to daughter Julia Bell
except $5 each to Alwin Bell and John Bell's heirs. Exec: Moses
McLendon. Wit: Isaac Stephens, Thomas A. Harrison. Probated
Jul Term 1860 Record Bk p 240.

(226) DANIEL REAGAN, exec. 13 Jul 1860. To wife Elizabeth; to
family until youngest son Robert D. comes of age; to son Joseph
E.; to two daughters Delilah Jane and Martha A., if they marry,
same amount as daughter Mary E. has had; two sons William H.H. and
Robert D. and two daughters Martha A. and Delilah Jane to have a
good house /sic/ or its equivalent to make them equal with Joseph
E. and Mary E. who have both had houses; slave "loaned to Mary E.
Kimbrough"; to son James E. Execs: sons Joseph E. and William
H.H. Wit: J.D. Jones, J.L. Grubb. Probated Sep Term 1860 Record
Bk p 262.

(229) JACOB PARKS, exec. 24 Jul 1858. To son James; to daughter
Susan Jackson; to daughter Sarah Parks in Ga., $10 if she comes
for it herself. Wit: R.P. Dunkin, John Vasser, Robert Hall.
Signed by mark. Probated Dec Term 1860 Record Bk p 300.

(230) PRESLEY CLEVELAND, exec. 13 Jan 1856. To children, Eliza A.
Johnston, Caroline Cleveland, Larkin, and Robert. Execs: S.J.
Martin, William E. Johnson. Wit: John Pennington, D.H. Cleveland,
H.B. Pennington. Signed by mark. Probated Jul Term 1861 Record
Bk p 387.

This half-filled book is apparently a copy of other records, with
the notices of probate added later. Pages 1-22 repeat the entries
copied in Will Book A.

(22) JOHN A. WRIGHT, exec. Jul 1861. To all children. Execs: N.
Magill and son John Wright. Wit: J.F. Magill, D.E. Lowry.
Probated Aug Term 1861 Record Bk P 397.

(23) JAMES DUNLAP, exec. 24 Jul 1861. Land for "support of afflic-
ted sister Martha Dunlap and Charity Ann Harrison daughter of
Nathaniel and Jane Harrison, Charity Emiline Harrison, Elizabeth
Harrison my sister in law"; to niece Mary E. wife of Orville R.
Carden; to the children of Nathaniel and Jane Harrison they being
William J., Mary E., Charity Ann, Sara M., Louisa I.W., and Sophrona
J. Harrison. Wit: Archibald Bacomb, William B. Grayson. Codicil,
24 1861. Probated Sep Term 1861 Record Bk P 400.

(25) JAMES A. HAIRE, exec. 23 Apr 1861. To wife Ann; to children
John T.M., James C., Eliza M.C. Houston, Anthon, Caroline M. John-
ston, Martha J.A. Smith. Exec: Joseph Johnston. Wit: J.I.
Wright, J.R. Stradly. Probated Sep Term 1861 Rec Bk p 400.

(27) JOHN SHEETS, exec. 26 Jun 1861. To son Decator; to girls
Rachel, Nancy, and Emiline as long as they stay single; all child-
ren, to wit, Jacob Sheets, Rachel and John, Henry and Margaret,
Nancy and Isabell, David and M__gen and Emiline. Execs: sons John
and Jacob and brother Henry Sheets. Wit: James Clibourne, Robert
L. Cockran.

(29) CASWELL L. WALKER, exec. 15 Dec 1861. To "all my children of
legitimate issue all money property &C that I have heretofore given
them"; Hamilton County Farm to be sold and proceeds paid to Dawson
A. Walker, Sallie Jane Morris, Mroclah C. McMahan, Nancy J. Blair,
David L. Walker, Seth J. Walker, and to Joseph Browder son of
daughter Polly H. Browder; other estate to be divided equally
between six legitimate children and two illegitimate children,
that is to say, Dawson A. Walker, Sallie J. Morris, Mroclah McMahan,
Nancy J. Blair, David L. Walker and Seth J. Walker and Albert H.
Walker (Alius) Albert H. Grayson and Miranda Greene daughter of
Sarah Bayles; land to Mroclah McMahan but not to be sold during
lifetime of her husband A.J. McMahan, he having squandered and
wasted; William C. Greene having neglected his business; Dawson A.
Walker and David L. Walker to be Trustees for Mroclah McMahan and
Miranda Greene, and to be Execs. Will examined 2 Mar 1862; above
Albert H. Walker alias Albert H. Grayson being in armies of C.S.A.

(33) NANCY GENTRY, exec. 27 Jun 1861. Land to daughter Mary Hawkins
and her husband E.C. Hawkins who have cared for me; they must pay
to remainder of heirs; to granddaughter Jane Gentry; to Nancy
Mullins. Wit: Edwin Hall, James Hunt, John Stephens. Signed by
mark.

(34) JOSEPH K. /JOSIAH K./ JOHNSTON, exec. 13 Aug 1861. To wife
Clarissa; to children; older children; Billie Prator Sneed to be
considered as one heir to be governed by charges against his father
and taken out of his part of the estate; great part of worth came
by wife. Probated Oct Term 1862 Rec Bk 517.

(35) ALFRED B. CLIFT, exec. 8 Jul 1862. To two children by first
wife, James Monroe and Polly Ann, when they come of age; their
deceased mother; to wife Nancy Caroline and children of her own
body, to wit, Hugh Peeler, Margaret, Matilda, Nancy Jane, and
Missoura Adaline. Exec: brother Cyrus H. Clift. Wit: E.E.
Griffiths, Jacob Sheets. Probated Sep 1862 Record Bk p 507.

(37) GEORGE W. MORGAN, exec. 25 Apr 1861. "in view of the disturb-
ances of the County and approaching war"; if I should die in service
of Country; to wife Martha K.; land owned jointly with Andw. L.
Rogers in Monroe Co., Tenn.; said Rogers having married my sister
Cherokee A. Morgan; equal division among children by said wife and
Olny S. Morgan, an illegitimate child of Viney Barnett; John A.
Stephens to have use of land during his life. Execs: William A.
Mayo, A.L. Rogers. Wit: J.I. Wright, Johnathan Thomas. Probated
Feb Term 1863 Record Bk P 544.

(39) ARMSTEAD BLACKWELL, exec. 9 Mar 1847. To wife Lucinda; to
son Samuel. Exec: friend Adam Mowry. Wit: David Mowry, Reuben
Russell. Signed by mark. Probated Feb 1863 Record Bk p 545.

(40) ISAAC TAYLOR, exec. 21 Dec 1862. Madisonville, Tenn. To
nephew Isaac Taylor; to Margaret Isabelle Taylor of the half blood,
land in Blount Co. being land owned by Berry Taylor at time of his
death adjoining lands of James Taylor, to be taken care of by Execs.
until sister shall marry or arrive at maturity; medical books to be
left with Dr. Joseph Upton. Exec: brother James Taylor. Wit:
J.I. Wright, Dr. Joseph Upton. Probated Feb 1863 Record Bk p 544.

(42) MARY A. McKENZIE, exec. 23 Jan 1861. To son Donald A., land
being one undivided seventh, but he is to pay $75 to William E.
Clarke, son of E.P. and Nancy Clarke, when he reaches twenty-one,
and $75 to Benjamin Casteel, son of B.J. and Elizabeth Casteel,
when he reaches twenty-one; to son John R.; to daughter Elizabeth
Casteel, and she may remain on farm with son D.A. McKenzie as they
are now living until she shall marry or removes. Exec: son D.A.
Wit: J.I. Wright, Isaac Taylor.

(43) JOSEPH BROWN, exec. 7 Mar 1863. To wife Matilda; $5 each to
daughters Sallie McSpadden and Harriet Stephens and to Mary
Elizabeth, child of daughter Margaret Jane Messimer, dec'd; $1 to
son John; $150 to daughter Elizabeth Hamilton; to daughter Lousanna
Brown; land to be sold and money divided between George Brown,
Nancy Wilson, Joseph N. Brown, Mary McSpadden's children, Louisana
Brown, Harvy Brown, and Matilda Brown. Execs. and Gdns. of Mary
McSpadden's children: George Brown, Franklin Magill. Wit: James
Forest, W.L. Rice. Codicil, same date.

(46) ZACHARIAH E. ROBERTS, exec. 21 Jun 1864. To daughter Nancy
Anderson; to two sons J.R. and William C. Exec: son-in-law A.J.
Anderson. Wit: Jason McMullin, John Erwin. Probated Oct 1864
Ledger P 6.

(47) ALFRED DENTON, exec. 20 Aug 1864. To wife; to all children
when youngest comes of age, except son John L. to have $5; sons
Charles and Jackson and daughter Malinda Burris have received money.
Exec: wife Dorcas. Wit: Jason McMullin, William Stapp. Signed
by mark. Probated Nov Ledger P 8. /no year given/

(48) C.N. HAWKINS, exec. 27 Apr 1863. To mother Susannah Hawkins and to brothers and sisters. Wit: M.M. Terry, A.L. Carson.

(49) WILLIAM PATTEN, exec. 6 Apr 1861. To four sons James Harvy, William Henry, Wily, and Thomas; to two daughters Elizabeth A. Porter and Margaret Jane Murry. Execs: sons James Harvy and Wily. Wit: B.C. Pettitt, Charles Cannon. Probated Nov 1864 Ledger p 7.

(50) MARGARET GRIGORY, exec. 9 Jun 1851. To sister Ann Grigory, interest in land as an heir of John Grigory; to brother Ephraim Grigory's four sons, William, John, Ephraim, and Altrotin Grigory; to John Grigory; to brother E.L. Grigory's two daughters Mary and Margaret Grigory. Exec: brother Ephraim. Wit: Robert Henderson, Danual White, A.J. Peace.

(51) JOHN WELDON, exec. 7 Jan 1864. J.L. Wilson to take charge of property and divide it among children and J.L. Wilson to be an equal heir. Wit: T.A. Henderson, B.P. Henderson. Probated May 8 1865 Ledger p 44.

(51) GEORGE C. HARRIS, exec. Dec 1864. To wife Sarah, land and all she possessed at our marriage; to the heir of daughter Rachel, that is, Amanda Wilson; to heirs of Jane Stephens; to daughter Lydia Harris; to heirs of Sarah Bayles; to heirs of B.J. Harris; to Elijah M. Harris; to Mary Lee and her heirs; to daughter Isabella; to Ez. C. Harris; to daughter Prisalla; to Rebeccah; to E.C. Harris, to pay debts that Ez. C. Harris paid for E.M. and E.C. Harris; to Zepperah Fry; any accounts I hold on my heirs or grand-children; to George W. Harris. Execs: Ez. C. and George W. Harris. Wit: Joseph E. Houston, McCamy McBride. Probated Aug 1865 Ledger p 73.

(54) THOMAS CLARK, exec. 6 Oct 1863. To wife Flora and two youngest sons Zachariah Taylor and Thomas Bendow; two sons Albert and James and two daughters Parthena Rogers and Buna Fryer; to sons William, Cornelius, and Greene; to daughters Amanda Elvira and Sarah Ann C.; to minor heirs of son Josiah formerly of Missouri; to grandson Josiah Fryer. Exec: A.C. Taylor. Wit: R.A. Ramsey, D.H. Dickey. Signed by daughter and acknowledged by me. Probated Aug 1865 Ledger P 74.

(56) JACOB B. WALL, exec. 10 Nov 1862. To wife Martha and daughter Mary Elender. Exec: Robert Russell. Wit: Telford Cannon, Joseph Johnston. Signed Jabac Wall.

(56) GEORGE BOWMAN, exec. 16 Aug 1865. Heretofore given to children Elizabeth Ault Browder Polly Tipton John P D Bowman Sarah Dole Hannah Ault James Bowman Fannie Richy and Susan Johnston /no punctuation/; to daughter Eliza Jane wife of John Blair; to wife Nancy B.; to daughter Susan wife of Louis Franklin Johnston. Execs: son James and son-in-law John D. Blair. Wit: John Dawson, J.C. Wyly.

(59) N.C. HIGDON, exec. 3 Feb 1866. "Brother Thomas if I should never get back"; Lida to have dower and at her death to brother Thomas; to Tomma. Probated Apr 1866 Ledger p 172.

(59) CALEB ROBINSON, not dated. Being wounded; mother Margaret Robinson to take my only child and raise it; money due from Capt.

Fred Falkerson and from John Russell; authorize Lieut. William
Whitlock, Co. A. 5 Tennessee Vol. Infty. to sign my name. Wit:
William Whitlock. Probated Sep 1865 Ledger p 89.

(60) MICHIAL FENDER, exec. 27 Mar 1858. To wife Winny; to lawful
heirs; to grandson John M. Stamper. Execs: friends John Ramsey
and Charles Owen. Wit: John Webb, P.T. Butler. Probated Jun
1866 Ledger P 199.

(62) CARTER HUGGINS, exec. 13 Dec 1851. Of Roane Co., Tenn.; to
wife Rachel; to granddaughter Martha Jane Forshea and son Eli
Huggins to keep her until she is grown or married; to granddaughter
Nancy Ann Forshea and son Derius Huggins to keep her; to grand-
daughter Martha Huggins, daughter of William Huggins; to son Ransom
Huggins and Virginia; to daughters Dicy Clarke and Lousia Grubb;
to sons James, William, Eli, Mathew, Derius, Edward. Exec: son
Edward. Wit: J.D. Jones, A. Allen. Probated Aug 1866 Ledger
P 218.

(64) KIZIAH TAYLOR, exec. 19 May 1866. To son David D. Taylor,
two shares in farm of which husband Leroy Taylor died possessed,
viz, the share bought by me from Barsheba Orr and her husband
James W. Orr being the one undivided sixth and the fifth of one
undivided eighth of said farm, also share bought by me from son
Isaac; to son Leroy Taylor, the share of son Garret R. Taylor
bought by me; so that said two sons will be sole owners of said
farm; son James; the children. Execs: sons David D. and Leroy.
Wit: James A. Coffin, E.L. Axley. Signed by mark. Probated Aug
1866 Ledger p 218 and 222.

(66) ELISHA JOHNSON, exec. 20 May 1864. Of Tellico Plains, Monroe
Co. To Mortimer F. Johnson; to daughter Julia M. Young of New York,
two lots of land in Buffalo; $50 each to William A. Young and
Emily Grant; to Mary A. Mumford, a widowed daughter now residing
with me; son M.F. to be paid annually 1/3 of funds, if he makes
no claims; daughter Mary A. Mumford to be Adminx. and Agent of
will. Wit: Lydia Bridges, Athens, Tenn., Mary Witt, Athens,
Tenn. Codicil, 4 Jun 1866. Joseph Johnston, merchant of Madisonville, to be a trustee to represent the interest of M.F. Johnson.
Wit: J.D. Abbot, T.R. Gibson. Codicil, 20 Jan 1866. In case of
death of Mary A. Mumford, Elisha J. Mumford is to be Adm. and son
M.F. if living is to be paid ½ instead of 1/3, on same conditions;
to Clancy Grant for his kind services; son M.F. has been kind and
dutiful altho for his particular habits has been a tax; to M.F.'s
heirs, if not amply provided for. Wit: T.F. Gibson, J.D. Abbot.
Probated Aug 1866 Ledger p 217.

(69) WILLIAM BOWERS, exec. 25 Aug 1865. To wife S. Elizabeth and
daughter Elizabeth and granddaughter Martha Samples, while they
live with wife; to daughter-in-law Jane Bowers during her widowhood;
to sons Alexander and James; to legal heirs. Exec: E.E. Griffith.
Wit: Thomas H.S. Smith, T.H. Richards. Probated Oct 1866 Ledger
p 252.

(70) ARCHIBALD SLOAN, exec. 27 Jan 1858. To wife Susan; to three
sons Madison J.C., George W., and William H.; their three sisters,
Sallie Peeler, Elizabeth Smalling, and Susan Sloan, my three
daughters now living; two oldest daughters, Polly Ann Mason and

Matilda Clift, both dec'd; three sons to pay their children, my
grandchildren, Sloan Mason, Polly Ann Clift, Monroe Clift. Execs:
sons Madison and George Sloan and Archibald Mason. Wit: John M.
Best, Jason McMullen. Probated May 1866 Ledger 503.

(74) JOSEPH MILLIGAN, exec. 19 Feb 1867. To daughter Arebella
Milligan and at her death to granddaughter Hannah Harrison and
grandsons Joseph and Francis Milligan. Execs: John H. and Thomas
A. Harrison. Wit: A. Howard, J.R. Latimore. Probated Jul 1868
Ledger p 536.

(75) SUSAN E. HENLEY, 25 Apr 1868. Noncupative Will. Guilford
Cannon "was requested to call at bedside of Mrs. Henley as she
requested to see me personally, Mr. Allen Broom and daughter Jenny
leaving the room"; to a sister in Indianapolis by name of McRoundals;
to Jenney Broom; to A.C. Broom. Probated Jul 1868 Ledger p 541.

(76) THOMAS CROWDER, exec. 15 Apr 1864. To children, James A.,
Atlas O.S., Stephens M., Uriah A., and Robert P. Crowder, Margaret
P. wife of Joseph B. Williams, and Bartley F. Crowder who is now
absent; to wife Mary A.G.; to grandson Robert P. Crowder, Jr., son
of Bartley F. Crowder, but bequest to be void if son Bartley F. is
yet living and returns to his County. Execs: sons James A. and
Robert P. Wit: E.E. Griffiths, J.S. Wooldrige. Probated Sep 1868
Ledger p 562.

(78) JOHN CARY, exec. 17 May 1868. To wife Elenor; to daughter
Nancy Ann Cary. Wit: Phillip Keller, N.J. Raper. Signed by mark.

(79) A.J. HUMPHREYS, 23 Dec 1868. Noncupative Will, made during
last sickness on 13 Dec 1868 in house of William Rogers at Belltown, Monroe Co., where he was surprised of sickness from home on
12 Dec 1868; witnessed by Thomas Harrison and Ben P. Reagan; to
sister Margaret and brother Joshua Jobe Humphrey. Exec: Thomas
A. Harrison. Probated Jan 1869 Record Bk p 5.

(80) THOMAS J. BALLARD, exec. 9 Jun 1869. To wife Mary; land wife
inherited from her father; to sister Sarah E. Ballard. Execs:
wife and James P. Galyon of Roane Co. Wit: W.P. and R.H. Jones.
Probated Aug 1869 Record B p 108.

(82) SQUIRE S. GLENN, exec. 7 Apr 1863. To wife Dorothy; to
children of daughter Martha Ann Donohoo, to wit, Dolly M., Nancy
M., Martha, Mary L., Francis, Squire T., Sarah, and Glenannah
Donohoo; to Dolly E. and Squire T. Glen, children of son G.T.
Glen, dec'd; Mary A. Glenn, widow of son George T., and her two
children to remain on farm. Execs: William B. Milligan, Jason
McMullen, John G_____, Michial Harrison, and wife Dorothy A.
Wit: Will written by W.B. Milligan by request. Codicil, 11 Mar
1867. To granddaughter N.M. Denton and her children if she has
any, three acres including house her husband O. Denton has just
built. Probated Jan 1871 Record Bk P 381.

(89) ROBERT SLOAN, exec. 5 Oct 1870. To wife Elizabeth; to four
sons now living, James, John, Bartley, and Isaac; to four daugh-
ters, Sarah Mason, Martha Best, Lucinda McSpadden, Mary Jane
Sloan; to son William's two children, Sarah Selena and Mary Jane
Sloan. Execs: sons James and John. Wit: M.J.C. Sloan, Henry
McSpadden. Probated Jan 1871 Record B P 374.

(92) EDWARD LEA, exec. 2 Jan 1871. To wife and family. Probated Feb 1871 Record B p 406.

(93) JOHN SUTTON, SR., exec. 12 Feb 1870. To wife; to two daughters Delilah Tallent and Elizabeth Sutton; equal division among heirs, William, Guilford, John Jr., Abraham, and O.P. Sutton, Anna Moses, Sinthey /sic/ Tallent. Exec: son William. Wit: P. Isbill, Joseph Huff. Signed by mark. Probated Feb 1871 Record B P 406.

(95) JACOB F. PECK, exec. Sep 1870. To lawful heirs equally to wit Mary A. Wilson, Mrs. S. Curd widow of Richard Curd, dec'd, Eliza E. wife of P.C. Edington, Virginia wife of Martin Williams, Nancy L. wife of Thomas Lesley, Margaret A. wife of Thomas Hightower, J.M., Joseph A., and William T. Peck; estate due me in Virginia. Execs: J.A. and William T. Peck. Wit: J.H. Patton, J.H. Kelso.

(97) JAMES A. COFFIN, exec. 11 Sep 1871. To six surviving children, all females, namely, Susan E., Sarah M., Margaret M., Nancy J., Mary Ella, and Julia A. Trustees of estate and Execs: daughter Susan E. Coffin, son-in-law John H. Inman, and brother Cornelius W. Coffin. Wit: R.J. McKinny, Samuel McKinny, W.N. Bicknell, J.W. Goddard. Probated Dec 1871 Record B P 563.

(100) ALEXANDER RIDER, exec. 13 Aug 1871. To wife Martha; five daughters Nancy Ann Hunt, Elizabeth, Mary, Martha, and Salina Rider; four sons at home and around me viz, S., Alexander, Robert, and Auston Rider; two sons and one daughter in the West viz, James and William Rider and Sarah E. Peck. Wit: Robert R. Winn, S.E. McCallum. Probated Feb 1872 Record B p 602.

(102) THOMAS BROWN, exec. 9 May 1861. To wife and children; already advanced to son Ignatius Cyprian. Execs: wife Jane McDonald Brown and sons Ignatius Cyprian and William Lunidas Brown. Wit: A.W. Cozart, Solomon Bogart. Probated May 1872 Rec p 20.

(105) JOHN RAMSEY, exec. 27 Apr 1872. To wife Susannah; to son John Eagleton Ramsey and daughter Martha Susannah Ramsey; to children of dec'd daughter Mary Jane Rowan; to little granddaughters Martha Ellen Ramsey and Susannah Elizabeth Rowan; my mother's part of my estate. Execs: wife and son and daughter. Wit: Charles Cannon, M.H. Biggs, N.P. Hight. Probated May 1872 Record p 19.

(107) GEORGE G. STILLMAN, exec. 22 Mar 1872. Of Sweetwater, Monroe Co.; to wife Julia H.; to daughter Ella, home with wife as long as she remains single; to Ella and son George at death of wife. Execs: wife and N.P. Hight. Wit: W.C. Clarke, N.T. Mays, J.W. Goddard. Probated Aug 1872 Record Bk P 56.

In this book, there are several pages missing and the last part
has been badly cut and torn.

In the abstracts below, the name of the deceased is given in
capital letters.

(15) (Index page) "Madisonville, Tenn. April 22/64 /sic7 know ye
in these presence that Joseph T. Linxwilder is appointed by this
assembly to serve as one of the deligates in the Convention of the
State of Tennessee to be held at knoxville knox County East Tenn.
on the Forth day of July in the year of our Lord one thous-eight
hundred and sixty one /sic7 . John Nicholson, Cleark of the
Convention."

(27,29,53,66) JACOB BAKER; 1 Jan 1853, Invt. and sale at his late
residence on Island Creek by I.N. Baker, Adm.

(31,281) STEPHEN PARSHLEY; 7 Feb 1853, Invt. and sale by John
Stanfield.

(31,95) JAMES SMITH; Invt. of sale held 6 Dec 1852 by William M.
Stakely and James A. Coffin, Execs.; J.A. Stephens Clk. by A.T.
Hicks, D. Clk.

(34) REUBEN WILHITE; 14 Jan 1853, Sale held 14 Feb 1852 by C.L.
Walker, Adm.; Jane Wilhite is a buyer.

(37,115) JOHN ROGERS; 28 Dec 1852, Invt. by John Key, Adm.; buyers
include David, J.C., and A. Rogers; 6 Jul 1854, Invt. by William
L. Eakin, Adm.

(41) JOSEPH McREYNOLDS; no date, Invt. of sale.

(43) DANIEL EVERETT; no date, Invt. of sale by W.B. Cowan and J.C.
McTeer, Adms.; buyers include Eppy and Signer Everett and Eppy
Everett Sr.

(44,46,103) SAMUEL DOUTHET; 7 Apr 1853, Invt., Sale, and Add. invt.

(46) JESSEE FORSHEE; 4 Apr 1853, Sale by David Lowry, Exec.

(55,179,189) JOHN HOLSTON; Sale held 18 and 19 Feb 1853, Add. invt.

(60) ANDREW VAUGHT, SR.; Sale held 26 Mar 1853 by John Vaught,
Adm.; buyers include Caroline, Rebecca, John, and Sarah Vaught.

(63) JOEL CASH; Invt. and sale held 11 Jun 1850 by J.J. Tipton, Adm.

(65,203,290) WILLIAM WALLACE (WALLIS), SR.; Sale held 25 Aug 1853
by William Wallace, Jr.; Sale and invt. by Thomas Wallis, Adm.; 12
Sep 1857, Add. invt. made by Thomas Wallis, Adm. with Will annexed,
after death of Tempy Wallis.

(73) FEREBY B. MALONE; 1 Aug 1853, Invt. of sale by John Cook.

(74) WILLIAM C. HUMPHREYS; 15 Sep 1853, Invt. and sale held 7 Sep
1853 by Solon McCroskey, Adm.

(75,80,154) ALLEN D. GENTRY; Oct 1853, Invt. and Sale, and Add.
sale by G.T. Glenn, Adm.; 4 Dec 1854. Notes coming into hands
from George T. Glenn, dec'd, by B.C. Pettitt, Adm. de bonis non.

(80) MARY VINCENT; 12 Sep 1853, Invt. by James Knox, Adm.

(80,103) ISAAC HAGLER; 19 Oct 1852, "valued to me by William Denton and Armstrong Morrow", not signed; 5 Jun 1854, Invt. by B.B. Hagler, Exec.

(83,170) JOHN M. ISBELL; 19 Nov 1853, Sale by William Isbell, Adm.; Amended Invt. Apr 1855.

(84) JOEL H. STRUTTON; Invt. by John Strutten, Adm. and sale held at residence of Wesley Davis 7 Sep 1853; buyers include J.W. and Elizabeth Strutten.

(87) ISAAC WEAVER; 14 Jan 1854, Invt. and sale.

(93) DAVID SMITH; no date, List of notes by Nat Watson, Adm.

(93) CHARLES KELSO; Invt. of property not devised in the Will, and sale held 23 Feb 1854 by James W. Kelso and F.T. Wadkins, Adms. with Will annexed.

(97) JOSEPH MERCER; no date, Invt. and sale by George Brown, Adm.

(98) DANIEL H. JONES; Invt., notes and accounts, and sale held 25 Feb 1854 by Hugh E. Martin, Exec.

(104) JAMES MITCHELL; no date, sale by Elihu Beals, Adm.

(105,114) GARLAND SMITH; sale held 19 and 20 May 1854 and list of notes, by Robert Carter, Adm.

(108,125) JOHN R. WILLIAMS; 5 Jun 1854, Sale and amended invt. by J.B. Williams, Adm.

(112,237) JOHN KEY; 5 Jun 1854, Sale by William Dyer, Adm.; 11 Feb 1856, invt. of sale.

(113) MARGARET S. WEAR; 27 May 1854, Sale by Joseph Wear, Exec.

(115) JAMES VINCENT; no date, Invt. by William H. Clemmer, Adm.

(116,164) MADISON CLIBOURNE; 2 Oct 1854, Sale and add. invt. by James Clibourne, Adm.

(118) WILLIAM JOHNSTON; 2 Oct 1854, Sale held after the death of the widow, by Henry Chesnutt and John Pennington, Execs.

(119) RICHARD STEPHENS; no date, Sale.

(123) JAMES P. MINIS; no date, Sale by Joseph Upton, Adm.

(126,249) WILLIAM GLASS; 6 Nov 1854, Notes and invt. and sale by Jefferson C. Glass, Adm.; buyers include Martha, M.A., James, and Anderson P. Glass.

(128) JOSEPH McREYNOLDS; no date, Notes.

(133,140,180) JAMES CHESNUTT; 4 Dec 1854, Notes and book accounts, money collected and stock sold, and add. list of accounts, by F.H. Gregory and Hugh Chesnutt; in the book accounts are those of N.E.O. Martin, Robert Cannon, Henry Chesnutt, all marked "deceased".

(142,143,168) JONATHAN PICKLE; 4 Dec 1854, Invt., sale, and add. invt., by James H. Pickle, Adm.

(145,147) BIDDY WALLIS; 4 Dec 1854, Invt. and sale by Sterling A. Wallis, Adm.

(149) WILLIAM GAY; Invt. and sale held 19 Oct 1854 by William M. Lowry, Adm.

(157,240) WILLIAM GADD; no date, Sales.

(161) H.H. CLEVELAND; 13 Oct 1854, Invt. by John Pennington, Adm.

(162) ABEL R. CHEYNE; Invt. and sale by Esther Cheyne, Adminx.

(163) DAVID STARRETT; 16 Dec 1854, Invt. and sale.

(165,166) WILLIAM WATSON; Invt. taken 10 Oct 1851 and Sale, by Josiah and Thomas McGuire, Adms.

(168) JOHN MOWRY; 5 Feb 1855, Invt.

(168) MARGARET ANN DEWITT; 19 Mar 1855, Invt. by William C. Dewitt, Adm.

(169) ALLEN WEST; Sale held 15 Dec 1854 by Mary A. West, Adminx.; buyers include Franklin West.

(171,282) JESSE BUTLER; no date, Sale and list of notes, and add. sale.

(177) JAMES BROWN; Sale held 27 Jan 1855 by Samuel T. and John N. Brown, Adms.

(189) WILEY JONES; 1855, Invt. by Readick Jones, Adm.

(190,191,245) JOHN CALDWELL; Invt. taken 2 Jul 1855, sale, and add. invt., by John E. Caldwell and James H. Johnston, Execs.

(198,206) WESLEY DAVIS; Sale held 16 Aug 1855 and add. invt., by William Stapp, Adm.

(199) THOMAS TALLENT; 27 Aug 1855, Sale by Elisha Tallent and Joseph Divine, Adms.; buyers include James, Mary Jane, Samuel, and William Tallent.

(201) P.H. WALKER; 5 Sep 1855, Sale by Elijah Cate, Adm.; buyers include Hiram Q. and Mary A. Walker.

(201) HENRY ELLIS; 1 Sep 1855, Sett. by Benedict Ellis, Adm.; nothing left after payment of widow's dower.

(202) ARTHUR H. HENLEY; no date, money received by David Henley, one of Execs., since 29 Mar 1854.

(206) ROBERT HUTCHESON; Sale held 10 Nov 1855 by E. Kimbrough, Adm.

(207) PATRICK ERVIN; 8 Jun 1855, Invt. and sale.

(207) ROBERT EVANS; no date, Invt.

(208) LEWIS CARTER; 7 Jan 1856, Invt. by ____ ____ Carter and A.H. Henley, Adms.; Sale held 26 Jan 1856; in list of notes due is "Jabe Carter- dead long since" and "Henderson Trim-Dead".

(211) SAMUEL W. MAGILL; "Mouse Creek, McMinn Co.," 19 Jan 1856, Invt. of sale by J.H. Magill and J.H. Shedden, Execs.

(213) JOHN HENDERSON; 5 Mar 1856, Sale by James H. Johnson, Adm.; buyers include Alexander, James, Nancy, and Samuel Henderson.

(214,298) DAVID F. SHELTON; Sale held on 14 Dec 1855 by Joab H. Terry and Mary Shelton, Adms.; 28 Dec 1857, Invt. received from former Adms. by Thomas Stephens, Adm.

(238) SAMUEL W. CARMICHAEL; 7 Mar 1856, Invt. received from George

W. Carmichael, Gdn. of Samuel W. Carmichael by F.P. Wadkins.

(238,290,301) ROBERT W. HICKS; Invt. and sale held 23 Feb 1856 by E.E. Griffith, Adm.; Isaac Hicks is a buyer; 8 Jan 1858, Invt. received from E.E. Griffith former Adm. by Washington Cannon, Adm.

(239) WILLIAM COLLAQUE; 18 Apr 1856, Invt. by Sampson Halcomb.

(240) SUSANNAH MESSIMER; 29 Apr 1856, Invt. and sale by W.B. and H.M. Messimer, Adms.

(245) ADALINE HUMPHRYS; 10 May 1856, Invt. by I.W. Beard, Exec.

(245) JOHN ROBINSON; Sale held 8 Aug 1856 by James E. Cole, buyers include Sally, Phil, Abbot, James, and Isaac Robinson.

(247,256) SARAH SUMMETT; 8 Sep 1856, Invt. and sale, and Add. sale by Eusabius Summett, Adm.; buyers include Francis, Eusabius, Peter, and Joseph Summett.

(250) ROBERT R. YOUNG; 6 Oct 1856, Notes and accts. by J.A. and T.J. Young, Execs.

(254) SUSAN GENTRY; 23 Aug 1856, Sale by B.L. White, Adm.; buyers include P.W., Polly, and Nancy Gentry.

(256) ISAAC HICKS; 30 Oct 1856, Sale by James A. Sharp, Adm.

(257,281) N.T. HUMPHREYS; 17 Nov 1856, Sale and add. sale by S.M. Henderson, Adm.

(258) ISAAC C. MARSHALL; no date, Sale by William H. Bowers, Adm.; given to widow Rebecca; buyers include William B., Orvill, Joseph E., R.G., and William N. Marshall.

(258) WILLIAM A. SHADDEN; 1 Dec 1856, Sale by John R. Gaines, Adm.

(263) SARAH BAYLESS; no date, Invt. and sale.

(264) ELISHA HICKS; 5 Jan 1857, Invt. by Richard Hicks, Adm., sold to Tabitha Hicks.

(264) JAMES TAYLOR; no date, Supp. invt. by John Stanfield.

(264) JOHN WOLF; Invt. sold 24 Oct 1856 in accord with his Will, by William M. Stakely and Robert Russell, Execs.

(269) F.A.PATTON; Supp. invt. by John Ramsey, Exec., 2 Mar 1857.

(269) WILLIAM GRAY; no date, Sale by Francis Gray, Execx.

(270) DAVID KELSOE; 2 Mar 1857, Sale by C.T.P. Davis, Adm.

(272) WILLIAM DENTON; Sale held 4 Dec 1856.

(277) N.G. BARKSDALE; Sale held 1 Nov 1856 by B.F. Barksdale, Adm.

(279,318) HUGH E. MARTIN; 6 Apr 1857, Invt. and Supp. invt. by John Ramsey, Exec.

(282,306) HENRY CLICK; 11 May 1857, Sale by C.R. Hartsell, Exec.; 26 Feb 1858, List of grain sold and account against Lewis A. Click for rent of farm in Cocke Co. for 1855-56.

(284) J.T. ROWLAND; 1 June 1857, Invt. by Louisa J. Rowland and M.F. Keith.

(286,304) MARY M. BLACKSTONE; no date, Sale by Archibald Bacomb, Exec.; 1 Mar 1858, Sale held 12 Dec 1857 of house and lot in Philadelphia, Monroe Co.

(287) JOSEPH B. GILBREATH; 4 Aug 1857, Sale by B.L. White, Adm.; buyers include Mrs. Gilbreath, John and William C. Gilbreath.

(291) THOMAS DIVINE; Sale held 20 Sep 1856 by J. Divine, Adm.

(292) ALEXANDER HART: 25 Oct 1857, Sale by W.T. Hart, Adm.

(296) JOHN FINE; Sale held 19 Nov 1857 by Peter L. Fine.

(297) POLLY FINE; 5 Dec 1857, Sale by Peter L. Fine, Adm.; buyers include Nancy and Martha L. Fine.

(302) OVERSTREET CROWDER; Jan 1858, Invt. and sale by B.P. Reagan, Adm.

(303) MARY FORSHEE; Sale held 16 Jan 1858 by Peter Moser, Adm.

(304) MARCELLUS C. WOOLDRIDGE; 1 Mar 1858, Sale by C.B. Taylor, Adm.

(307) MILLY SIMMS; 1 May 1858, Sale by Joseph Upton, Adm.; Elijah Simms, Mary and Elizabeth Gentry are the only buyers.

(308) VALENTINE THACKER; 5 Jul 1858, Invt. by James L. Thacker, Adm.

(312,320) JAMES HALL; Sale held 10 Jun 1858 and 1 Nov 1858 by Samuel P. Hall, Adm.

(316) OSCAR E. DOUGLASS; 28 Jul 1858, Sale and invt. by Jane C. Douglass, Adminx.

(317) GEORGE BREEDWELL; 4 Oct 1858, Sale by Robert Russell, Exec.

(318) There is much scribbling on the pages of this Record Book, apparently done by Civil War soldiers. On this page there is the following: "Madisonville, Tennessee. Absalom B. Hudson James Hudson Co E C 5 Regt Ind volr In Care of Capt Baker".

(319) JOHN DAUGHERTY; 16 Oct 1858, Sale and invt. by A. Daugherty, Exec.

(321) PLEASANT KITTRELL; 21 Oct 1858. Invt. by W.P. Kittrell, Adm.

(321,325) JOSEPH CUNNINGHAM; 8 Jan 1859, Sale and list of notes.

(326) ADAM BARR; 3 Jan 1859, Sale.

(328,333) JONATHAN TIPTON; no date, Invt. not complete, and Sale continued.

(333) MRS. ELIZABETH YOUNG; Sale held 16 Oct 1858.

(335 to end of book) Pages torn and cut; names on the scraps are Robert McReynolds, dec'd, Adm. of Sarah Hart, dec'd.

The name of the deceased person is given in capital letters.

(0,17) JOHN SIMPSON; 7 Oct 1864, Invt. of notes by Eli C. Johnston, Adm.; 12 June 1865, Add. invt.

(18) ALFRED DENTON; Invt. 1 Dec 1864.

(19) WILLIAM SHAFFER; Invt. and sale held 22 Dec 1864 by Daniel T. Shaffer.

(22) WILLIAM C. MOORLOCK; Invt. 2 Jan 1865 by Jourdin Carden, Adm.

(26) ABIJAH FOWLER, JR.; Invt. taken 17 Dec 1864 and sale by Samuel Edington, Adm.

(28,151) JAMES H. JOHNSTON; 3 Apr 1865, Invt. by John H. Johnston and Henry Kile, Adms.; exempt articles in hands of widow Elizabeth for use of herself and C.W. Johnston; Sale held 19 Jan 1865; buyers include John H., James H., Sam M., Mrs. Elizabeth, Miss Caroline, and Miss Sallie Johnston; 6 May 1867, Invt. and sale.

(42,142) THOMAS McCAULEY; Invt. taken 29 Jul 1865 by J.J. Swanner, Adm.; Sale.

(43) PRESLEY CLEVELAND; Sep 1865, Invt. and sale held 30 Aug 1861 by William E. Johnston and S.J. Martin, Execs.

(52) RACHAEL HUTCHESIN; 8 Sep 1865, Invt. and sale by D.W. Latimer, Adm.; buyers include W.J., Samuel, and Savan Hutchesin.

(55,161) GEORGE C. HARRIS; 4 Sep 1865, Invt. and sale by Ez. C. and George W. Harris, Execs.

(65) PETER MOSER; 4 Sep 1865, Invt. by Eusebius Summit, Adm.

(66) RUTH HALL; Invt. and sale held 12 Oct 1865 by James C. Hall, Adm.

(69) J.B. WALL; Sale held 21 Oct 1865 by Robert Russell, Exec.

(71) J.K. JOHNSTON; Invt. sold 30 Sep 1865 by D.A. Browder, Adm.

(76) THOMAS CLARK; 23 Oct 1865, Invt. by W.G. Clark, Adm.

(77) ZACHARIAH ROBERTS; Invt. sold 3 Dec 1864 by A.J. Anderson, Adm.

(79) A. FORREST and SAMUEL J. EDWARDS, trading under the name of Forrest & Edwards at Mouse Creek Depot, McMinn Co.; no date, Notes and accounts due, signed by William M. Edwards; notes due 1860-62 include "Allen Dotson Dec'd" and "C.M. Presswood Dec'd."

(86,99,217) JOSEPH DIVINE; 1 Jan 1866, Invt., Sale, and Sale of leather received of Joseph E. Houston, by William Burris, Adm.

(87) CHARLES McDONALD; Sale held 23 Dec 1865 by B.J. Harrell, Adm.

(88) PATRICK T. TROTTER; Invt. taken 15 Dec 1865 by Edwin Hall, Adm.; Sale.

(91) JOSEPH HENDERSON; Invt. of sale 4 Oct 1865 by John H. Johnston, Adm.

(93) MARGARET D. SHAFFER; Invt. and sale held 20 Dec 1865 by Jacob M. Shaffer.

(98,229) JAMES C. EDWARDS; Invt. taken 2 Dec 1865 by S.J. Martin, Adm.

(101) E.G. MAYO; no date, Sale.

(102) ROBERT EAKIN; 7 May 1866, Invt. by James M. Eakin, Adm.; statement by John R. Leonard and Larkin Webb, Adms., that foregoing can be collected out of estate of James M. Eakin.

(104,201) THOMAS ARP; 2 Apr 1866, Supp. invt. and sale by Alfred C. Arp; Invt. sold 18 Apr 1868 by Joseph B. Humphreys, Gdn. to minor heirs.

(105) ROBERT D. RAGAN; 12 Apr 1866, Invt. by S.J. Martin, Adm.

(106) WILLIAM DUNCAN; 8 Feb 1866, Invt. by John E. Duncan, Adm.

(107,138) WILSON WEATHERS; 19 Mar 1866, Invt. and sale by J.L. Weathers, Adm.

(109) SAMUEL W. WHITE; 9 Apr 1866, Invt. by Jacob Sheets, Adm.

(109) WILLIAM HALL; 5 Feb 1866, Invt. by Edwin Hall, Adm.

(110) GEORGE BOWMAN; no date, Invt. and sale.

(112) JOHN ROY; Sale held 23 May 1866, and invt. of notes, by Joseph Sands and Joseph A. Roy, Adms.

(121) FRANCIS MOSER; Sale held 19 Dec 1865 by J.H. Worthy, Adm.

(124) J.C. BOYD; Sep 1865, Invt. of accts. due, by Thomas G. Boyd, Adm.

(144) PHILIP STEPHENS; 26 Aug 1865, Invt. of notes by Thomas Stephens, Adm.

(146) JAMES DODSON JOHNSON; 5 Mar 1866, List of accts. by James R. Robinson, Adm.

(162) LARKIN CARDIN; 7 Jan 1867, Invt. by Jordan, James, and Leonard Cardin.

(171) THOMAS CROWDER; 22 Sep 1868, Sale by Robert P. Crowder, Exec.

(177,214) JUDIATH M. KIMBROUGH; Sale 19 Jan 1867 by Josiah Wright, Adm.

(179) WILLIAM HUNT, SR.; no date, Invt. by G.W. Williams, Adm.; notes dating back to 1826; Sale 23 Dec 1868.

(194) LEWIS BLANKINSHIP; 7 Sep 1868, Sale by J.H. Worthy, Adm.

(197) CARTER HUDGINS; 24 Aug 1868, Invt. by Edward Hudgings, Exec.

(199) W.W. STEPHENS; 7 Dec 1868, Sale by William M. Smith, Adm.; allowance to widow.

(200) Mrs. Jane Cook, a lunatic /not deceased7; widow of late Jacob Cook, dec'd; 25 Jul 1868, Invt. by L.M. Blackman, Gdn.

(203) FRED DEAN; 7 Dec 1868, Invt. by J.H. Kelso, Adm.

(205,220,238) JAMES GHORMLEY; Sales held 28 May 1867, 5 Sep 1868, and 8 Mar 1869 by Jason McMullen and T.A. Henderson, Adms.

(206) G.C. MONTGOMERY; 12 Aug 1868, Report by J.C. Montgomery, Adm.

(206) JOHN BRYANT; 17 Feb 1869, Report by M.F. Johnson, Adm.

(207) GEORGE PATTERSON; Sale held 25 Jan 1867 by G.W. Patterson, Adm.

(208,235) MICHAEL FENDER; 1 Mar 1869, Invt. after death of his widow Winney Fender on 19 Dec 1868 by John Ramsey, Exec; 5 Nov 1866, Return by John Ramsey and Charles Owens, Execs.

(211) MARY (POLLY) HUMPHREYS; Sale held 22 Dec 1866 by C.W. Hicks, Adm.; former Adm. was A. Humphreys.

(230) JAMES MASON; 2 Sep 1867, Invt. and sale by Arch Mason, Adm.

(239) THOMAS J. BALLARD; 6 Sep 1869, Invt. by Mary Ballard, Exec.

(242) J.W. KELSO; 25 Oct 1869, Invt. by William J. Fowler, Adm. with Will annexed.

(245) JAMES GASTON; 1 Nov 1869, Sale by J.V. Gaston, Adm.

(246) LODUSKY WALKER; no date, Invt. 4 Oct 1875 by N.P. Hight, Exec.

INVENTORY 1868-1877

The inventory reports from 1871 to 1877 are outside the scope of this book, and are not included.

The name of the deceased person is given in capital letters.

(2) A.L. WILSON; 6 Jul 1868, Sale by W.W. Porter; B.C. Pettit, Clk.; interesting and detailed list of books sold and the purchasers.

(7) SAMUEL HENDERSON; 28 May 1867, Sale by G.L. Henderson, Exec.

(11) JACOB GIVENS; 18 Jun 1867, Invt. by Sarah Ann Givens, Admix.

(12) THOMAS J. ALLEN; Invt. and sale held 26 Oct 1866 by A. Hawkins, Adm.

(17) REPS JONES; 28 Dec 1866, Invt. and sale by Daniel Jones, Adm.; sales made by widow before letters of Administration; buyers include Reps, C.H. and Mrs. Delila Jones.

(22) LARKIN CARDIN; 7 Jun 1867, Sale.

(29) JOSEPH C. BOYD; Notes and sale held 28 Nov 1865.

(30) A.S. MASON; 2 Sep 1867, Invt. by Arch Mason, Adm.

(30) WILLIAM C. MORELOCK; 9 Jan 1866, Invt.

(32) JOSEPH F. ALLISON; 2 May 1868, Invt. by C.W. Hicks, Adm.; property not exempt for the widow.

(33) G.C. MONTGOMERY; Invt. and sale held 24 Aug 1866 by J.C. Montgomery, Adm.

(35,49) BENJAMIN JOHNSON; 1 Apr 1867, Invt. by John Grant, Adm.; 13 May 1867, Sale; the only buyers are Perry and W.R. Johnson, William and Minerva Williams, and Eveline Grant.

(36) GEORGE PATTERSON; 6 Jan 1868, Invt. and sale by G.W. Patterson, Adm.

(38) JOHN McCROSKY; no date, Invt. and notes due; Claims against U.S. Government.

(41) JOHN SCRUGGS; 3 Feb 1868, Invt. and sale by James Scruggs, Adm; buyers include T.N., James, M.L., Emmet, and R.F. Scruggs.

(48,124) GEORGE C. HARRIS; Sale for 1866 and 1867; 3 May 1869, Invt. of rents.

(50) A.L. CARSON; 30 Apr 1869, Sale and notes by Lucretia P. Carson, Adminx.

(52) JOSEPH CUNNINGHAM; Oct 1867, Invt. delivered to Robert Cunningham, Adm., by Joseph D. Jones, Adm. of Joseph Walker, dec'd.

(54) WILLIAM CARTER; 2 Mar 1867, Invt. and sale by W.N. Purdy and Randolph Carter, Gdns. of William Carter.

(55) SUSAN J.E. HENLY; 8 Jul 1868, Invt. by Guilford Cannon, Adm.

(56) JOHN REDMAN; 2 Apr 1866, Invt. by Isaac Lindsey, Adm.

(57) JAMES CURTIS; Invt. and sale held 13 Feb 1868 by S.C. Curtis.

(60) R.R. CLEVELAND; 4 Jul 1868, Invt. by Frank K. Berry, Adm. and Sidney G. Cleveland, Adminx.; receipt from Sidney G. Cleveland and Caroline Cleveland Berry, the only heirs.

(77) ELISHA JOHNSON; 3 Sep 1866, Invt. of assets and liabilities by Mrs. Mary A. Mumford, Adminx. with Will annexed; 3 Jun 1867, E.J. Mumford, Exec.

(86) SAMUEL W. WHITE; 11 Feb 1867, Invt. and sale by Jacob Sheets, Adm.; amount in hands of Floyd S. White, former Adm.

(87) WILSON WEATHERS; 19 Dec 1866, Supp. invt. by James L. Weathers, Adm.

(88) MARGARET D. SHAFFER; Sale held 20 Dec 1865.

(92) N.C. HIGDON; Sale 7 Dec 1866 by Thomas A. Higdon, Adm; allowed the widow.

(94,179) ISAAC COLE; 25 Jan 1868, Invt. and sale by John R. Cole, Adm.; 8 Apr 1870, Invt. by W.P. Cole, Gdn. to Mary M. and Rebecca E. Cole, minor heirs.

(96,147,181) GREGORY F. HAWKINS; 7 Feb 1868, Invt. and sales by J.R. Burchfield, Adm.; 9 Mar 1869, Invt. of rents by Edwin Hall, Gdn. to minor heirs.

(100) KEZIAH TAYLOR; 3 Sep 1866, Invt. and sale by Leroy Taylor, Exec.

(103) ALFRED UPTON, Col.; Sale 16 Nov 1867 by Joseph Upton, Adm.

(104,207) JACOB COOK; 2 Dec 1867, Invt. and sale by Hugh K. Lowry, Adm.; buyers include James, S.B., Margaret, A.M., and Hetty Cook; Supp. invt.

(110,156) A.B. CLIFT; Invt. 11 Mar 1867 by John L. Cline, Adm. with Will annexed; 14 Dec 1869, Invt. of sale of farm products by Thomas Ross, Gdn. to minor heirs.

(112) JESSE BOONE; 26 Jan 1867, Sale by C.T.P. Davis by order of County Court of Monroe Co.

(114) T.L.D. TROTTER; 5 Feb 1866, Invt. by E.M. Trotter and Joseph Cathcart, Adm.

(116) MRS. PRUDENCE MARTIN; 3 May 1869, Invt. by Joseph Martin, Adm.

(117) JEREMIAH BOYD; 20 May 1869, Invt. of sale and notes by E. Summit and J. Boyd, Adms.

(125) THOMAS TALLENT; 30 Apr 1869, Invt. by Isham Avans and E. Tallent, Gdns. to minor heirs.

(126) SARAH WARREN; 3 Jun 1869, Invt. of sale held 26 Jun 1867 by W.N. Purdy, Adm.

(128) J.K. JOHNSTON; Invt. 10 Jan 1866.

(129) JOSEPH BROWN; Sale 15 May 1863 by his Execs.

(135) JOHN FINE; Feb 1868, Invt. by E.A. Taylor, Adm. with Will annexed; according to the Will, P.L. Fine of Missouri was made Exec. and after the sale he appointed Joseph Walker of Monroe Co., now deceased, as his agent.... said Peter L. Fine and Joseph Walker, both deceased during the late War and Adms. have been appointed on both their Estates, viz: Joseph D. Jones on Estate of Joseph Walker.... and William L. Scruggs of Missouri on Estate of Peter L. Fine; vouchers from heirs of Mahala Walker, dec'd, alias Mahala Fine.

(138) FRANCIS GRAY; 3 May 1869, Invt. by M.F. Johnson, Adm.

(139) THOMAS McCAULEY; no date, Invt. of sale.

(140) RUTH HALL; 4 Oct 1865, Sale.

(143,148,173) HENRY MARSHALL; 3 May 1869, Notes due, by James A. Dyre, Adm.; Sale held 18 Mar 1869; Sale held 22 Jan 1870.

(145,151) JAMES H. JOHNSTON; 31 Mar 1869, Report by James Harvy Johnston, Gdn. to Sallie M. and C.M. Johnston, minor heirs; no date, motion to amend report filed 3 Apr 1865.

(152) THOMAS CROWDER; Sale Dec 1868.

(152,170) JAMES GHORMLY; 5 Apr 1869, report by Hannibal McSpadden, Gdn. to Mary Ghormly, a minor heir; Invt. of sale of corn 3 Feb 1870.

(153) MATTHEW HUDGINS; 1 Dec 1869, report by Chesley C. Carter, Adm.; all property to widow Louisa.

(154) ALEXANDER HENDERSON; Sale 6 Nov 1869 by W.F. Hudson, Adm.

(158,163½,164) MARGARET C. DAVIS; 3 Jan 1870, report of Commissioners in division of property jointly owned by N.P., M.C., and C.T.P. Davis on 14 Dec 1869; Invt. of property by John R. Henry, Adm.; report of property sold 30 Dec 1869; buyers include Nancy P., Thomas C., C.T.P., and N. Ellen Davis.

(166) JOSEPH FORSHEE, SR.; 18 Dec 1869, Sale held 1 Jul 1865 by Evan S. Forshee, Exec.

(169,194) WILLIAM WATKINS, SR.; 7 Mar 1870, reports by William D. Watkins, Adm.

(171) F.K. BERRY; 3 Jan 1870, Invt. by F.K. Berry, Adm.; receipt from F.K. Berry, S.E. Caldwell, and E.E. Molleston, the only heirs,

lawful and of age; they acknowledge that the personal property formerly administered upon by Thomas Laughlin, dec'd, was divided to their satisfaction.

(172) JOHN RIDER; Invt. 7 Mar 1870 and sale by M.M. Tipton, Exec.

(174) PHILLIP KELLER; Invt. and sale held 25 Jan 1870 by E.S. Forshee, Adm. with Will annexed.

(176) J.W. MITCHELL; Invt. and sale held 12 Mar 1870 by J.G. Mitchell, Adm.

(180) ABIJAH FOWLER; 25 Apr 1870, Invt. by Samuel Edington, Gdn. to minor heirs; year 1869.

(182) PETER and ELIZABETH MORRIS; 3 Jan 1870, Report of sale by W.N. Purdy as Gdn. of Caroline, Sarah, John, George, and William Morris, children and heirs.

(185) JOSEPH BROWN; 9 Jun 1870, Sett. by George Brown and J.F. Magill, Execs.; Invt. filed having been destroyed by the late war.

(186) MARTHA LEONARD; 6 Jun 1870, Invt. by J.H. Leonard, Gdn. to minor heirs.

(187,195) BENJAMIN HOWARD; 3 Jun 1870, Invt.; Sale held 28 May 1870 by Asa B. Young, Adm.; buyers include Caroline, Joseph, J.B., John, Kern, and Mrs. Joe Howard.

(198) SIMEON GRIFFITH; 23 Jul 1870, Report by James Cook, Gdn. to minor heirs; received pension money.

(199,213) L.M. CARTER; Sale held 13 Aug 1870 and Invt. of notes, by William Dyer, Adm.

(200) MARY DYER; 4 Oct 1870, Invt. of notes by William Dyer, Adm.

(204) H.P. DICKEY; 3 Oct 1870, Invt. by D.A. Browder and A.J. Dickey, Adms.

(205) JAMES GIVENS; no date, Sale.

(207) JOHN TRUE; 5 Nov 1870, Invt. by J.N. Johnston, Adm.

(209) WILLIAM BRAKEBILL; 28 Dec 1870, Invt. of notes arriving from sale, by William Dyer, Adm.

(212) WILLIAM L. EDWARDS; 2 Jan 1870, Invt. by S.J. Martin, Adm.

(214) B.D. CLIFT; Invt. sold 24 Dec 1870 and 7 Jan 1871 by D. McLemore, Adm.

Date	Deceased	Administrator or Executor
Nov 1864	William Patten	J.H. Patten, Exec.
Nov 1864	C.N. Hawkins	Edward E. Hawkins, Adm.; Will annexed.
Aug 1865	J.C. Boyd	Thomas G. Boyd, Adm.
Apr 1865	A.F. Carson	J.L. Carson, Adm.
Jun 1865	James C. Edwards	Saml. J. Martin, Adm.
Aug 1865	Geo. C. Harris	Ez. C. and Geo. W. Harris, Execs.
Aug 1865	Thomas Clark	W.G. Clark, Exec.
Apr 1865	James W. Pardue	James Knox, Jonathan Summett, Adms.
Oct 1864	Ezachriah Roberts	A.J. Anderson, Exec.
May 1865	Josiah K. Johnston	David A. Browder, Exec.
Sep 1865	John Rausin	David Rausin, Adm.
Sep 1865	Rachael Hutcherson	Daniel W. Lattimore, Adm.
Nov 1865	William Duncan	John E. Duncan, Adm.
Oct 1865	William Hall	Edwin Hall, Adm.
Nov 1865	Joseph Devine	William Burriss, Adm.
Dec 1865	Margaret D. Shaffer	Jacob M. Shaffer, Adm.
Dec 1865	Charles McDonald	B.J. Herrell, Adm.
Dec 1865	Samuel W. White	Jacob Sheets, Adm.
Dec 1865	Frank Mosier	James H. Worthy, Adm.
Dec 1865	Patrick T. Trotter	Edwin Hall, Adm.
Dec 1865	Nathaniel C. Cuthbertson	Mrs. M.L. Cuthbertson, Adminx.
Jan 1866	John Fine	E.A. Taylor, Adm.
Jan 1866	James D. Johnson	J.R. Robertson, William F. Johnston, Adms.
Jan 1865	James H. Johnston	Henry Kile, John H. Johnston, Adms.
Feb 1866	John Redman	Isaac Lindsey, Adm.
Jan 1866	Samuel J. Edwards	William M. Edwards, Adm.
Feb 1866	Wilson Weathers	James L. Weathers, Adm.; Will annexed.
Feb 1866	George Bowman	James B. Bowman, John D. Blair, Execs.
Feb 1866	T.L.D. Trotter	E.M. Trotter, Joseph Cathcart, Adms.
Feb 1866	Thomas Arp	Alfred Arp, Adm.
Feb 1866	R.D. Ragon	S.J. Martin, Adm.
Mar 1866	E.G. Mayo	W.W. Kile, Adm.
Apr 1866	John R. Flemming	James G. Flemming, Adm.
Apr 1866	Noah C. Higdon	Thomas A. Higdon, Exec.
Apr 1866	Robert Eakin	John R. Leonard, Larkin Webb, Adms.
May 1866	John Roy	Joseph Sands, Joseph A. Roy, Adms.
May 1866	George C. Montgomery	Mrs. A.R. and J.C. Montgomery, Adms.
May 1866	G.W. Wiggins	Eligah Wiggins, Adm.
May 1866	James Gaston	J.V. Gaston, Adm.
May 1866	Reps Jones	Daniel Jones, Adm.
Jun 1866	William Parker	James J. Byers, Adm.

Date	Deceased	Administrator or Executor
Jun 1866	John R. Johnston	Jesse F. Jones, Adm.
Jun 1866	Michael Fender	John Ramsey, Charles Owen, Execs.
Aug 1866	Elisha Johnson	Mary A. Mumford, Execx.
Sep 1866	Thomas Devine	Willey Lasster, Adm.
Sep 1866	John McCracken	William Fowler, Adm.
Oct 1866	Thomas J. Allen	Anderson Hawkins, Adm.
Aug 1866	Kiziah Taylor	Leroy Taylor, Exec.
Dec 1866	Larkin Cardin, Sr.	Leonard, James C., and Jourdin Cardin, Execs.
Dec 1866	A.L. Wilson	W.W. Porter, Exec.
Dec 1866	Samuel Johnston	Josiah N. Johnston, Adm.
Dec 1866	Mary Humphreys	Abraham J. Humphreys, Adm.
Jan 1867	A.B. Clift	John L. Cline, Adm.; Will annexed.
Jan 1867	Judiath M. Kimbrough	Josiah Wright, Adm.
Jan 1867	Carter Hudgins	Edward Hudgins, Exec.
Mar 1867	Larkin Cardin, Sr.	Jordan Cardin, Adm. pendente lite.
Apr 1867	Samuel Henderson	George L. Henderson, Exec.
Apr 1867	James Ghormly	Jason McMullin, Thomas A. Henderson, Adm.
Apr 1867	John Weldon	Thomas A. Henderson, Adm.; Will annexed.
Apr 1867	Houston Clift	Elisha Tallant, Adm.
Apr 1867	Jacob Givens	Sarah A. Givens, Adminix.
Apr 1867	James L. Henderson	W.N. Bicknell, Adm.
May 1867	William Carter	Thomas F. Carter, Adm.
Nov 1866	Andy Millsaps	John Carringer, Adm.
May 1867	Elisha Johnson	E.J. Mumford, Exec., Will annexed to succeed Mary A. Mumford, Execx., dec'd.
Jun 1867	A.S. Mason	Arch Mason, Adm.
Jun 1867	John Coltharp	Andrew J. and John H. Coltharp, Execs.
Jun 1867	Floyd S. White	Mary A. White, Adminx.
Jun 1867	Sarah Warren	W.N. Purdy, Adm.
Aug 1867	James Mason	Arch Mason, Adm.
Oct 1867	Elizabeth Martin	Joseph A. Bildeback, Adm.
Oct 1867	George Patterson	George W. Patterson, Adm.
Oct 1867	Fredrick Dean	James H. Kelso, Adm.
Dec 1867	Adam Garren	Thomas G. Boyd, Adm.
Nov 1867	Jacob Cook	H.K. Lowry, Adm.
Dec 1867	John Scruggs	James Scruggs, Adm.
Jan 1868	John Pennington	John C. Pennington, Lewis F. Bryant, Execs.
Jan 1868	Isaac Cole	John R. Cole, Adm.
Feb 1868	James Curtis	S.C. Curtis, Exec.
Apr 1868	Joseph F. Ellison	Charles W. Hicks, Adm.
May 1868	R.R. Cleveland	F.K. Berry, Sidney G. Cleveland, Adms.
Jun 1868	Toliver White	Edwin Hall, Adm.

Date	Deceased	Administrator or Executor
Jun 1868	Thomas McColley	J.J. Swanner, Adm.
Jul 1868	Susan J.E. Henly	Guilford Cannon, Adm.
Oct 1868	Thomas Crowder	Robert P. Crowder, Exec.
Oct 1868	John R. Johnston	Joseph D. Jones, Adm.
Nov 1868	William Hunt	G.W. Williams, Adm.
Nov 1868	W.W. Stephens	William M. Smith, Adm.
Dec 1868	William Reynolds	Hugh Chesnutt, Adm.
Dec 1868	Prudy Martin	Joseph Martin, Adm.
Feb 1869	Polly Humphreys	Charles W. Hicks, Adm.
Mar 1869	Henry Marshall	James A. Dyer, Adm.
Mar 1869	William H. Jones	Charles W. Hicks, Adm.
Apr 1869	Goldman Bryson	S.H.M. Bryson, Adm.
May 1869	Jeremiah Boyd	Eusebus Summit, Jeremiah Boyd, Adms.
Jun 1869	Moses J. McLendon	Margaret J. McLendon, Adminx.
Aug 1869	F.D. Blankinship	C.B. Taylor, Adm.
Aug 1869	Thomas J. Ballard	Mary Ballard, Adminx.; Will annexed.
Sep 1869	F.K. Berry	F.K. Berry, Adm.
Oct 1869	J.W. Kelso	William J. Kelso, Adm.; Will annexed.
Oct 1869	A.W. Hutcherson	J.M. Hutcherson, Adm.
Oct 1869	Mathew Hudgins	Chesley C. Carter, Adm.
Oct 1869	Alexander Henderson	William F. Hudson, Adm.
Dec 1869	Elizabeth M. Lowry	David H. Lowry, Exec.
Dec 1869	Irvin Roddy	James H. Worthy, Adm.
Dec 1869	Margaret C. Davis	J.R. Henry, Adm.
Dec 1869	John West	John J. Crippen, Adm.
Dec 1869	John Knox	James Knox, Adm.
Jan 1870	Elizabeth Kelso	William J. Fowler, Adm.
Jan 1870	Phillip Keller	E.S. Forshee, Adm.; Will annexed.
Feb 1870	John Rider	Malcom M. Tipton, Adm.; Will annexed.
Feb 1870	J.W. Mitchell	James G. Mitchell, Adm.
Feb 1870	W.W. Stephens	Fildelia A. Stephens, Adminx.
Feb 1870	William Watkins	William D. Watkins, Adm.
Mar 1870	Frances L. Lowry	David H. Lowry, Adm.; Will annexed.
Apr 1870	Joseph R. Osborne	Thomas Osborne, Adm.
May 1870	Benjamin Howard	Asa B. Young, Adm.
May 1870	J.M. Grubb	T.E.H. McCroskey, Adm.
Jul 1870	Gilbert Blankinship	J.R. Burchfield, Adm.
Aug 1870	Lewis M. Carter	William Dyer, Adm.
Aug 1870	Jesse F. Jones	William F. Hudson, Adm.
Sep 1870	Mary Dyer	William Dyer, Adm.
Sep 1870	William Brakebill	William Dyer, Adm.
Sep 1870	H.P. Dickey	D.A. Browder, A.J. Dickey, Adms.
Oct 1870	John True, Sr.	J.N. Johnston, Adm.
Oct 1870	James Givens	J.R. Birchfield, Adm.
Oct 1870	William L. Edwards	S.J. Martin, Adm.

Date	Deceased	Administrator or Executor
Dec 1870	Benjamin D. Clift	A.D. McLemore, Adm.
Dec 1870	Elizabeth Redmond	James Redmond, Adm.
Dec 1870	N.J. Spillman	Grimes A. Spillman, Adm.

The Letters from 1871 to 1877 are outside the scope of this book.

(1) 6 Dec 1864 Abijah Fowler, Gdn. to Mary Fowler now Mary Hatsey.

(2) 1 Jul 1865 William Dyer, Gdn. to minor heirs of John Wolf, dec'd, namely, John P., James M., and Sarah C. Wolf; Credits: Jane B. Wolf's receipts 24 Mar 1865.

(3) 1 Jul 1865 William Dyer, Adm. of John Strutten, dec'd; a receipt of John W. Strutten.

(5) 1 Sep 1865 J.W.J. and M.W. Niles, Gdns. to minor heirs of Andrew R. Humes, dec'd; Paid for Miss Billie /sic7 J., Thomas H., and Miss Andrea R. Humes; Bettie J. and Thomas H. Humes having come of age, and Margret Humes having married S.D.E. Niles.

(9) 5 Feb 1864 J.E. Reagon, Adm. of Daniel Reagon, dec'd; settlement made 13 Feb 1863 with former clerk A.T. Hicks; receipts for equal amounts from D.J. Reagon, John M. Kimbrough and wife Mary E., M.A. Reagon, R.D. Reagon, W.H.H. Reagon, and self, one of the heirs.

(10) 4 Jan 1865 John B. Wilson, Gdn. to Isaac N. Barr, minor heir of Adam Barr, dec'd; final settlement with ward.

(11) 25 Sep 1865 William Dyer, Gdn. to minor heirs of John Wolf, dec'd.

(12) 21 Oct 1865 Mary Ann Ross formerly Spillman, Adminx. of N.J. Spillman, dec'd.

(13) 26 Aug 1865 Thomas Stephens, Gdn. to Minor heirs of George Stephens, dec'd, to wit, Samuel and J.C. Stephens.

(15) 14 Oct 1865 William M. Stakely, one of Execs. of James Smith, dec'd, and Gdn. of Martha A. Smith; Settlement from 2 Feb 1863.

(17) 28 May 1866 Jefferson Glass, Gdn. to Sylvester Glass; settlement from 21 Jan 1862; receipts include those from Mary and A.P. Glass.

(18) 9 May 1865 Jacob Sheets, Exec. of John Sheets, dec'd; Inventory filed 21 Dec 1861; B.C. Pettitt, Clk., by J.C. Winkler, D.C.

(19) 11 Oct 1865 Thomas Laughland, Adm. of F.K. Berry; paid tuition at Bat Creek, 1860 and 1861, for Franklin K. Berry; paid Sidney Berry 1862-1865.

(20) 9 May 1865 C.P.T. Davis, Adm. of David Kelso; settlement from 15 Dec 1858.

(22) 11 Dec 1865 Samuel Edington, Adm. of Abijah Fowler; Mary A. Fowler receipt.

(23) 23 Apr 1866 G.W. Vincent, Gdn. of minor heirs of Hiram Vincent, dec'd, namely Hiram Vincent; settlement from 7 Jan 1858; final settlement.

(24) 27 Oct 1865 James Sharp, Adm. of Joseph Sharp; sale held 25 Oct 1862.

(25) 12 Dec 1865 James M. Robenett, Gdn. to minor heirs of Elizabeth Young, dec'd; Gdn. allowed for three years service.

(26) 13 May 1865 Elizabeth Phillips formerly Mosier, Adminx. of Phillip Mosier; interest on sale notes from 17 Oct 1854.

(28) 20 Jul 1865 F.M. Rowan, Gdn. to Mary Jane Rowan.

(29) 7 Jul 1865 John O. Roy, Gdn. to Mary A. Roy, daughter of Joseph Roy, dec'd; ward of age and full amount paid 8 Feb 1865.

(30) 23 Sep 1865 J.J. Witt, Gdn. to minor heirs of John Walker; settlement from 25 May 1860; vouchers to M. Witt, Manury J. Witt, and Daniel L. Witt.

(31) 8 Jan 1866 A.T. Hicks in regard to funds in his hands belonging to Charles McClure.

(31) 5 Feb 1866 F.M. Phillips, Gdn. to minor heirs of Peter Moser, dec'd; note on John and Noah Moser; board and clothing for two of wards for two years, one aged seven years.

(32) 5 Jun 1865 D. Walker, Adm. of John Cunningham, dec'd; asks to be released from any further responsibility and Court so orders.

(33) 3 Apr 1866 Ez. C. Harriss, Gdn. to Nancy Ritchy, who is of unsound mind; settlement from 3 Apr 1862; receipts of Sarah and Cyntha Ritchey.

(34) 3 Mar 1866 Solen McCrosky, Gdn. to James Humphreys.

(35) 3 Mar 1866 Eusebus Summut, Adm. of Peter Moser, dec'd.

(36) 25 Mar 1866 Daniel L. Stephens, Gdn. to Abraham and Thomas Denton; sett. from 25 Sep 1861; A. Denton's receipt 23 Dec 1862.

(37) 8 Jan 1866 W.B. Grayson Gdn. to Martha Dunlap; received sum from Adm. of James Dunlap, dec'd.

(38) 3 Feb 1866 Thomas Stephens, Adm. of Phillip Stephens, dec'd; Inventory was filed 27 Aug 1863.

(40) 17 Jan 1866 John Ramsey, Exec. of F.A. Patten, dec'd; final settlement; in 1862 paid wards: E.A. Taylor, Gdn., Amanda A. Bicknell, H.F. Patten, Charles Owens by Charles Owens, Sr.

(41) 4 Sep 1865 Nathan Magill and John Wright, Execs. of John A. Wright, dec'd; sett. with former clerk A.T. Hicks 24 Jul 1863; receipts from William M. Edwards, Adm. of S.J. Edwards, dec'd, 2 Dec 1864, and Madison Wright.

(42) 2 Oct 1866 M.F. Johnson, Adm. of Noah Graves, dec'd; final sett.; receipts from Nancy Graves; paid expenses to Chattanooga and return.

(43) 2 Oct 1866 M.F. Johnson, Adm. of William R. Pressly /sic/, dec'd; sett. from 23 Jul 1863; paid to Mrs. Presnell /sic/ for her yearly support; money found in Presnell's possessions; James Presnell receipt; paid Margaret Pressnell, ward of dec'd.

(45) 1 Sep 1866 Dawson A. Walker, Exec. of Caswell L. Walker, dec'd; sett. from May 1862.

(46) 25 Aug 1866 Absolum Harrell, Gdn. to minor heirs of Charles McDonald, dec'd; Gdn. has received nothing and is released.

(46) 30 Nov 1866 E.L. Griggory, Exec. of Margaret Griggory, dec'd;

receipt showing he has satisfied the parties named in Will in full;
Ann Gregory recpt. 29 Nov 1865; John F. Gregory receipt Nov 29,
1865 for "property left to him in the last will and testament of
my Aunt Margaret Gregory deceased"; Margaret S. and Mary S. Gregory
receipt 29 Nov 1865 "for our Aunts cloathing".

(48) No date. James Cook, Gdn. of Robert, David, and James
Griffith, minor heirs of Simeon Griffith, dec'd; money received from
M.M. Young collected from the United States; paid for boarding
wards for one year.

(49) 8 May 1867 F.M. Rowan, Gdn. to Mary Jane Rowan.

(50) 22 May 1867 W.N. Purdy and Randolph Carter, Gdns. to William
Carter, a man of unsound mind.

(51) 29 May 1867 John D. Boring, Gdn. to minor heirs of Bartley
Boring and John D. Boring, dec'd; sett. from Mar 1863.

(52) 28 Feb 1867 Nathaniel Magill and John Wright, Execs. of John
A. Wright, dec'd.

(53) 1 Mar 1867 Josiah Wright, Gdn. to minor heirs of John H.
Dobson, dec'd.

(54) 3 Jan 1867 D.W. Latimore, Adm. of Rachel Hutcheson, dec'd;
insolvent estate; all persons to file claim before 10 Sep 1866;
paid to Samuel J. Hutchenson; funds received are sufficient to pay
costs and claims made to date.

(57) 26 Apr 1867 W.N. Bicknell, Treas. of Boliver Academy; settlement.

(60) 30 Apr 1867 Jeremiah Calfee, Adm. of Elizabeth Ritchey, dec'd;
sett. from 1862; equal amounts paid to Elijah Lee, Ez. C. Harris,
John M. Ritchey, Thomas Lesley, Samuel Ritchey, Sarah Ritchey,
Margaret Randolph, Mary Boring formerly Ritchey (her receipt "taken
out of my house when the rebels robbed my house Sept 1st, 1862").

(61) 12 Nov 1866 J.D. Robinson, Gdn. to minor heirs of James
Robinson, dec'd.

(62) 3 Jul 1866 D.P. Walker, Adm. of Thomas Harmon, dec'd; sett.
from 11 Sep 1849.

(64) 20 Nov 1866 E.C. Johnson, Adm. of John Simpson, dec'd; paid
many Atty. fees and judgment costs.

(70) 11 Dec 1866 Samuel Edington, Adm. of Abijah Fowler, dec'd.

(71) 17 May 1867 S.J. Martin, Adm. of Robert D. Reagin, dec'd;
received from U.S. Government, William H. Reagin, Delilah J.
McGuire, Nicholas M. McGuire, J.E. Reagin; equal amounts paid to
J.E., William H.H., and Martha A. Reagan, D.J. McGuire, Mary E.
Kimbrough.

(73) 20 Jun 1867 Solen McCroskey, Gdn. to James Humphreys, minor
heir of William Humphreys, dec'd.

(74) 16 Dec 1867 John H. Johnston and Henry Kile, Adms. of James
H. Johnston, dec'd; receipts from Elizabeth, John H., Betsey, E.C.,
Clara, and John C. Johnston, and later, Clara Forkner; "Above
settlement and all papers... handed to S.P. Hale, Clerk & Master,

This 23d day of April 1870. H.C.P. Horton, Dpty. Clk."

(77) 6 Feb 1867 Elizabeth Cleveland, Gdn. to minor heirs of Robert
Cleveland, dec'd; sett. from 6 Oct 1862; received from Clerk and
Master, Hamilton Co. and from Execs. of Pressly Cleveland; receipts
for equal amounts from W. and P. Cleveland, and M.E. Patton; paid
for R.S. Cleveland.

(78) 30 Nov 1866 Julian Brannum, Gdn. to minor heirs of William
and Ellender Brannum, dec'd; sett. from 24 Dec 1861.

(79) 5 Dec 1867 John H. Johnston, Adm. of Joseph Henderson, dec'd;
notes on Alexander, William M., and Samuel Henderson; receipts from
John H., Margaret A., Scynthia, and F.M. Johnson.

(81) 22 Jun 1867 T. Butler, Adm. of Jessee Butler; sett. from 5
Nov 1859; equal amounts paid to F.C. and George W. Butler.

(82) 23 Jun 1866 Josiah Wright, Gdn. to minor heirs of John H.
Dobson.

(83) 3 Mar 1868 Isaac Lindsey, Jr., Adm. of John Redman; cash
received from Mrs. Redman.

(85) 5 Oct 1867 James L. Weathers, Adm. of Wilson Weathers, dec'd.

(87) 28 Dec 1867 W.W. Kile, Adm. of E.G.A. Mayo; Inventory was
filed 2 Apr 1866.

(88) 22 Nov 1867 James L. Weathers, Adm. of Wilson Weathers; final
sett.

(89) 15 Jan 1868 J.S. Russell, Gdn. to Matilda Denton, minor heir
of William Denton; paid said ward for contingent fee and rail
road fare.

(91) 14 Nov 1865 William Dyer, Gdn. to minor heirs of John Wolfe;
received $48, the interest on $800, from Stakely & Co., "amount
allowed the said heirs in the Will annaly"; paid Jane B. Wolfe
$46 and costs $2.

(92) 14 Nov 1866 William Dyer, Gdn. of minor heirs of John Wolfe;
same report as 1865.

(93) 14 Nov 1867 William Dyer, Gdn. of minor heirs of John Wolfe;
same report as 1865 and 1866.

(94) 1 Aug 1867 J.W.J. Niles and M.W. Niles, Gdns. to minor heirs
of Andrew R. Humes, dec'd; sett. from 1 Sep 1865; included in
receipts are those from V. and E. Smith, 19 Jun 1866, and Miss
Andra R. Humes for similar amounts.

(96) 5 May 1867 David A. Browder, Adm. of J.K. Johnston; sett.
from 4 Dec 1865; paid Callie Johnston 2 Oct 1865 and Henry C. and
Callie Peck 1 Jan 1866; paid Josie C. Lacky.

(98) 14 Nov 1867 William Dyer, Gdn. to minor heirs of John Wolfe.

(99) 19 Jun 1866 J.J. Swanner, Adm. of Thomas McColly, dec'd.

(100) 1 Jan 1867 Joseph Upton, Gdn. to minor heirs of N.J. Spillman; several amounts received from G.A. Spillman; paid to John H.
Bruner for William Spillman's board; expense to Cleveland and
return.

(102) 20 Sep 1867 D.W. Latimore, Adm. of Racheal L. Hutchinson.

(104) 22 Nov 1867 Eli C. Johnson Adm. of John Simpson.

(107) 25 Sep 1867 Ez. C. and George W. Harris, Execs. of George C. Harris.

(111) 2 Oct 1866 M.F. Johnson, Adm. of Daniel Ratlidge; expenses to Knoxville and return to draw back pay from the Rebel Government.

(112) 1 Sep 1866 Dawson A. Walker, Exec. of Caswell L. Walker; sett. from May 1862; cash paid for coffin and burial clothes 7 May 1862; paid Clerk of Cherokee Co., N.C.; paid A.H. Walker alias A.H. Grayson; paid S.J. Blair and wife; paid S.J. Walker, S.J. Morris, D.L. Walker, and retained for myself; paid W.S. Morris for M. Wilhite; paid Joe Wilhite; paid M.C. Mahan; paid Miranda Green; paid M.M. Wilhite.

(118) 10 Dec 1867 Elisha Tallant and Isam Avans, Gdns. of minor heirs of Thomas Tallant, dec'd; paid M.D.L. and G.W. Tallant.

(120) 30 Jan 1868 Edwin Hall, Adm. of P.T. Trotter; Inventory and sale on 20 Dec 1865.

(122) 28 Aug 1866 J.J. Prater, Gdn. to minor heirs of John Simpson; Sale.

(125) 30 Oct 1866 J.J. Prater, Gdn. to minor heirs of John Simpson; amounts paid for Bowman G., James C., David F., Sarah T., and John T. Simpson, and Theressa Simpson now Jackson.

(129) 1 Jan 1868 J.J. Prater, Gdn. to minor heirs of John Simpson.

(133) 22 Sep 1867 William P. Kittrell, Adm., with Will annexed, of Pleasant Kittrell; sett. from 22 Oct 1861.

(134) 21 Jan 1868 Jacob Shaffer, the security of Dannel Shaffer, Adm. of William Shaffer, dec'd; Inventory was filed 2 Jan 1864.

(136) 25 Sep 1867 Dawson A. Walker, Exec. of Caswell L. Walker; received cash from estate of James Walker; cash paid Miranda Green, M.M. Wilhite, McClu McMahan; paid B.C. Pettitt, Clk., for settlement with R. Wilhite's heirs.

(138) No date. D.A. Walker, Exec. of C.L. Walker made settlement and following sums due the heirs of Reubin Wilhite; paid A.C. Wilhite as per return of C.L. Walker, Gdn. 24 Jun 1859; paid M.M. Wilhite as per same; paid Joseph M. Wilhite as per return of D.A. Walker Exec; one-third of $5130.12 is due ward, A.C. Stalcup /she/ now A.C. Raper, M.M., and Joseph M. Wilhite.

(139) 25 Sep 1867 Dawson A. Walker, Exec. of Caswell L. Walker who was Gdn. of minor heirs of Reubin Wilhite, dec'd; sett. made 24 Mar 1862 and Clerk allows C.L. Walker for his services for six years; paid Ann C. Stalcup formerly Wilhite, Miss Mollie M. Wilhite, and Joe Wilhite.

(143) 30 Aug 1867 Jacob L. Cline, Adm. of John Cline.

(144) 29 Aug 1867 James C. Hall, Adm. of Rutha Hall.

(145) 24 Jun 1868 W.W. Porter, Exec. of A.L. Wilson.

(146) 21 Jan 1868 Jacob M. Shaffer, Adm. of Margaret D. Shaffer, dec'd.

(149) 12 Feb 1868 Robert Russell, Exec. of J.B. Wall; Inventory filed 21 Oct 1865; receipt from Deania Wall.

(151) 4 Sep 1868 Joseph Sands and Joseph A. Roy, Adms. of John Roy, /page 151 is on reverse of page 158. There are no pages numbered 152 through 157.

(158 and 159) Entries crossed out and "See Page 180, 81, & 82" is written on margin.

(160) 8 Jun 1868 J.C. Montgomery, one of Execs. of G.C. Montgomery; "Register fees Sent to the freedmans Bureau to Secure the lands that had been Confiscated".

(162) 17 Jul 1868 John Ramsey, Exec. of Hugh E. Martin; James G. Martin, one of the heirs; Thomas C. Harris and wife Maggie A., a portion of their distributive share.

(163) 16 Sep 1868 E.A. Taylor, Adm. with Will annexed, of John Fine; $200 each paid to M.C. Taylor, Nancy Fine, M.L. and J.C. Starrett, and $1100 to Sarah Beard, and varied amounts to Joseph H. Walker by O.P. Hill, Mary C. and John Letteral by O.P. Hill, and M.C. and G.W. Messer by O.P. Hill.

(165) 11 Sep 1868 Leroy Taylor, Exec. of Kiziah Taylor; Inventory was filed 30 Sep 1866; paid to James P. Taylor, Burshaba and J.W. Orr, D.D. Taylor, and Leroy Taylor's distributive share paid to G.G. Stillman, Express Agent at Sweetwater on Express to James P. Taylor.

(167) 16 Sep 1868 E.A. Taylor, Adm., with Will annexed, of John Fine; made an exhibit of the last settlement of P. L. Fine by his agent Joseph Walker, on 13 Jun 1862.

(169) 25 Jan 1869 Josiah Wright, Adm. of Judiath M. Kimbrough.

(171) 29 Mar 1869 Ez. C. Harris, one of Execs. of George C. Harris; paid Isabella Morris, James W. Stephenson, W.C. Green, E.M. Wilson, and others; paid "E.C. Harris share willed to Ez. C. Harris".

(173) 22 Mar 1869 T.A. Henderson, Adm. with Will annexed of John Weldin; final settlement; paid equal amounts to A.B. Welding, Sarah S. and James M. Greenlee, Sophira A. and Archibald W. McNabb, Louisa A. and Pinkney S. McNabb, John S. Wilson, E.A. McCrary, Emaline and John D. Hamilton.

(175) 4 Jun 1869 Daniel Jones, Adm. of Reps Jones; Inventory was filed 28 Dec 1866; paid J.D. and Reps Jones.

(177) 8 May 1869 George Brown and J.F. Magill, Execs. of Joseph Brown; Sale was held 15 May 1863; paid to Samuel E. McSpadden, Gdn., Harvy H. Brown, Elizabeth Hamilton, Joseph N. Brown, Matelday Roy, Louisa Terry.

(179) 30 Jun 1869 W.N. Purdy, Adm. of Sarah Warren.

(180) 4 Sep 1868 Joseph Sands and Joseph A. Roy, Adms. of John Roy; varied amounts paid to J.B. and Mary E. Roy, J.A. Roy, Matilda Roy, H.H. Roy, Robert Cunningham, Gdn., and $350 each paid to J.R. Cunningham, Jackson and Lucinda McDaniel, William Roy, and Jonathan Roy.

Pages in last half of book, from page 184, are blank.

LOUDON FREE PRESS, published at Loudon, Tennessee:

I-5, 11 Dec 1852: At his residence in Philadelphia, Tenn. on 1st
inst, Mr. Mathew Nelson, aged 74 years, 1 month, and 14 days.

I-26, 13 May 1853: At Cannon's Store in Sevier Co. on 1st May,
Mrs. Mary Trigg Cannon, wife of Mr. William H. Cannon and daughter
of Col. William Heiskell of Monroe Co.

II-12, 14 Feb 1854: Two miles north of Madisonville on Friday the
10th inst, of congestion of the brain, Rev. John Key, aged about
56 years.

II-18, 28 Mar 1854: On Friday 17th, Wiley B. McNabb was found
dead in the field where he was plowing, one or two miles from
Balplay, in Monroe Co., having been killed by lightning.

II-21, 18 Apr 1854: At his residence in Monroe Co. on 9th inst,
Mr. Garland Smith in the 34th year of his age... left wife and six
small children.

II-22, 25 Apr 1854: In Monroe Co. on Wed. 19th inst, Jonathan
Davis in the 72nd year of his age.

II-26, 23 May 1854: On Monday 8th inst at the residence of his
brother-in-law, Henry Denhoe's /Donohoo7, Ball Play, Monroe Co.,
Mr. George T. Glenn, son of S. Glenn, Esq., in the 25th year of
his age.. brain fracture from fall.. born and raised in Monroe Co.
.. leaving wife, two children, parents, and an only sister.

II-26, 23 May 1854: On Bat Creek in Monroe Co. on 18th inst, of
consumption, Mr. Henry Y. Mosier, aged about 24.

II-28, 13 Jun 1854: At Sweetwater on 19th ult of scarlet fever,
Samuel Hogg Lenoir, aged 3 years, second son of I.T. and M.C.
Lenoir.

II-31, 5 Jul 1854: At Coyatee in Monroe Co. on 30th ult of Cholera
Morbus, infant child of Mr. John and Nancy Campbell.

II-33, 19 Jul 1854: At his residence two miles east of Philadelphia on Friday, Robert Cannon, Esq., an old citizen of this county.

II-34, 2 Aug 1854: Of cholera on 29th Jul at Coyatee, Monroe Co.,
Mrs. Elizabeth, wife of Abraham Hicks, second daughter of Elizabeth
and John Blair of Miller's Cove, Blount Co., aged 41 years 4 months
and 24 days... left husband and eight children.

II-35, 9 Aug 1854: On 26th of cholera, Mrs. Dialtha, wife of
Charles Donohoo, aged 35 years 5 months and 12 days.

II-41, 20 Sep 1854: J.A. Hare, Esq. of Madisonville informs us
that the health of that place is now good. The last case of
cholera was Capt. A.R. Chaynie who died about the 13th.

KNOXVILLE REGISTER, published at Knoxville, Tennessee:

X-503, 10 Apr 1826: At his residence in Philadelphia, Monroe Co.,
Saturday, 1st inst, John Lavender, esq., aged 52 years... left
five children.

XII-583, 24 Oct 1827: On 6 Oct Mrs. Eliza McCoy, wife of Dr.

Cummings McCoy of New Philadelphia, E.T. aged about 22 years and
the Doctor her husband on the 14th of same month, aged about 28
years leaving a son less than two years old... members of Presbyterian Church.

XII-614, 28 May 1828: On 18th ult at her residence in Monroe Co.,
Mrs. Carey, wife of Thos. Carey.

XII-620, 9 Jul 1828: At his residence in Monroe Co. on 27th ult,
Mr. Richard Cobbs, in the 30th year of his age... native of
Albemarle Co., Va.... left wife and three children.

XIII-660, 15 Apr 1829: On Tues. 7th of this month, in Monroe Co.,
Mrs. Betsy J. McGhee, aged 27 years, wife of John McGhee, Esq. and
daughter of Col. Charles McClung of this county.

XIV-710, 17 Mar 1830: On 14th inst in the 20th year of his age,
at his father's in Tellico, Mr. William F. Bicknell.

XIV-719, 19 May 1830: On 27 Apr last in 39th year of his age, at
house of Mrs. Mary Woods, in Garrard Co., Ky., Mr. William S.
Blair of Monroe Co... Clerk of Pleas and Quarter Sessions... Bank
Agent.

XV-762, 9 Mar 1831: Lately in Monroe Co., Mr. Westley Swanson.

XV-765, 30 Mar 1831: On 11th inst, Mrs. Hannah Glass, consort of
Capt. Jesse Glass, of Monroe Co., aged 27 years.

XV-769, 27 Apr 1831: On 15 Apr at residence of William Kimbrough
in Monroe Co., his wife Elizabeth Kimbrough.

XV-770, 4 May 1831: On 22d Apr at her residence on Tennessee
River, Monroe Co., of the prevailing epidemic, Mrs. Nancy Callaway,
aged 47, consort of Joseph Callaway, Esq... husband and four
children left to mourn her.

XVI-824, 16 May 1832: On 8th inst at Wright's ferry, Mr. Daniel
H. Haynes, a merchant of Philadelphia... aged about 32... interred
at Maryville.

XVII-850, 7 Nov 1832: At her father's in Monroe Co. on 20 Oct,
Miss Caroline Russell.

XVII-850, 7 Nov 1832: On Sunday 28th ult at his own residence in
Monroe Co., Mr. Joseph Callaway, Esq... victim of cholera... aged
53... native of N.C... Surveyor General of Hiwassee District.

XVII-853, 28 Nov 1832: In Monroe Co. on 18th inst, Mr. Isaac W.
Price in the 32d year of his age, leaving wife and three children.

XVII-855, 12 Dec 1832: Of consumption in Philadelphia, Tenn. on
28th ult, Albert C. Price, aged 21 years.

XVII-872, 10 Apr 1833: At Rockville, Monroe Co., on 21 inst /sic/,
Mrs. Lucinda Ann McCroskey, consort of John McCroskey.

I-22, 20 May 1840: At his boarding house on Fork Creek, Monroe
Co., on Monday the 13th Apr, Fisher C. Turner, asst. teacher in
Fork Creek Academy, in 31st year of his age... born and raised in
Roane Co.

I-22, 20 May 1840: At his residence at Blair's Ferry, Tenn. on

Tues 12 May, Mr. John Carmichael senr. in 61st year of his age.

V-216, New Series, 5 Feb 1845: At his residence in Monroe Co. on
Friday 24 ult, Rev. B.H. Mayo, in the 52 year of his age.

V-216, New Series, 5 Feb 1845: On Tues 14 ult at his residence in
Monroe Co., James Upton, Esq. in the 79th year of his age... one of
earliest emigrants to Tenn.

VII-316, New Series, 6 Jan 1847: On Monday 21 Dec at residence of
his father, Thos. L. Upton of Monroe Co., Mr. James H. Upton in
23rd year of his age... native of Blount Co. but his father moved
to Monroe Co. when James H. was quite young.

XLI-46, 19 Nov 1857: In Monroe Co. on 26th ult James Harrison,
son of Isaac and Anna M. Stevens, after an illness of about seven
months, in 18th year of his age.

XLI-46, 19 Nov 1857: On 4th inst in Monroe Co. of Apoplexey, Mrs.
Anna McCubbins, consort of Isaac Stevens in the 59th year of her
age.

KNOXVILLE ENQUIRER, published at Knoxville, Tennessee:

I-45, 26 May 1825: On Thurs 19 inst at Col. Charles McClung's,
Jane McGee, infant daughter of John McGee, Esq. of Monroe Co.

II-101, 26 Jul 1826: At New Orleans, sometime last month, Mr.
Robert Browder, of Philadelphia, Tenn.

KINGSTON GAZETTEER, published at Kingston, Tennessee:

I-22, 2 Sep 1854: At Madisonville on 23 inst Mrs. Sarah Bayless,
aged ninety nine years and some months. Mrs. B. was the widow of
a revolutionary soldier.

I-30, 28 Oct 1854: On Thurs 24 inst at Hiwassee College, A.M.
Clark of Loudon. Mr. Clark was a student at the College.

I-33, 18 Nov 1854: At his residence in Monroe Co. on 20th Sep
after a lingering illness of several months, Mr. Jonathan Pickel,
in the 66th year of his age.

HIWASSEE PATRIOT, published at Madisonville, Tenn. from Jan 1839
until 14 May 1839, then moved to Athens, Tenn.

I-4, 12 Feb 1839: On Wed. 6th inst, Mrs. Mary P. McConnell, Consort of Mr. Wm. P. McConnell of this place, aged 66 years 6 days...
member of Methodist Episcopal Church.

I-6, 26 Feb 1839: On Sunday 24th inst, Emily Theadotia, daughter
of A.W. and Susan I. Elder, aged 3 years, 9 months, 6 days.

I-7, 5 May 1839: On 2nd inst Mrs. Mary Ann wife of Mr. Guilford
Cannon, merchant of this place... member of the Presbyterian
Church.

I-7, 5 Mar 1839: On Tues. 1st inst, of scarlet fever, Susan
Rebecca, aged 1 year, 8 months, 4 days, daughter of A.W. and
Susan I. Elder.

I-10, Athens, 14 May 1839: In vicinity of Madisonville, 17 April,
Mrs. Caroline Cannon, consort of John O. Cannon, Esq. and daughter
of Matthew Nelson, Esq. of Philadelphia, Tenn., former Treas. of
East Tenn.

I-10, 14 May 1839: On 1st May, Guilford Newton, son of John O.
and Caroline Cannon, aged 4 years 10 months.

I-50, 20 Feb 1840: In Madisonville, Friday 1st inst Mary Jane
Victoria, infant daughter of William and Sara Ann Williams.

II-3, 26 Mar 1840: In Madisonville, Thurs. 19th inst, Col. E.H.
Weare, Clerk of Circuit Court.

II-16, 30 Jun 1840: Chancery at Madisonville- Caswell Torbett, of
lawful age, and Marcena, James W., Mahala, Teresa, and Rachel
Torbitt, minors by gdns. Charles Kelsoe and John Torbitt VS Robert
McReynolds, Marvell Duncan, John Hall, John McGhee, John O. Cannon,
Mahala Upton, and William Upton. In 1828 complainants father James
Torbitt died and within a few days their mother also died...
administration granted in Monroe Co. to Robert McReynolds, William
S. Blair, and Marvell Duncan. Marvell Duncan is now a citizen of
Georgia. Said Blair afterwards died and respondents Cannon and
McGhee were appointed Adms. and respondent Mahala Upton (then
Mahala Blair) Adminx. of Blair's estate... James Hall, complainants
grandfather, took negro girl with Adms. consent and kept her until
a short time before his death when he moved to his son John Hall's.

II-16, 30 Jun 1840: Chancery at Madisonville- Solomon Stow and
Parella Stow VS John Friddle, Mary Friddle, John Huson, Andrew
Allen and his son John Allen, William Huson, Daniel Heiskell, and
Angeline, Mason, and Perella Huson, minors, and children of Thomas
Huson, dec'd... Angeline, Mason, and Perella Huson are of Missouri.
In 1817 Mason Huson died, testate, leaving widow Mary who has since
married John Friddle... property to be divided when youngest child
reached maturity... son Thomas Huson moved to Mo. and died.

DATE OF MINUTES	ITEM
First Sat Dec 1832	John Crisp stated that he once belonged to Baptist Church in Chester Dist., S.C.
2nd Sat May 1839	Caroline Walker died
2nd Sat Jun 1839	Nancy Harrell died
3rd Sat Sep 1841	Katherine Harrill, deceased
3rd Fri Oct 1851	Mary Stephens deceased Oct 10, 1851, at 8 o'clock in evening, the wife of George Stephens (senior)
3rd Sat Mar 1853	March 1853 Brother George Long deceased
Sat Jun 1853	Sarah Herrell deceased 18 June 1853 at 3 o'clock a.m.
4th Sat Nov 1857	Deaths of members Sarah Hightower, Catherine Herrill, Polly Ann Barker in the A.D. 1857 & 8
Between 4th Sat Jan 1859 and 4th Sat Feb 1859	Polly Hightower departed this life Feb 16th, 1859, the wife of John Hitower
Between 4th Sat Apr 1859 and 4th Sat May 1859	Jahugh Cunningham Deceased May 3rd 1859 (Deacon) Polly Stephens Departed this life May 15th 1859 (Daughter of S. Stephens) N.B. George A. Stephens Deceased June /sic7 25th 1859
Between 4th Sat Aug 1862 and 4th Fri Oct 1862	Henry W. Cartwright deceased
4th Fri Oct 1862	J.R. Lane deceased
4th Sat Nov 1862	Sister Barnette deceased
Between 4th Thur Dec 1862 and 4th Sat Mar 1863	Isaac Ingram Died at Vicksburg Nancy Warrick, Deceased Winney Renfroe, Deceased A.J. Presley, Deceased at Vicksburg
4th Sat Jul 1863	Member of building committee appointed to replace Brother Joseph Walker deceased
4th Sat Oct 1864	R.M. Stephens departed this life
Jan to Aug 1865	Sarah Weathers, deceased
Sep 1866	John McBride departed this life in 1866
Between 4th Sat Feb 1867 and 4th Sat Mar 1867	Sister Newcom departed this life 4th March
Between 2nd Sat May 1867 and 2nd Sat Jun 1867	Sister A. Carle Departed this life May 23/67 Sister Sarah Cunningham Departed this life June 9/67
2nd Sat Feb 1870	James Weathers departed this life in Calafoind

The County Court Minute Books before this date have evidently been
destroyed. These abstracts are made from two books, October 1858
to March 1863 and June 1864 to December 1868. This is not a
complete abstract of the books. All items not found in other
records or those which give an earlier date for an event have been
copied. Court met on the first Monday of the month and usually
continued for several days.

October 1858

(1) Greene Co., Mo.: Bond, 16 Aug 1858, of Isam Watson, father
and Curator of Martha S., Nancy Melinda, and Barnet H. Watson,
minors; securities are Barnet and Spencer Watson; Isam and children
have removed to Greene Co., Mo. from Monroe Co.

November 1858

(4) J.I. Wright appointed Adm., Will annexed, of Sarah Hart.

(5) Commissioners appointed to lay off year's support for widow of
Abraham Hull.

December 1858

(8) Settlement made 6 Nov by John H. Milligan, Gdn. to Dolly Jane
Grant.

(8) Settlement made 6 Nov by Michael A. Harrison, Gdn. to William
R. and C. Grant.

(8) Settlement made 13 Nov by J.L.H. Cunningham, Gdn. to minor
heirs of Miles Cunningham.

(8) Settlement made by Joseph R. Rudd, Gdn. to minor heirs of V.A.
Harris.

(8) Samuel D. Simms, orphan, apprenticed to S.D. Axly.

(9) Will of Jonathan Tipton presented for probate; handwriting of
witness John McClain, who is dead, is proven and handwriting of
Jonathan Tipton is proven; Will held up for probate to secure
proof by John Rider, witness; J.B. and Q.A. Tipton enter into bond
as Execs. as named in Will.

(9) Will of Joseph Roy proven and Execs. named make bond.

(10) Elisha Kimbrough app. Adm. of Adam Barr.

(12) Comm. app. to lay off year's support for Margaret Roy, widow
of Joseph Roy.

(12) Comm. app. to lay off year's support for Elizabeth Barr, widow
of Adam Barr.

(16) J.W.J. and Margaret W. Niles app. Gdns. for Bettie J., Thomas,
Margaret, and Andrea R. Humes, minor orphans of A.R. Humes.

January 1859

(18) Settlement by James M. Browder, Gdn. to Samuel W. Pickle.

(18) Settlement by James Forest, Gdn. to Harriet W. McGill.

(18) Settlement by John Minis, Gdn. to Elvira and Martha Everett.

(19) Will of William Watson proven.

(20) Court pays for coffins for Richard Sherlin, Caswell Alred, John Wimberly, James Cook, and Aaron Waller.

(21) Court pays for coffin for Polly Buchannan.

(21) Court pays for burial clothes for John N. Patterson.

(22) John O. Shields, aged 15, apprenticed to John Gibson.

(22) Thomas O. Shields, aged 12, apprenticed to John Stakely.

(23) Joseph Divine, Adm. of Thomas Divine; petition to sell land; Comm. laid off dower for Elizabeth Divine, widow of Thomas, on 6 Sep 1856.

(28) Samuel M. Haun, Adm. of William Watson, moves the Court to rescind the indenture binding two orphan boys, John O. and Thomas O. Shields, to William Watson, who has died.

(29) In Tax List for 1858, Alexander Biggs, Robert Harrill, J.M. Samples, Jonathan Roy, James A. Roy, and William Land are all listed as deceased.

February 1859

(37) Settlement by E.E. Johnston, Gdn. to minor heirs of O.H.P. Caldwell.

(38) Settlement by J.A. Cline, Gdn. to Archibald Comer.

(38) Settlement by J.D. Robinson, Gdn. to minor heirs of James Robinson.

(38) Polly Humphrys app. Gdn. to Elizabeth E., A.J., John R., David W., Alfred C., Margaret R., and Joshua J. Humphrys, minor orphans of N.T. Humphrys.

(40) Will of Jonathan Tipton further proven by John Rider and ordered to be recorded.

(40) Court pays for burial clothes for child of Richard Shirling.

(41) Court pays for burial clothes for Alfred Carter and J. Shirling.

(43) Comm. app. to lay off year's support for widow of James Raper.

(47) Reuben Giles declared not guilty of being father to a bastard child of which Emily Donnelly was delivered.

March 1859

(48) James R. Webb app. Adm. of Larkin Webb.

(49) E.E. Johnston resigns and William M. Stakely is app. Gdn. to James A., Samuel J., and Mary Caldwell, minor orphans of O.H.P. Caldwell.

(49) Hiram McGinty makes bond to support a child begotten by him upon the body of Clarissa Smith.

(50) Comm. app. to lay off year's support for Margaret Raper,

widow of James Raper, make their report.

(55) Robert Russell, Adm. of Washington Breedwell, required to file report.

April 1859

(56) Settlement by Toliver White, Gdn. to William White.

(57) Settlement by Charles McDaniel, Gdn. to minor heirs of Gates McDaniel.

(58) Hugh Chesnutt app. Adm. of Tabitha Chesnutt.

(59) Court pays for burial clothes for Newton King.

(60) John Thomas allowed sum for holding inquest over body of Montvale Lee.

(60) Court pays for burial clothes for Daniel Moses.

(69) In Tax List for 1859, Thomas Skidmore and John Lindsey are listed as deceased.

(74) John Carson app. Adm. of Hannah Steele.

(75) Tribute of Respect, to memory of Newton J. Spillman.

May 1859

(77) Settlement by William M. Stakely, Gdn. to M.C. and B.R. Haun.

(77) Settlement by Hannah Jones, Adminx. of Daniel H. Jones.

(78) E.E. Griffith app. Adm. of William Hicks; Comm. app. to lay off year's support for Rosannah, the widow.

(79) J.C. Tipton app. Gdn. to Margaret and Mary Ann Wilkerson.

June 1859

(84) A.B. Clift app. Adm. of Shelton Levens.

(84) John A. Rowan app. Adm. of Jehu A. Cunningham.

(85) Charles McDaniel, Gdn. to Charles and George McDaniel, renews bond.

(86) Mary Ann Walker, Gdn. to minor heirs of P.H. Walker; Power of Atty. from Elijah Cate, Big Spring, Tenn. to Mr. Hicks, County Court Clerk, to sign Cate's name to bond.

(92) Settlement by A.W. Cozart, Gdn. to Joseph H. Cozart and others.

(92) Settlement by A.W. Cozart, Gdn. to Charles Y. Caldwell.

(92) Settlement by Reps Jones, Gdn. to Mary and Reps Jones, Jr.

July 1859

(93) Settlement by C.L. Walker, Gdn. to minor heirs of Reuben Wilhite.

(93) John Hicks, orphan apprenticed to Jasper Webb.

(94) Will of Wilson Weathers proven and recorded.

(95) Comm. app. to lay off year's aupport to Sampson and J.C. Stephens, minor children of George Stephens, dec'd.

(101) Registry of Martin Van Buren Cansler, a Free Boy; dark mulatto, aged 20, son of Catharine Cansler, a free white woman; said boy was born and raised in Monroe Co., and now is in employ of G.M. Cuson.

August 1859

(106) Will of Jesse Rhea proven.

(107) Will of James Ewing proven.

(108) Permilia (Amelia) Rhea, widow of Jesse Rhea, who died Jul 1859, dissents to Will and requests dower.

(109) Jefferson Etter app. Adm. of Sarah Ann Messimer.

(112) David Gaston and wife Mary VS George W. Reynolds and wife Elizabeth; petition for dower; Mary Gaston the widow of William Watson; right of the Reynolds in land assigned to Mary Gaston.

September 1859

(114) Will of Valentine Mayo proven.

(114) Noncupative Will of William Henderson proven; widow Amanda L. Henderson app. Adminx. with Will annexed and O.C. Henderson app. Adm.

(115) Abijah Fowler renews bond as Gdn. to Mary Fowler, minor.

(116) Samuel (Daniel) T. Shaffer surrenders apprenticeship of James Williams to his mother Peggy Jane Williams.

(117) Petition of John Lillard VS James Lillard, both of Monroe Co.; Jury finds that James Lillard is insane; present condition has only existed for five or six months; said James Lillard has a wife Mary Ann and one child Amanda Tennessee; David Lowry app. Gdn. to James M. Lillard.

(119) Comm. app. to lay off year's support to Sarah Ann Isbill, widow of Thomas M. Isbill.

(123) Sarah Ann Isbill app. Adm. of Thomas Martin Isbill.

October 1859

(124) Settlement by Milly Roddy, Gdn. to minor heirs of Samuel Roddy.

(125) Settlement made 31 Aug by John E. Grigsby, Gdn. to minor heirs of William Gammon.

(125) Settlement by F.M. Rowan, Gdn. to Mary Jane Rowan.

(125) Settlement made 1 Aug by Alexander Daugherty, Gdn. to minor heirs of William Daugherty.

(125) Settlement by E. Kimbrough, Gdn. to minor heirs of John Rogers.

(126) Settlement by E.G.A. Mayo, Gdn. to minor heirs of B.H. Mayo.

(127) B.P. Hankins, Joseph Divine, Edward Hankins, Jonathan M. Hankins, Allen and Amelia Broome, Isaac and Ann Stephens, Susan Hankins, N.C. Hankins by his Gdn. VS James B., Elizabeth, John H., Jane, Nancy, and James Wilson; all litigants except Joseph Divine are heirs of John Hankins, dec'd; lands sold on 22 Aug 1857.

(131) Nancy Henson app. Adminx. of Lazarus Henson; Comm. app. to lay off year's support to Nancy, the widow of Lazarus Henson.

(132) J.H. Montgomery app. Adm. of Eliza Scott.

(132) Will of Sterling Ragsdale proven and recorded.

(133) Moses Robinett app. Gdn. to Thomas M., James K., and William H. Young, minor orphans.

(134) Calvin C. Webb, petition to affirm adopted name; Calvin C. is as well known by name of Calvin C. Webb as of Calvin C. Ball; Martin Webb is the father of petitioner and recognized as such.

(134) Court pays E.D. Malone for transcribing Book K /Deed Book K/ at 30¢ per deed.

(134) Worthy A. Isbill allowed sum for burial clothes for Charity Watts.

(139) John McBride and wife Nancy McBride VS Lazarus Smith and wife, J.H. Johnston, Houston and Jane Johnston; petition for dower; Nancy McBride the widow of William E. Johnston.

(145) Purchase money for land of John Hankins, dec'd, all paid and proceeds ordered to be distributed to J.M. Hankins, Allen C. and Amelia Broome, Isaac and Ann Stephens, and Edward Hankins, the distributees of said estate.

November 1859

(146) John W. Howard app. Gdn. to George Cobb, minor orphan.

(146) Judith M. Kimbrough app. Gdn. to William I., Elizabeth C., Nancy W., Josiah, and Mary D. Kimbrough.

(148) Settlement by Robert Russell, Adm. of G.W. Breedwell.

(148) John A. Wimpy granted certificate to obtain law license.

(149) Indentures binding Miller Lankford to Thomas J. Young are rescinded.

(151) Court grants freedom papers to Jasper Patty, aged twenty-nine, born a free boy of color to Martha Patty, a free woman of color.

December 1859

(153) Louisa Malone, orphan, apprenticed to Mordecai Walker.

(153) Will of Eli Cleveland proven.

(154) Will of Paulina Taylor proven and recorded.

(154) Ansel Gadd app. Gdn. to minor heirs of Tabitha Gadd.

(155) Josiah Wright app. Gdn. to Mary C. and John H. Dobson, minors.

(157) Resignation of William W. Lillard as Adm. of Abraham Hull.

January 1860

(163) Court pays for burial clothes for John Cagle and George Snider.

(163) Court pays for burial clothes for J.W. Mullins, a mute.

(165) Court pays for burial clothes for Samuel Cartwright and John Linsey.

(165) Court pays for burial clothes for Nancy Bradford.

(173) Bond of L.D. Tipton as Gdn. to G.P. Tipton, minor orphan.

(174) John P. Hampton, orphan, apprenticed to John C. Vaughn.

February 1860

(178) Certificate for law license granted to H.A. Hood.

March 1860

(181) John R. Cole app. to take possession of any property devised to Tabitha Forshee, dispose of the same, and pay proceeds to the Committee of the Asylum of the poor.

(185) A boy bound to Jasper Webb be returned to his father James Hix.

(185) Certificate for law license granted to G.M. Hicks.

(186) Settlement by W.A. Robinson, Gdn. to minor heirs of John Robinson; entry entitled Sarah and Rhoda Robinson.

April 1860

(204) Charles Bogart app. Gdn. to L.M., Margaret A., Elizabeth F., Charles H., Susan C., Mary, Nancy C., Sarah E., and Aikin C. Bogart, minor orphans and his own children.

(204) Joseph McClure resigns as Gdn. to Francis, Samuel, Newton A., Mary, Elizabeth, and John McClure; said Joseph McClure to pay to Newton A. McClure his distributive share in estate of Samuel Douthit, dec'd, and also pay to him the distributive share of John McClure a minor child of Samuel McClure, dec'd, his distributive share in the estate of the said Samuel Douthit, dec'd, the said Joseph having produced in open court records from the County Court of Dade Co., Missouri, showing his authority for that purpose; said Joseph to pay into the hands of the Clerk of this Court the several amounts due Francis and Samuel McClure.

May 1860

(221) J.W. Howard app. Gdn. to Thomas and Adaline Aikin, minor orphans.

(221) Henry Kile app. Gdn. to Josephine Scott, minor orphan.

(223) John Halcomb, orphan, apprenticed to John Ramsey.

(224) Comm. app. to lay off year's support to Nancy Mashburn.

(225) John Stratton app. Gdn. ad litem to minor heirs of Jehu Stephens.

(225) Certificate for law license granted to Robert E. Houston.

(225) Judith M. Kimbrough VS William I., Elizabeth C., Nancy W., Josiah A., and Mary D. Kimbrough, minor children of Duke Kimbrough, dec'd.

June 1860

(226) Settlement by Thomas G. Harvy, Gdn. to minor heirs of Jesse Forshee.

(226) Settlement by G.W. Carmichael, Gdn. to S.W. Carmichael.

(226) Settlement by Michael A. Harrison, Gdn. to Catharine Grant.

(226) Settlement by James Erwin, Gdn. to Alexander Erwin.

(226) Settlement by William T. Hart, Adm. of Alexander Hart.

(226) Settlement by William Stapp, Gdn. to Nancy Stapp.

(227) Settlement by J.J. Witt, Gdn. to minor heirs of John Walker.

(227) Settlement by Jefferson Glass, Gdn. to Sylvester Glass.

(237) Comm. app. to lay off year's support to widow and minor heirs of Jeremiah Holloway.

July 1860

(240) Will of Mary Bell proven.

(245) Report made by Comm. app. to lay off year's support for Susan Holloway, widow of Jeremiah Holloway.

(250) Settlement by Thomas Laughlin, Adm. of F.K. Berry.

(252) E.D. Malone, Register, to be paid for transcribing Deed Books A and B to a new book, and a book be secured to transcribe the books from A to K.

August 1860

(255) E.A. Taylor app. Gdn. to F.A., Anne E., and J.P. Patton, minors.

(256) Jacob Givens app. Adm. of Zachariah Givens.

(257) Joseph Simms, orphan, apprenticed to J.P.T. McCrosky.

(257) Settlement of Michael Girdner, Gdn. to Lucinda E. Gardner and others.

(259) Court orders Sheriff to bring in the minor children of James Smith in the 10th Dist, Dugan, Clark, and Joseph Smith, and the other about 7 or 8 years old, also a mulatto child of Elizabeth Thompson, also a mulatto child of Mary Kiser.

(260) Resignation of R.H. Wells as Gdn. to Penelope, Olivine, Elizabeth, and Dorcas Shadden.

September 1860

(262) Will of Daniel Reagan proven.

(263) Jeremiah McGuire app. Adm. of Josiah McGuire.

(263) Thomas Elkins app. Adm. to Martin Bilderback.

(264) Elizabeth Cleveland app. Gdn. to William, Pressly, Mary E.,
and R.S. Cleveland, minors.

(265) Jane Bilderback app. Gdn. to William J., Keziah W., Joseph
A., and Isabella J. Bilderback, minors.

(265) David Smith, orphan, apprenticed to Isaac Robinson.

(265) John W. Thompson, a mulatto child, apprenticed to Phillip
Keller.

(266) Martha Kizer, a mulatto child, apprenticed to J.H. Johnston.

(266) Sheriff ordered to bring in three children of Martha Hurst
to be bound out.

(267) Comm. app. to lay off year's support to Sarah, widow of
Josiah McGuire.

October 1860

(271) Jeremiah Calfee app. Adm. to Elizabeth Richey.

(272) William A. Cline app. Gdn. to Margaret H. and Martha M.
Cline, minors.

(273) D.W. Latimore app. Gdn. to Isaac N. Barr, minor.

(280) Indenture apprenticing David Smith to Isaac Robinson vacated.

(282) David Smith, orphan, apprenticed to William Atkins.

(282) Court pays for burial clothes for Vina Cansler.

(288) Alexander Erwin found not guilty of a charge of bastardy
brought by Margaret Allgood.

(289) Comm. app. to lay off year's support to Jane, widow of Martin
Bilderback.

(291) S.P. Hall, Adm. to pay into court the share of Jack Hall.

(291) William M. Stakely, who was appointed Gdn. to Clementine H.
and Barbera R. Haun at Jan Term 1857, petitions Court to transfer
estate to Lawrence Co., Mo., where Minerva Clementine and Barbara
R. Haun, minor orphans of Abraham Haun, live and where they, being
over 14, have selected Newton W. Haun as Gdn.

December 1860

(298) G.W. Lawrence app. Gdn. to minor heirs of P.H. Walker, having
married Mary A. Walker, the former Gdn.

(300) Will of Jacob Parks proven.

(301) Mary Emory, orphan child, apprenticed to T.D. Clayton.

(305) William Roberts resigns as Adm. of Bazell Roberts.

January 1861

(306) Elijah Lea app. Gdn. to Fanny Lea, a lunatic.

(308) Ez. C. Harris app. Gdn. to Nancy Ritchey, an idiot.

(309) Joseph Divine, Gdn. to Marcus and L.D. Tallent, minor heirs of Thomas Tallent.

(311) R.J. White app. Adm. of Nancy White.

(312) Wily Harden, a boy of color, apprenticed to William H. Taylor.

(312) Mary Serrat, orphan child, apprenticed to William H. McKeehan.

(312) John William Serat, orphan, apprenticed to G.H. Coltharp.

(312) Miller Lankford, a boy of color, apprenticed to W.N. Bicknell.

(314) Court pays for burial clothes for Mary Ann Hacker.

(317) Report made by Comm. app. to lay off year's support for Esther Cheyne out of estate of Zachariah Givens, her deceased husband.

(324) Petition of Charles M. McGhee to be appointed Gdn. of Elizabeth M., Anne E., Margaret W., John, and Lavinia McGhee, minor children of B. McGhee, dec'd; the mother of Elizabeth M. is also dead, and Mary K. Parker, the mother of the other said minors, is Adminx. with Will annexed of Barclay McGhee, and was appointed 6 Oct 1856, but has made no settlement. Charles M. is the only surviving brother of Barclay McGhee, dec'd.

(325) Jasper Webb to bring the minor children of Lucretia Wallis to Court.

February 1861

(331) A.P. Glass app. Gdn. to Sylvester Glass, a lunatic.

(332) Eliza Brown, orphan, apprenticed to Samuel McCallie.

(332) Leonidas Horn, orphan boy, apprenticed to E.D. Heiskell.

(332) Joseph McConkey, orphan, apprenticed to G.W. Lane.

(338) Ordered that Sheriff bring to next Court the minor children of Jonathan Milsaps, dec'd, Clinton aged 10, Campbell 8, Bettie 4 or 5, and Andrew 1, at Jesse Milsaps. The girl at Richard Wallons; also the children of Anna Cochran to wit Mary age 8, Minerva at James Cochran's.

March 1861

(340) D.B. Curtis app. Gdn. to James W. Curtis, a minor.

(343) Mary B. Cockram, orphan, bound to John Wilson.

(343) Elizabeth and Rachel McConkey, orphans, bound to G.W. Lea.

(343) Lazarus Patterson, orphan, apprenticed to George Lane.

(343) Mary Serat, orphan, apprenticed to Benjamin Kirkland.

(348) Alexander Cochran found guilty of begetting a bastard child

on the body of Malvina Bradford and makes bond for the support.

(350) Benjamin Kirkland applies for release as security on bond of Equilla Mills as Gdn. to James W. Roberts.

April 1861

(353) Court pays for burial clothes for James Dyer.

(356) Court pays for burial clothes for Roland Murray.

(356) Joseph Simms, orphan, apprenticed to William Duncan.

(356) Mary E. Millsaps, orphan, apprenticed to D.B. Cunningham.

(357) Minerva J. Cochram, orphan, apprenticed to William H. Roberson.

(357) John McConkey, orphan, apprenticed to John McConkey, Sr.

(357) Campbell Millsaps, orphan, apprenticed to B.P. Hankins.

(357) John O. Roy app. Gdn. to Harrison, Mary A., Louisa, Caroline, and Margaret Roy, minors; John O. Roy resigns as one of Execs. of Joseph Roy.

May 1861

(377) R.J. White app. Adm. of Isaac Lindsey.

(377) Jonathan Hicks, orphan, apprenticed to J.E. Houston.

(377) Indentures apprenticing Louisa Malone to Mordecai Walker rescinded.

June 1861

(381) S.S. Glenn app. Adm. of G.T. Glenn.

(384) John Dodson declared guilty of being the father of a bastard child of which Ann Secrest was delivered in Monroe Co. on the 12 Dec 1860.

July 1861

(387) Will of Pressly Cleveland probated.

(388) William C. Julian app. Adm. of Thomas Reagan.

(389) Court pays for coffin for George Brewer.

(389) Court pays for burial clothes for Allen Gentry.

(390) Court pays for coffin for Leonard Morris.

August 1861

(393) Petition of J.C. Tipton, Gdn. to minor heirs of John Wilkerson, dec'd, to transfer gdnship. to Bradley Co.; heirs are Margaret and Mary Ann Wilkerson.

(394) Invt. by B.L. White, one of Execs. of William Gray.

(394) Thomas Stephens app. Adm. of Phillip Stephens.

(395) Thomas Stephens makes bond as Gdn. to Sampson and J.C. Stephens minor orphans.

(397) Will of John A. Wright probated.

September 1861

(400) Will of James Dunlap probated.

(400) Will of James A. Haire proven by J.I. Wright and signature of the other witness, John R. Stradly, who is beyond the limits of the State, is proven; Will recorded.

(401) Report by Comm. to lay off year's support for Rachel, widow of Thomas Reagain.

(403) The number of free white male inhabitants residents of Monroe Co. on 1 Jan 1861 was 2409.

(403) Jury finds that Martha Dunlap is of unsound mind and has been for many years; she has no property except a small bequest from her deceased brother James Dunlap.

(405) Indentures apprenticing William Sitzler to Daniel Daily are rescinded.

October 1861

(411) Will of John Sheets probated.

(411) F.M. Phillips app. Adm. of Thomas Phillips.

(412) Thomas O. Shields, orphan, apprenticed to Joseph Cathcart.

(412) Samuel Henly app. Adm. with Will annexed of A.H. Henly, to succeed Thomas Henly who has gone beyond the limits of the State of Tenn. and is beyond the jurisdiction of the Government of the Confederate States of America.

(413) Court pays for burial clothes for Jonathan Milsaps.

(414) List of inspectors for election to be held for president and vice-president of the Confederate States of America and for Confederate Congress of America in November 1861.

(415) Comm. app. to lay off year's support for Elizabeth, widow of Thomas Phillips.

(418) Indentures apprenticing Thomas O. Shields to John Stakely are rescinded.

December 1861

(424) Peter, Harrison, and Cass, negroes, apprenticed to Isaac Cole; entry entitled Peter, Harrison, and Cass Richeson.

(425) Indentures apprenticing orphan John Hicks to J.E. Houston are rescinded.

January 1862

(427) John A. Burris app. Adm. of Jacob T. Burris.

(429) Noah Orton app. Gdn. to John Murphy, minor orphan.

(429) James Montgomery app. Adm. of Boyd Bales.

(432) Court pays for burial clothes for Mrs. Mary Forshee.

(432) Court pays for burial clothes for George White.

(438) James Givens allowed sum for caring for his son John, lunatic.

(441) W.L. Eakin app. Adm. of William M. Brown.

(445) Harrold Hicks app. Adm. of Russell Hicks.

February 1862

(447) Clarissa Johnston VS James A. Wright and others; Will of Josiah K. Johnson /Note that in Will Book B, this name is Joseph K. Johnson/ presented by widow Clarissa Johnston for probate; Copy of Will dated 13 Aug 1861; E.C., C.J., and Esther S. Johnston, minor children of Josiah K. Johnston, W.P. Snead, grandchild of said deceased and also a minor, and J.A. Wright and wife Luticia J. Wright contest the Will; James A. Wright app. Gdn. ad litem of said minors; purported Will and all papers certified to Circuit Court; Clarissa Johnston appointed Special Adm.

March 1862

(450) Settlement by Gdn. to minor heirs of Eusebius and Sarah Summitt.

(452) Thomas Lesly app. Gdn. to Elizabeth Daugherty, lunatic.

(453) Court pays for burial clothes for Joseph Malone.

(454) Court pays for burial clothes for E. Fortner.

(455) Court votes Tax for support of indigent families of Volunteers.

April 1862

(458) Court pays for burial clothes for Mariah Slayton, pauper.

(474) William Isbill, Sr. app. Adm. of William Isbill, Jr.

(477) Persons appointed to enroll militia in their respective districts.

May 1862

(479) Martha Ann Henson app. Adminx. of Joseph Henson.

(479) David M. Lindsey app. Gdn. to David, Mary E., Martha, and Tennessee Lindsey, minor orphans.

(480) Joseph Walker app. Adm. of John A. Cunningham.

(480) Thomas J. Allen app. Adm. of Polly M. Brown.

(481) Will of C.L. Walker probated.

(482) S.Y.B. Williams app. Agent for Monroe Co. to attend to the purchase of salt and the distributing of same, according to regulations that may be adopted.

June 1862

(483) William M. Edwards app. Adm. of S.J. Edwards.

(483) Milly J. Saffell app. Adminx. of H.N. Saffell.

(484) George Chesnutt app. Adm. of William Reynolds.

(484) David Cunningham app. Adm. of Margaret Cunningham.

(485) M.F. Johnson app. Adm. of Noah Graves.

(489) Contract between Stuart Buchanan & Co. of Saltville, Va.,
and S.Y.B. Williams, Agent for Monroe Co. for purchase of 5000
bushels of salt of 50 pounds to the bushel, receivable at Saltville, Va.; salt is to be paid for before it is removed at rate of
$1 per bushel, not including sacks; contract dated 28 May 1862 and
salt to be furnished monthly for twelve months.

July 1862

(490) M.F. Johnson app. Adm. of J.H. Swaney.

(491) James Tate app. Adm. of John A. Tate.

(491) Madison Harris apprenticed to Josiah Wright.

(493) Comm. app. to lay off year's aupport for Lucinda Cagle from
estate of her deceased husband.

August 1862

(496) Settlement made with J.C. Montgomery; titled "Addie Grubb".

(496) Robert Russell elected Sheriff by the Court to fill the
vacancy caused by the death of A.B. Clift; Russell swears to
uphold the Constitution of the Confederate States of America.

(499) David Lindsey resigns and Matilda Lindsey is appointed as
Gdn. to Martha J. and Tennessee Lindsey.

(499) John D. Boring appointed Gdn. to Amos, Alexander, Tryphena,
Malinda, and Thomas Boring, minor orphans.

(500) William Bowers app. Adm. of A.M. Bowers.

(501) E.W. Boring app. Adm. of J.D. Boring; Comm. app. to lay off
years's support to minor children.

(501) Comm. app. to lay off year's support to Jane, widow of A.M.
Bowers.

(501) Comm. app. to lay off year's support to Lucinda Cagle, widow
of Willis Cagle, make their report.

September 1862

(506) Nicholas Boring is app. Gdn. to Lewis F., N.J., Mary, and
G.W. Boring, minor orphans.

(506) Narcissa Harrill is app. Adminx. of Robert Harrill.

(507) Will of A.B. Clift is probated.

(508) John Minis app. Adm. of Stanhope Belt and Comm app. to lay
off year's support for widow Sarah Belt.

(508) William Dyer app. Adm. of John Stratton.

(509) Comm. app. to lay off year's support for Narcissa Harrill,
widow of Robert Harrill.

(510) Henry Presnell admits guilt in begetting a bastard child upon the body of Betsy Ann Harriss.

October 1862

(513) Settlement by Solomon Wilson, Gdn. to minor heirs of David Wilson.

(513) James A. Sharp app. Adm. of Joseph Sharp.

(514) D.P. Walker app. Adm. of Jehu Cunningham.

(515) Petition for dower by Elizabeth Webb widow of Larkin Webb who died 2 Mar 1862; Mabury, Missouri, Mary O., and Jasper Webb are minor heirs.

(516) Comm. app. to lay off year's support to Clarissa, widow of Daniel Ratlidge.

(516) Comm. app. to lay off year's support for Eliza, widow of Joseph Sharp.

(516) Margaret P. McKenzie, an orphan aged 13 years, is apprenticed to Dennis S. Smith.

(517) Will of Nancy Gentry proven by Edwin Hall, one of witnesses, and held up for proof by other two witnesses who are absent.

(521) E.E. Griffith app. an Agent of Monroe Co. to visit Saltville, Va. and have power to negotiate with McClung and Jaques & Co. for salt, as well as Stuart Buchanan & Co.; he has power to surrender former contract if he can make satisfactory arrangements for salt.

November 1862

(523) Margaret McGowan app. Adminx. of Thomas McGowan.

(524) Floyd S. White app. Adm. of Samuel White and Comm. app. to lay off year's support for widow Nancy; Samuel White died in summer of 1862.

(525) John B. Wilson app. Gdn. of I.N. Barr to succeed D.W. Latimore, Gdn. resigned.

(525) Report of salt commissioners.

December 1862

(529) William McCaslin app. Adm. of William C. McCaslin.

(529) Sarah Maxwell app. Adminx. of Robert Maxwell.

(530) Jury of inquisition app. to report on lunacy of Peyton Hudson finds that he is of weak mind, has not been capable of managing his affairs for the last twenty-five years and has had great injustice done him in the purchase and sale of lands; Thomas H.S. Smyth app. Gdn.

January 1863

(536) Alsey A. Isbill app. Adm. of John M. Isbill.

(536) G.W. Bales, orphan boy aged two years, is apprenticed to Samuel T. Sharp.

(538) A.T. Newman admits guilt in begetting a bastard child on the body of Betsey Smith.

(541) County scrip to be issued.

(543) Ordered that Clerk pay to William Carter an amount paid into Court by William Carter, Sr., his Gdn., said William having proved to Court his identity; money paid by William Carter, Sr. as Gdn. of minor heirs of Robert Carter.

February 1863

(544) Will of G.W. Morgan probated.

(544) Will of Isaac Taylor probated.

(545) Indentures apprenticing Eliza Brown to Samuel McCauly are rescinded and she is apprenticed to Jonathan Thomas.

(545) Will of Armsted Blackwell probated.

March 1863

(548) Settlement by James McTeer, Adm. of Daniel Everett.

(548) Settlement by Louisa M. Gay, Gdn. to minor heirs of William Gay.

(551) County officers swear to support the Constitution of the Confederate States of America.

(552) Jury of inquisition finds that Lucinda Forshee, wife of John Forshee, is of unsound mind and wholly incapable of caring for her family; the Forshees have no land and live by hard labor.

(553) Comm. app. to lay off year's support to widow of C.A. Gurly.

(554) William Samples resigns as Gdn. to James H. and Malinda Brannon.

June 1864

(1) Elisha Tallant app. Adm. of Samuel Tallant, dec'd.

October 1864

(4) Comm. app. to lay off dower for Matilda Brown.

(4) J.J. Prator and Eli C. Johnson app. Adms. of John Simpson.

(6) Will of Zachariah Roberts proven.

November 1864

(7) Will of William Patten proven.

(8) Will of Alfred Denton proven; Dorcas Denton, Execx.

(8) Daniel T. Shaffer app. Adm. of William Shaffer, dec'd.

(9) Joseph Divine app. Adm. of James L.J. Persen, dec'd.

(9) James H. Carmichael app. Gdn. of John B.F. Carmichael and one younger not named, minor orphans.

(10) Report by Comm. to lay off dower to Delilah Tallant, widow of Samuel Tallant, dec'd.

December 1864

(24) Mathew Cagle app. Adm. of Jonathan Hankins.

(27) Settlement by Abigah Fowler, Sr. as Gdn.; said ward Mary Fowler is of age and has married and lives in Virginia; he is ready to pay her off whenever the way is open so that he can get to see her.

(27) E.E. Hawkins app. Adm. of C.N. Hawkins.

January 1865

(29) Comm. app. to lay off dower for widow of Joseph Brown.

(29) Comm. app. to lay off dower for widow of Peter Mosier.

(30) Comm. app. to lay off year's support for widow of J.H. Johnston.

(30) Bond of James Talent as Gdn. to Lucinda, Samuel H., Eliza, and Mary Tallent, minor orphans of Samuel Tallent, dec'd.

April 1865

(38) Comm. app. to lay off year's support for the three minor children of James W. Pardue, dec'd.

May 1865

(42) Plat of dower land laid off for Mrs. Matilda Brown, widow of Joseph Brown.

(43) Plat of dower land laid off to Mrs. Elizabeth Phillips, widow of Peter Mosier.

(44) Comm. app. to lay off year's support for widow of Houston Clift.

(44) Will of John Welden proven.

(44) Application for dower by Elisabeth Johnston, widow of James Harvey Johnston who died Dec 1864.

(45) David A. Browder app. Adm. of Josiah K. Johnston.

June 1865

(46) William M. Edwards app. Adm. of Samuel J. Edwards.

(51) William E. Sneed app. Gdn. to E.S. Johnston and William P. Snead, minors.

(52) William L. Edwards app. Gdn. to Kiziar, John J., Asa, Atlas (Allas), Clara, and Marion Edwards.

(54) Ephram L. Gregory app. Adm. of Margaret Gregory.

(54) Comm. app. to lay off year's support for Elizabeth, widow of James C. Edwards.

July 1865

(57) Rates set for J.W.J. Niles ferry.

(58) Comm. app. to erect a prison.

(58) Application for dower by Nancy C. Morelock, widow of William C. Morelock who died 1 Sep 1864.

(59) James R. Robinson app. Gdn. ad litem of Mary J., Monroe, and Samuel H. Morgan, minor children of Mary J. Morgan, dec'd, in suit of Elisha Tallent, Adm. of Samuel Tallent VS Widow and Heirs. Samuel Tallent died Feb 1864.

(66) Court to pay Tellico Lodge No. 8 $75 for use of large room in basement of Masonic Hall to be used as Court Room and Clerk's office for one year.

August 1865

(72) A.T.W. Pain app. Adm. of John C. Pain.

(73) J.L. Cline app. Adm. of John Cline.

(73) Will of George C. Harris proven.

(74) Will of Thomas Clark proven.

(75) Margaret Cline app. Gdn. to James M. Cline.

(75) Settlement by John O. Roy, Gdn. to Mary A. Roy.

(75) Isaac Linsey, Jr. app. Gdn. to John C. Mull, minor orphan.

(76) Thomas G. Boyd app. Adm. of Joseph C. Boyd.

(77) Elisha Tallant, Adm. of Samuel Tallant VS Delilah Tallant widow, William Cochran and wife Elizabeth, Sarah L., Malinda, Samuel H., and Elizan Tallent, and James Tallent Gdn. of minor children of Samuel Tallent, dec'd, and Mary J., Monroe, and Samuel H. Morgan, heirs of Samuel Tallent, dec'd.

(79) Elizabeth A. Brown, aged 12, bound to J.J. Swanner.

(85) Court pays for coffin for Jacob Doyal and child, and for Mrs. Stafferd.

September 1865

(88) J.L. Cline app. Gdn. of George and Isaac Wilson, minor orphans.

(91) Court finds that Rachel Caldwell is an idiot and has been since her birth about 1827, is entitled to some lands in Blount Co., has never married and has no children, and is now and has been living with Nathaniel Ewing who has cared for her for last twenty years; Ewing is app. her Gdn.

October 1865

(96) William Roberson app. Adm. with Will annexed of Caleb Roberson, dec'd.

(97) J.V. Gaston app. Adm. of John Jacobs.

(97) Bond of Isam Avens and Elisha Tallent, Gdns. to Marcus D. Lafayet and G.W. Tallent, minor orphans.

(98) John H. Houston app. Adm. of Joseph Henderson.

(99)Will of Jacob B. Wall proven.

(100) Comm. app. to lay off year's support for Lodusky Walker,
widow of Joseph Walker.

(101) Lodusky Walker VS Jesse F. Jones, Gdn. of Caroline Elizabeth
Emeline and Lolly Walker /sic/.

(105) Settlement by J.J. Witt, Gdn. to Manery July and Daniel L.
Witt.

November 1865

(109) Comm. app. to lay off year's support for Nancy Divine, widow
of Joseph Divine.

(109) Comm. app. to lay off year's support for Elizabeth Redman,
widow of John Redman.

(116) Nancy Divine, widow, VS William Burris, Adm., and Jane
Pearson, James, Mathew E., Lucinda, Jacob, and Julia Ann Divine,
heirs; Joseph Divine died Jan 1865.

(116) Comm. app. to lay off year's support for Mrs. M.L.
Cuthbertson.

(116) Comm. app. to lay off year's support for Mrs. Frank Mosier.

(116) Comm. app. to lay off year's support for Nancy, widow of
Thomas Arp.

(117) John M. Best app. Gdn. to Hiram J., Mary F., Martha A., and
John Jefferson Cunningham, minor heirs of Thomas Arp, dec'd;
titled "Hiram J. Cunningham & others".

December 1865

(117) James McLeary app. Gdn. to Nancy A., Sarintha W., Isaac,
Mary Jane, and William Thomas Arp, minor heirs of Thomas Arp.

(118) Absalom Herrell app. Gdn. to Mary Thomas Abbott G. Josephine
George and Martha A. McDonald, minor orphans of Charles McDonald.

(119) Jane Noland app. Gdn. to Catharin, Henry, and Nancy Jane
Partin, minor orphans.

January 1866

(126) Petition of Samuel Henderson and F.M. Johnson to have Will
of Joseph Henderson transferred to Circuit Court; Samuel Henderson
is brother and F.M. Johnson is nephew to said Joseph who died
without issue and whose mother and father are dead; Court rules
that Will be transferred.

(127) Matilda Roy and husband John Roy VS George Brown and
Franklin Magill, Execs. of Joseph Brown, Louisiana Terry and hus-
band John Terry, Harvy H. Brown, Thomas W., Joseph W., Mary C.,
John T., Catharine M., and George McSpadden, devisees in Will of
Joseph Brown who died 1863; Matilda Roy was widow of Joseph Brown
and is applying for dower.

(127) Penelope Hicks and husband Mark M. Hicks VS Benjamin J.

Herrell, Adm., Absalom Herrell, Gdn., and Mary A., Thomas A.,
Albert G., Sarah E., George H., and Ellen McDonald, only heirs of
Charles McDonald, dec'd; Penelope Hicks was widow of said Charles
McDonald and is applying for dower.

(130) James Green app. Gdn. to Rebecca, Samuel, Joseph, and Sarah
Roberson, minor orphans of Phillip Roberson.

(131) Henry Sheets app. Gdn. to John and Sarah Upton Sheets, minor
orphans of Mrs. Henry Sheets.

(137) Court ordered that all claims issued against the County from
6 May 1861 to April 1865 or until the reorganization of the Civil
Law be null and void.

February 1866

(139) W.J. Hutcherson app. Gdn. to Robert Hutcherson, minor orphan
of Robert Hutcherson.

(139) John C. McSpadden app. Gdn. to Charles and George McDonald,
minor heirs of Gates McDonald.

(140) Samuel J. Hutcherson app. Gdn. to Leathy J. Hutcherson,
minor child of Robert Hutcherson.

(141) Sampson Stephens app. Gdn. to Sampson and J.C. Stephens,
minor orphans of George Stephens.

(145) Will of George Bowman probated.

(146) Joseph Marr app. Gdn. ad litem to Larkin, Hetty Ann, John,
William J., George, and Lafayette Morelock, minor heirs of William
C. Morelock.

(146) Court pays for coffin for Emaline Morrow, pauper.

(148) Comm. app. to lay off dower for widow of William Wadkins.

(149) Thomas A. Ball and wife Elizabeth, Thomas J. Waddle and wife
Mary VS Samuel McClure; Samuel McClure late of Missouri is dead
and the complainants are the only surviving heirs and are granted
funds in hands of Clerk belonging to said Samuel McClure.

(149) William McDonald, orphan, bound to D.H. Joines.

(150) Martha J. McDonald, orphan, bound to D.H. Joines.

(150) Settlement made with former Clerk A.T. Hicks in regard to
funds in his hand belonging to heirs of Charles McClure.

(151) Martha K. Morgan, widow of George W. Morgan, VS Mary S.,
Gideon, Frank, Elizabeth M., Wash, Ella, and Olney Morgan, devisees
of George W. Morgan, and Andrew L. Rogers, Exec. George W. Morgan
died Nov 1862.

March 1866

(154) Elizabeth A. Brown, orphan, bound to Samuel J. Henderson.

(154) Eli C. Johnson granted certificate to obtain law license.

(158) Comm. app. to lay off year's support for widow of E.G.A.
Mayo.

April 1866

(168) Mary C. Mayo app. Gdn. to William Tate and S.A.B. Mayo, minors of E.G. Mayo.

(169) Luke M. Carter app. Gdn. to James Marion Jesse J. and E.S. Carter, minor orphans of Mrs. L.M. Carter.

(170) Joseph Sands app. Gdn. to Millie C., John W., Nancy E., Samuel R., William, James, and Robert Orr, minor orphans of Erby Orr and his wife Nancy.

(171) Will of Noah C. Higdon probated.

(173) Lydda Higdon dissents from Will of her dec'd husband N.C. Higdon and Court orders that she receive dower.

(174) Court released John N. Griffith from working on the Public Roads on account of his only having one hand and not able to work.

(174) Coroner and Jury allowed sum for holding inquest over body of John Duncan.

(174) Comm. app. to lay off year's support for Mrs. Robert Eakin.

(175) Comm. app. to lay off year's support for Lydia Stratton, widow of John Stratton.

(177) Jury of inquest over body of Frank Mosier.

(177) Jury of inquest over body of George C. Montgomery.

May 1866

(187) James Cook app. Gdn. to Robert, David, and James M. Griffith, minors of Simeon Griffith.

(188) John A. Ragains app. Gdn. to Jeremiah, Nancy N., and Jabe Stephen Ragains, minors of Thomas Ragains.

(194) Comm. app. to lay off year's support to Matilda Roy, widow of John Roy.

(195) Settlement by G.W. Vinsant, Gdn. to Hiram Vinsant.

(195) Settlement by G.W. Vinsant, Gdn. to William W. Vinsant, a minor of Hiram Vinsant.

(196) Plat of dower laid off to Mrs. Mary C. Mayo, widow of E.G.A. Mayo.

June 1866

(199) Will of Michael Fender proven.

(200) Application for dower: Matilda Roy widow of John Roy VS Jonathan, Joseph A., William, Calvin, Lewis, Esther, Sarah, James A., and Hiram E. Roy, Betsy Ann Sands and husband Joseph Sands, William Harris Cunningham, Linda McDaniel and husband Jack McDaniel, and Evaline Roy and husband Joseph Roy, all of the heirs that reside in the State; John Roy died Apr 1866.

(201) Thomas G. Boyd app. Gdn. to minor Alice L. Leath.

(201) Thomas G. Boyd app. Gdn. to minors Annie and Julia McCrackin, orphans of John McCrackin.

(202) Application for dower: Martha E. Jones VS George Hide and wife M.J., Susan M., Samuel H., James M., Mariah E., John C., and Cornealus Jones; Williams H. Jones died 186 /sic/.

(202) John Ramsey released from bond for a bound boy named John Shields who was decoyed off by his mother.

(204) Margaret Roberson, Adm. of Caleb Roberson, ordered to appear.

(205) Report by comm. appointed to lay off year's support for Elizabeth Moser, widow of Francis Mosier.

July 1866

(206) Serena Leonard paid $72 for waiting on sick with small pox for 36 days.

(207) Court orders that a jail be built from the brick now in the walls of the old Court house.

(208) Court pays for burial clothes for pauper John Williams.

(214) Report by committee appointed to lay off year's support for Mrs. Alpha R. Montgomery, widow of George C.

(214) John Loftis released from charge of bastardy brought by Eliza Roy.

(216) Toliver White app. Gdn. to Mariah, Caroline, Saphira, Calafornia, Dorothy, John, and Isabela Mullens, Minor orphans of Joseph Mullens.

August 1866

(217) Will of Elisha Johnson proven.

(218) Will of Carter Huggeons proven.

(219) Petition of J.J. Byers to be released as Adm. of William Parker because assets of estate are mostly in Knox Co.; Mary K. Parker is entitled to the personal estate.

(219) Eliza Roy accused Alex Ritchey of bastardy; case quashed.

(221) Allen Presly released from liability for bound children, James and Martha Presly.

(222) Will of Caleb Robinson set aside, widow entitled to all property and to claims due from United States.

(222) Will of Kiziah Taylor proven.

September 1866

(224) William Burris app. Adm. of P.L. Watson.

(225) Daniel H. Joines app. Gdn. to Mary A., Thomas E., Albert G., Sarah E.G.H., and Martha E. McDaniels, minor orphans of Charles McDaniels.

(226) Martha Watson accuses Lot Cagle of bastardy.

(227) Joseph Spencer app. Gdn. to Susan Sewell, minor.

(227) Clarance Bell, aged 8, bound to Samuel Carr.

(228) Application for dower: Eliza J. Roberson, widow of James Roberson VS Sarah, Adline, Thompson, Jacob, and John Roberson, the only heirs.

October 1866

(242) Jourdin Carden, Adm. of William C. Morelock VS Nancy Morelock widow, Margaret A., Hetty Ann, John, George, and Lafayett Morelock, citizens of Monroe Co., and Samuel and Larkin Morelock, citizens of Georgia.

(251) Comm. app. to lay off year's support for Elizabeth Jacobs widow of J.J. Jacobs.

(252) Will of William Bowers proven.

(253) Plat of dower land assigned to Mrs. Eliza Jane Roberson in real estate of James Roberson, dec'd.

(254) W.J. Hutcherson app. Gdn. to L.S. and L.J. Hutcherson, minors of Robert Hutcherson, dec'd.

(255) List of insolvences, removed, overage, and over tax for year 1865 in twenty districts of Monroe Co. includes George and Lafayett Morrow as dead.

November 1866

(259) Jane A. Roy app. Gdn. to Calvin W., Lewis W., Esther L., Sarah A., and James A. Roy, minor orphans of James Roy.

(261) Petition for dower: Polly Gaston, widow of James Gaston VS Joseph, George, and J.V. Gaston, Rachel Kiser, Malinda Kiser, the only heirs.

(261) Comm. app. to lay off year's support for Rebeca Millsaps widow of Andrew Millsaps.

(262) Enos D. Shields released from bond for bound boy John Gilley who ran away.

(265) Williams Carter declared of unsound mind and his wife Susan aged 82 and heirs Jackson Carter aged 50, Nancy Wilson aged 48, Anderson Carter aged 46, Elizabeth Carter aged 44, Calvin Carter aged 40, Martin Carter's heirs to wit Nancy Carter 18, heirs of Martha Leonard to wit Anderson Leonard 15, Thomas Leonard 14, Sam Leonard 12, David Leonard 10.

December 1866

(267) Samuel McSpadden, Sr. released from bond for a bound boy William A. Williams who was taken by father of said child.

(268) James Devine app. Gdn. to Martha, Lucinda, Jacob, Margaret, and Julia A. Devine, minors of Joseph Devine.

(269) Will of A.L. Wilson proven.

(269) Will of Larkin Cardin, Sr. proven.

(272) Edwin Hall petitions to be released as security for Samuel J. Hutcherson "who has emigrated" and released guardianship of Leathy J. Hutcherson.

(272) Resignation of C.M. McGhee, who has moved to Knox Co., as Gdn. of Bettie, Magill, and John McGhee and other minor children of his dec'd brother Barclay McGhee.

(274) Orphan boy named William L. Selvy apprenticed to Allen C. Broome.

(274) Petition for dower: Rebecca Millsaps widow of Andrew Millsaps VS Henry S., William, Martha, Mary, Joseph, Houston, Bartlett, and Andrew Millsaps, the only heirs.

January 1867

(285) Will of Daniel Bain proven.

(286) Comm. app. to lay off year's support for Julia Hankins, widow of Edward Hankins.

(286) James R. Cunningham released from liability for bound boy Samuel Wyric who left by persuasion of his mother.

(287) Samuel Edington app. Gdn. to Fannie, Samuel, and Mary Fowler minors of Abijah Fowler.

(287) John Grant app. Adm. of Benjamin Johnson.

February 1867

(297) Will of John McCroskey proven.

(297) Application for dower: Renah Allen widow of Thomas J. Allen who died 1866 VS Anderson Hawkins, Adm., Henderson and D.B.S. Allen, Anderson Hawkins and wife E.A., the only heirs.

March 1867

(301) George W. Ervine and wife Sophia and Caroline Evans contest Will of Larkin Carden; papers certified to Circuit Court; Sophia and Caroline are children of Larkin.

(302) Madison G. Wright app. Gdn. to Sela E. and Sarah Glass, minor orphans of William Glass.

(302) Will of John McCroskey probated.

(303) Samuel M. Haun app. Gdn. to Robert H. Allen, minor orphan of T.J. Allen.

April 1867

(308) Court pays for coffin for McCazy Brewer, pauper.

(309) Court pays for burial clothes for Pegy Cardin, pauper.

(318) Will of Samuel Henderson probated.

(320) Ann R. Dobson app. Gdn. to Mary C. and John H. Dobson.

May 1867

(331) J. Harvy Johnston app. Gdn. to Sallie M. and C.M. Johnston, minor children of James H. Johnston, dec'd.

(332) James T. Baker app. Gdn. to Jesse B. Grubb, minor of John Grubb.

(334) Comm. app. to lay off year's support for Susan, widow of William Carter.

(336) Settlement by Henry Sheets, Gdn. to minor heirs of Henry Sheets, Jr.

(337) Mary A. Mumford, who was app. Execx. of Elisha Johnson Aug 1866, has died; Elihu J. Mumford app. Exec. in her stead.

June 1867

(340) Will of John Coltharp probated.

(344) A.J. Wilson found guilty of begetting a bastard child on the body of Eliza Ball.

July 1867

(346) Court pays for coffins for John Edwards, Ephraim Clark, William Beakman, and James Hampton, paupers.

(347) Court pays for coffin for Alex Williams, pauper.

(348) Court pays for burial clothes for Thomas Swaggerty, pauper.

(351) Margaret Clift, widow of Houston Clift VS Elisha Tallent, A.B. Clift, M.J. Lankford, S.N., L.M., A.T., J.B., J.D., and C.H. Clift; petition for dower.

(351) Certicate to William Fowler for application for license to practice law.

(352) Osias Rhea app. Gdn. to Thomas & George Rhea, minor orphans of Osias Rhea.

(359) W.L. McSpadden app. Gdn. to William T. McSpadden, minor orphan of Thomas T. McSpadden.

August 1867

(362) Samuel Carr released from bond for bound boy Clarence Bell, who has been decoyed away by the boy's mother.

(365) Nancy C. Cline VS J.L. Cline and others; A.B. Clift died in summer of 1862 and C.H. Clift the Exec. did little towards winding up said estate, and died; Jan 1867: J.L. Cline app. Adm. de bonis non; Nancy C. Cline dissents from Will of said A.B. Clift, her former husband, for purpose of having dower assigned.

September 1867

(368) Petition for dower: Elizabeth Ghormly, widow, VS J.L., W.H., and A. Ghormly, Thomas A. and Rachel A. Henderson, Jason McMullin and wife Sallie M., E.B. Ellis and wife E.J., the only heirs of James Ghormly, dec'd.

(368) Petition for dower: Renah Allen, widow VS Anderson Hawkins
and wife E.A. Allen, and David and Robert W. Allen, heirs of Thomas
J. Allen, who died Aug 1866; Anderson Hawkins is also the Adm.

(369) Comm. app. to lay off year's support to Aquilla, widow of
Richard Mills.

(369) Robert Cunningham app. Gdn. to William H. Cunningham, a
minor orphan of Allice Cunningham.

(370) Nancy C. Cline VS John L. Cline, T.B. Ross and wife Polly
A., James M., Hugh P., Margaret M., Mary J., and Missouri A.
Clift, the only heirs of Alfred B. Clift, who died in summer of
1862.

(371) Comm. app. to lay off year's support to Eliza, widow of John
W. Bruster.

October 1867

(376) James A. Caldwell granted certificate to obtain license to
practice law.

(376) Joseph Elledge released from working on public roads because
of loss of one arm.

November 1867

(394) Comm. app. to lay off year's support for Caroline widow of
Toliver White, Jane widow of Jacob Cook, Susan widow of George
Patterson, and Martha E. widow of Samuel G. Maxwell.

(397) Joseph Upton app. Adm. of Alfred Upton (Colored).

December 1867

(400) Comm. app. to lay off year's support for Teressa N., widow
of John Scruggs.

(400) George Brown and J.F. Magill decline to serve as Gdns. to
the children of Samuel E. McSpadden and Mary his wife formerly
Mary Brown, under the Will of Joseph Brown. Samuel E. McSpadden
is app. Gdn.

(402) Samuel E. McSpadden app. Gdn. to Thomas W., Joseph W., Mary
E., John T., Catharine M., George, and Inos McSpadden, minor
children of S.E. and Mary McSpadden, and minors of Joseph Brown,
dec'd.

(403) Thomas B. Ross app. Gdn. to James M., Hugh P., Margaret M.,
Nancy J., and Missouri A. Clift, minor heirs of A.B. Clift.

(409) Nancy C. White widow of Toliver White.

(410) Mrs. Nancy Caroline White, widow, VS Clift Henry and wife
Sarah formerly White, Marion Breeden and wife Caroline formerly
White, David Lovley and wife Harriett formerly White, and Jane
and George White; Petition for dower.

January 1868

(419) Comm. app. to lay off year's support to Lucretia, widow of
Lafayette Carson.

(420) Elisha Tallent, Adm. of C.H. Clift VS A.B. and S.N. Clift, Taylor Lankford and wife and others: Gdn. ad litem app. for A.B., S.N., L.M., A.T., J.B., J.D., and C.H. Clift, minor children and heirs of C.H. Clift; Margaret Clift and M.J. Lankford have been served with processes; publication has been made as to Taylor Lankford who absconded or is now a non-resident; defendants are heirs of C.H. Clift.

(422) Comm. app. to lay off year's support for Rebecca, widow of Isaac Cole.

(424) Will of John Pennington probated.

(424) Registered voters of Monroe Co., Jan 6, 1868, number 1060 white and 283 colored.

(425) James R. Cunningham app. Gdn. to Alice J., Merand F., and Thomas C. Renfro, minor orphans of Melvin Renfro.

February 1868

(429) Will of James Curtis probated.

(430) D.W. Latimore app. Gdn. to James W. and Joseph D. Curtis, minor heirs of William R. Curtis, and to William A. and Isaac B. Curtis, minor heirs of Burton Curtis.

(431) B.P. Rogers app. Gdn. to Sarah A. Tallent, minor heir of John Tallent.

(434) Will of Mary Young probated.

(436) Martha Millsaps, widow, VS Heirs of Michael Millsaps; application for dower.

(436) Mary Trotter, widow, VS Heirs of Phillip Trotter; application for dower.

(438) Specifications and plans for new Court house.

March 1868

(445) Edwin Hall app. Gdn. to Margaret M., Susan C., Martha S., Betty C., D.H., John F., and Polly A.I. Mullins, minor heirs of Joseph Mullins, in place of Toliver White, dec'd.

(447) Petition for dower; Elizabeth Hawkins, widow, VS J.R. Burchfield, John Hawkins, Elizabeth Smith and husband Thomas Smith, Sarah Jane Millsaps and husband Eligah Millsaps, Rachel C., Adline D., Gregory F., and Nancy M. Hawkins, and other personal and real representatives of Gregory F. Hawkins, who died about 10 Sep 1867.

(452) Mrs. M.E. Sloan formerly Mrs. T.L.D. Trotter, a citizen of Cass Co., Ga., who was app. as one of Adms. of T.L.D. Trotter in Feb and has since married T.M. Sloan, petitions to be released as Adm.; Petition was filed at Oct Session 1867 and was mislaid.

April 1868

(469) Court pays for coffin for Martin Dunkin and Henry Snider, paupers.

(498) Proposal to erect new Court house, by John Minis; specifica-

tions. ̲/̄On back cover of this book is a small drawing of a building which appears to be the new Court hous̲e̲/̄.

(498) Oliver Ragsdale app. Gdn. to Robert, James, John, Amanda,
and Martha Jacobs, minor orphans of John Jacobs.

May 1868

(501) Sidney G. Cleveland, widow, VS Frank K. Berry and wife
Caroline Berry formerly Cleveland, the only heirs of Robert R.
Cleveland who died 7 Apr 1868.

(501) Petition to sell land of Sarah Warren, dec'd; W.L., William,
and Sarah Edwards, Margaret and William Lowry, Elizabeth and James
Lillard, John W. and John Edwards, heirs; five shares in land;
W.L., John W., and John Edwards one share each, Elizabeth and James
Lillard one share, William and Sarah Edwards 1/3 of one share each,
and Margaret and William Lowry the remaining 1/3 of one share.

(503) Will of Archibald Sloan probated.

July 1868

(525) Court pays for coffins for Elizabeth Miller and F.M. Felts,
paupers.

(530) Martha J. Messimer app. Gdn. to Mary E. Messimer, minor
orphan.

(535) J.H. Worthy app. Adm. of Lewis Blankenship.

(536) Will of Joseph S. Milligan probated.

(538) Jury finds Mrs. Jane Cook, widow of Jacob Cook, of unsound
mind since her husband's death about 22 Oct 1867; report titled
"Eve Mills, Monroe Co."

(541) Will of Mrs. Susan J.E. Henly probated.

(546) Settlement by J.D. Roberson, Gdn. to Sidney E. Wilcoxen, a
minor heir of James Roberson.

August 1868

(552) Petition to sell land; David M. and Isaac Lindsey, 3rd, VS
Thomas, George, and Ozias Rhea, Matilda, David, Mary E., Martha,
and Tennessee Lindsey, heirs of Isaac Lindsey.

September 1868

(557) Petition to sell land; J.V. Gaston, Adm. of James Gaston, VS
Mary, Joseph, and George W. Gaston, and Eli, Malinda, Jonas, and
Rachel Kizer, and Thomas, James, and Margaret Gaston, George and
Jane Snider, Jacob and Malinda Rhines, and Russell Gaston. Publi-
cation ordered in the "Philadelphia Pilot" published in Philadelphia,
Tenn.

(559) Nancy Saffle, widow, VS James, Samuel, Mary, Thomas, Washington, John, and Nancy Jane Saffle, children of Thomas Saffle who
died 1867; petition for dower.

(560) Certificate to Charles W. Hicks to apply for law license.

(561) Francis J. Lillard, orphan girl, apprenticed to John W. Cloninger.

(561) Sarah McConky, wife of John McConky, and widow of James W. Rogers, renounces her right to dower.

(562) Will of Thomas Crowder probated.

(563) Nancy Blankenship, widow, VS W.B., I.E., Lewis H., James H., and John S. Blakenship, minor heirs of John T. Blankenship, Mary E. and James H. Worthy, Nancy A. and John B. Lillard, Francis J. and C.E. Pardue, and James H. Worthy, Adm.

(564)T.J. Hunt app. Gdn. to John A., Mary A., Nicholas, Martha, and N.B. Rogers, minor orphans of James W. Rogers.

October 1868

(573) Will of John Cary probated.

(573) Rachel Kinnaman app. Gdn. to Mary J. and Robert Kinnaman, minor orphans of Samuel Kinnaman.

(574) Aquilla Presly app. Gdn. to Jane, Christian, Roland, Marshall, and Thomas Mills, minor orphans of Richard Mills.

(574) James I. Phillips, orphan, apprenticed to Isaac Phillips.

(587) Court pays for coffins for Isabella Freeman and for the wife of Josiah Atkins, paupers.

(588) Court pays for coffins for Isaac Jones, Rebecca Lyons, and Caroline Bell, all paupers.

November 1868

(598) Comm. app. to lay off year's support for Lavenia A., widow of William Hunt.

(598) Comm. app. to lay off year's support for Fidelia A., widow of W.W. Stephens.

(598) Samuel Henderson released from bond for bound girl named Eliza Brown who has been given up to her stepfather, Edward Smithwick.

December 1868

(605) Comm. app. to lay off year's support for Louisa, widow of John R. Johnston.

(607) W.P. Cole app. Gdn. to Mary M. and Bexsey E. Cole, minor orphans of Isaac Cole.

(608) Thomas G. Boyd app. Gdn. to Wattata Wesly Alexander Dulasha minor orphans of Dulasha dec'd. /sic/

(608) Joseph Martin app. Adm. of Prudy Martin (Colored).

Only those cases which have historical or genealogical interest
have been abstracted or noted.

(1) Circuit Court held for Monroe Co. at house of William Dickson
on South bank of Tennessee River on 1st Monday of May 1820...
holden by Hon. Charles F. Keith, Judge.... John B. Tipton appointed
Clerk; William B. Warren, J.P.; Daniel D. Foute, Deputy Clerk;
John McCrosky, Sheriff.

(4) May 1820; next Court to be held at Kelsoe's; on 21 Feb 1814 in
Monroe Co., Peter Upshaw bound himself to deliver a trunk of goods
at house of Isaac Ball in Roane Co.

(12) Sep 1820; In 1818 in what is now Monroe Co. but was Indian
Territory, Andrew Taylor sold land to James Anderson.

(23) Nov 1821; Petition of Mary Castel by next friend Henry Whitten-
burg for divorce from husband Abraham Castel, whom she married 1
Aug 1818; in Jun 1819 he went to Ky.; in winter of 1820 he was in
this country and when he left he took with him Polly Heartgrave,
and petitioner has been informed they have married.

(32) Jun 1821; In Oct 1815 in Pendleton District, S.C., John M.
Dooly obtained judgment against Poledore Naylor; Naylor has removed
himself out of Tennessee.

(37) Dec 1821; Court to be held at Caldwell's in May 1822; in Feb
1819, John Grigsby in possession of a lease of land on East side
of Big Pigeon River in Cocke Co. and transferred said lease to
Harris Dewitt, but Dewitt was sued and ejected from said land.

(39) Mar 1823; Benjamin Neal recovered judgment against James Todd
in McMinn Co., where Todd was then living.

(41) May 1822; Andrew Taylor, a white man, registered for reservation 1 May 1818 in Hiwassee District at Citico Old Town, as head
of an Indian family, but the Treasurer of East Tenn. sold said
land, registered to Andrew and David Taylor, and Mathew W. McGhee
was highest bidder.

(47) Sep 1822; In Feb 1819 in Wilkes Co., Ga., Andrew Ruddle for
use of John Carmichael recovered judgment against Joseph Phillips
as garnishee of Robert Browder; Robert and William Browder were
partners.

(71) Jun 1822; William Henry and Absolem Beck became bail for
Thomas Harvey 20 Aug 1821 (debt); claim that Beck was under 21
and that Harvey died in Georgia is denied by plaintiff and requires
proof.

(80) Sep 1822; John Walker, Sr. indebted to John Lowry for "going
into the Cherokee Nation to the residence of Charles Hicks and
settling and liquidating the accounts existing between the said
John Walker and the said Cherokee Nation..."

(86) Nov 1823; Petition of Benjamin Clark; warrant issued on him
in Lincoln Co., N.C. 20 Apr 1815.

(100) May 1824; Samuel McTeer is Coroner.

(107) Oct 1824; In Jan 1823, James Starr, Wenanchee his wife,

Tasanchih otherwise Tasanchih Maw, Nelly otherwise Nelly Maw, Eubeche otherwise Eubeche Maw, leased land to John Den who then leased to Richard Few.

(155) May 1825; George Selvage granted divorce from wife Mary formerly Mary Catlet, whom he married in Cocke Co. in 1807; in Dec 1818 she left him and family of small children in Roane Co.; he has lived in Monroe Co. for more than a year.

(228) On 15 Mar 1820, Jesse Butler was of Morganton, Blount Co., and now is of Monroe Co.

(229) May 1826; Eleanor Melton by next friend James Edington petitions for divorce from husband Jesse Melton of Sevier Co.; married 4 Jun 1805, lived in Sevier, Blount, and Monroe Counties until 1825 when Nancy Bell, a young woman who had lived with them for more than two years became pregnant by Jessee and bore his child; Eleanor dismisses her suit.

(243) Nov 1826; John Den Lessee VS Eli Cleaveland et al; Joseph Routh admitted to defend in room of Solomon Barker and it is ordered that William Dillard and William Patton jointly with Yrpts Mayberry be Gdns. of Solomon, John, Polly, and Betty Routh.

(302) Dec 1824; Death of Josiah Payne of Blount Co. is suggested; Samuel Patterson leased 9 Apr 1823, of Samuel Douthit of Blount Co., a certain ferry boat and land situated at the old crossing place near Morganton.

(316) Apr 1826; John Miller a citizen of Cherokee Nation is Atty. in fact for Telaskaki, who took reservation in Monroe Co. and was run off through fear of white men, but left a white man as Lessee; John Isbell was granted same land.

(338) May 1828; Joseph McCoy granted guardianship of Francis McCoy, infant son of Cummings McCoy, dec'd; in Dec 1827 Malinda Kenner was appointed Gdn. by Court of Pleas and Quarter Sessions and Joseph McCoy appealed.

(341) Nov 1827; George Selvage and wife Nancy VS Buckner Walker and Mary Selvage, Execs. of Jeremiah Selvidge, dec'd; writ against Mary issued to Roane Co.; in Dec 1825 Joseph Selvage was indebted to Nancy Selvage, then Nancy Oaks, a single woman.

(388) Apr 1828; Anderson & Foute VS William Bayless, Debt; defendant disputes the account on the ground that his wife had left his bed and board and he did not feel liable for any of her debts, but he offered no evidence to prove that this was a matter of notoriety; suit dismissed.

(414) Mar 1828; Mark Phillips VS Michael Carroll, and John Lowry, Nicholas S. Peck, Joseph R. Henderson, Minter Cantrell, Adms. and Elizabeth Cantrell formerly Elizabeth Bradley, Adminx. of James Bradley, dec'd; in Nov 1825 Michael Carroll and James Bradley executed covenant; the Adms. and Adminx. appointed 1826 and afterwards said Elizabeth married said Minter Cantrell.

(459) Nov 1828; Samuel A. McKenzie, Alexander Hart, and Isaac Humble, Adms. of Samuel Loughmiller, dec'd.

(521) Sep 1829; in Dec 1823, Joseph Alexander assignee of William

Utter of Blount Co. recovered judgment against Joshua Parsons.

(536) In Nov 1821 Henry Coil executed note to Jesse Kerr of Blount Co. who was on his way to Georgia; in 1829 arbitrators meet at home of William Henry in Blount Co.

In this book, depositions were ordered to be taken of the following persons, with page number denoted:

1824

(107) Johnathan Kerkendoll of Alabama; Joseph McMinn, John McCarty, and John Spears who live near the Agency in McMinn Co.

1825

(142) David Hays of Haywood Co., N.C.; Harmon Little of Humphreys Co.

1826

(107) William Lea of Washington City.

(142) William Novell and George Wate of Bedford Co.

1827

(207) Benjamin Catlett of Sevier Co.

1828

(195) William Tipton of Blount Co.; Robert Rhea who is old and infirm of Monroe Co.

(412) William, Elizabeth, and Emeline Irby.

(452) James C. Mitchell of McMinn Co.

CIRCUIT COURT RECORDS 1821-1830
STATE CASES

(2) May 1821; John B. Tipton, Clerk, by Daniel D. Foute, Deputy Clerk; William Upton, Deputy Sheriff.

(6) Nov 1821; A conviction of horse stealing; the sentence consisted of twenty lashes on bare back, sitting in pilory two hours on three several days, being branded on inside of left hand with the letter H.T., and imprisoned in jail of Monroe Co. for six calendar months, and charged with costs of the prosecution.

(37) May 1823; Hamon Helton found guilty of mortally wounding John Cross at Tellico, causing his death on 11 Apr 1823; John Helton charged with aiding; witnesses: Betsy Helton, Joseph Phillips, Samuel Colquith, William Williams, George Loftis.

(43) May 1823; William Clinton of Monroe Co. found not guilty of the murder of a Cherokee Indian named Cumberland at Tellico, who died 23 Feb 1823; John Wilkerson, Atty. Gen. for third solicitorial District.

(71) Jun 1823; James Baker, Polly Daniel, Hiram Vincent and his

wife Polly are accused of beating Mrs. Polly Harvey.

(104) Dec 1824; Elizabeth Brumly indicted for persuading Lewis Davis to murder James Thompson; she is found not guilty.

(115) Nov 1824; Solomon Barlow of Illinois is put in jail because he is a suspicious character.

(118) May 1825; True Bill; Lewis Davis otherwise called Lewis Brumley otherwise called Lewis Humley late of Monroe Co., labourer, on 13 Nov 1824 at Tellico River shot and killed James Thompson.

(131) Jun 1825; Warrant: Commissioners appointed by County Court to collect and preserve the goods and chattels of Absalem Smith, dec'd, complain that they have reason to believe that Samuel Patterson, labourer, hath been accessary and instrumental in the death of Absalem Smith, dec'd, and has taken the personal property, and has forged an instrument of writing purporting to be a Will, and has taken on himself the management of the estate; defendant is discharged.

(157) Mar 1825; Arrie Stover, single woman, accuses John Jobe of being father of her bastard child; John Jobe found to be a resident of Washington Co.; Arrie dismisses her suit and Jobe pays costs.

(162) Nov 1826; Keziah Mize alias Keziah Vance of Monroe Co., spinstress, at home of Arthur Orr on Big Creek, did cut with a knife James W. Meek; nolle prosqui.

(176) Jul 1826; Warrant: Edmond Lyons makes oath that John Mize, Sr. of Monroe Co., labourer, has intermarried with one Keziah Vance in Monroe Co., but he has another wife now living to whom he has not been divorced; James W. Meek deputized to execute warrant; nolle prosqui.

(190) Nov 1826; Jones Griffin late of Monroe Co.; May 1827 Capias executed on Jones Griffin in McMinn Co.; Nov 1828, Jones Griffin not to be found in McMinn Co.

(232) Nov 1827; Russell Lawson indicted for mortally wounding Wilson Duggan with a knife at Fork Creek on 3 Nov 1827; Duggan died 5 Nov 1827; James Lea and John Lawson indicted for aiding; found not guilty.

(272) Nov 1828; Harrison S. Ragsdale of Monroe Co. indicted for mortally wounding by a stroke with a gun, on 27 Sep 1828 at the Tennesse River, John L. Hopkins, who died 30 Sep 1828; James Rollins, Absolem Strutton, Hiram Murry, and Moses Roberts, all of Monroe Co. indicted for aiding; not a True Bill against Moses Roberts; Jury after a trial lasting eight days finds Ragsdale guilty; nole prosqui entered as to Absalem Strutton; James Rollins found not guilty of murder but of "feloneous slaying", after a four day trial; Ragsdale sentenced to be hanged on 13 Feb 1829 and appeals to Supreme Court; James Rollins sentenced to be branded with letter M on left hand, confined in jail for two months, and pay costs of prosecution; case of Hiram Murry continued. Transcript of record for Supreme Court: Court ordered the Sheriff to summon a jury of fifty one including the original panel and to summon the most respectable men he could find in the court yard to which latter direction by the Court the defendant excepts; witness

Joseph Milikan states that he was at house of William Harrison in
Monroe Co. that is near the Muster Ground of Capt. Smith's company
which had paraded there before the fight; he heard deceased Hopkins
talk of killing the son of McIntosh of Georgia in a duel; Major
Stephens tried to squash the affray; witnesses for State are Joseph
Milikan, John Wilson, Samuel Hensley, William Williams, Thomas
Harrison, Dr. Nathan Harris, Samuel Yates, Richard Roberts, Lewis
Smith, James Wright, William Flanigan, Moses Roberts, James Harri-
son, Edward McEldry, Stephens Rhea (who is cousin to wife of
deceased); witnesses for defentant are John Strutton (brother of
Absalem Strutton), Jackson Pannell, Elijah Kelly (who waded the
river going to muster and drank some spirits while there and waded
the River when he went home and slipped and fell in), Thomas
Hensly, Jonathan Poland, Anderson Millsaps, Elisha Freshour,
Jeremiah Carver, Daniel Russell, Valentine Harris, James Rose, J.
Campbell Carsier, William Culver, William Wheeler, Benjamin Prater
(defendant had rented land of him), Lewis Miller, William Murry
(has known defendant for many years and his son is one of defendants); /all or most of these witnesses were at the muster ground at
the fight/; nolle prosqui entered against Hiram Murry. /This trial
and transcript cover forty-three pages in the book./

(338) Jun 1829; Ann Wilson, single woman, accuses George Worthy,
Jr. of Monroe Co. of being father of her male bastard child born
28 Nov 1828.

(345) Sep 1829; Narcissa R. Cary makes oath that Hugh Twomey did
assault John E. Cary, Jr.

CIRCUIT COURT RECORDS
STATE AND CIVIL ENROLLMENT 1830-1831

May Court 1830

(38) Apr 1828; William Bayless charges Able and Jacob Pearson with
persuading his wife Sarah Bayless to remove herself from his residence and taking his slaves with her.

(106) 13 Feb 1829; John Browder, Adm. of Robert Browder, dec'd,
VS Samuel H. Crawley and Mary Carden, Adms. of Robert Carden,
dec'd.

November Court 1830

(140) Nov 1829; Sarah, wife of William Ainsworth.

(142) In November 1824, John Menifee entered into covenant with
John France, both of Monroe Co.; John France to build a two story
house.

(168) Petition Dec 1829: Abel Stow of Monroe Co. died 182 /sic/
leaving the following children, to wit, John Stow, Jarrett Stow,
Martha Smith formerly Martha Stow who married Joseph Smith, Sally
Carter formerly Sally Stow who married Charles Carter, all of whom
are of age.

(175) Deposition to be taken of Frank Bounds of Knox Co.

May Court 1831

(214) George Duggan of Monroe Co granted divorce from wife Celia
Duggan formerly Celia M. Baugard of Monroe Co.; they were married
25 Jan 1827; Celia eloped Mar 1828 with William Mills to Kentucky.

(223) James Spears of Monroe Co granted divorce from Sophia Spears
formerly Sophia Heston whom he married 24 Dec 1824; lived in
Monroe Co. for four years; in Sep 1829 Sophia eloped with one John
Sexton, taking most of her husband's possessions and his horse
with her; petitioner is informed that Sexton said they were going
to Illinois.

(226) Elenor Melton by her next friend Hardy C. Tatum, granted
divorce from Jesse Melton; for many years Jesse treated Elenor with
respect but four or five years ago began repeated acts of adultery
with a certain Miss /sic7 and has had several children by her.

November Court 1831

(316) John Morris of Roane Co. petitions that on 24 Mar 1829 his
brother Israel Morris executed note.

CIRCUIT COURT STATE & CIVIL ENROLLMENT 1852-1866

May Term 1852

(9) Avery Van Miller, Elizabeth Inlaw and husband Philip Inlaw,
Alfred Miller, Lucinda Adair and husband Calvin L. Adair, Almira
Paiden and husband Benjamin Paiden, Andrew J. Miller, and Isabella
Hicks leased the Andrew Miller reservation to John Den.

(22) 4 May 1847, Thomas White, who made note, is a resident of
Ohio; attachment levied on 5000 acres of land he owns in 16th and
17th Districts of Monroe Co. on both sides of Citico Creek.

(25) Joel Cash died 1850 in Monroe Co., leaving the following as
heirs: Shadrak Cash who is summoned in Knox Co., Benjamin, John,
and Barkley Cash, Mary wife of Samuel Duggan, Tabitha wife of
Abraham Tipton, Keziah wife of Thomas Gibson, all of whom are
nonresidents, and Joel Cash, Nancy and Lazarus Henson, Susan and
Robert Aiken (Eakin), and Jacob J. Tipton, and the last named was
appointed Adm.

(30) Christopher Boston died in Monroe Co. in 1849, leaving a
widow Elizabeth, and one or two minor children, whose names are
unknown to Benjamin Arp, Adm., all of whom left Tenn. a short time
after the death of Christopher and are now residents of N.C.

September Term 1852

(47) William Griffith died in Monroe Co. 19 Mar 1848 leaving no
issue, but brothers and sisters: John Griffith, Rebecca Marshall
formerly Griffith wife of Henry Marshall, Edward, Jane, and Delila
Griffith, all of Monroe Co.

January Term 1853

(88) Copy of Will of Samuel Douthet.

(111) Sarah S. Jordan formerly Scruggs granted divorce from John Jordan; married in 1845 in Monroe Co.; they removed to Lumpkin Co., Ga. in Sep 1846 and remained there until Sep 1848 when said John abandoned her; she returned to her father's home in Monroe Co. in Aug 1849; she is given control of their infant daughter.

(96) Deposition to be taken of Ralph Hagler of Texas, 1850.

(113) Adra Bowman dismisses her petition for divorce from Edwin Bowman; married Oct 1841; he abandoned her in Oct 1844; it is suggested and admitted to the Court that since filing the petition Adra has married James M. Cannon.

(119) William G. Bogle has been Gdn. of Margaret E. and Lucretia P. Wear for several years, both are still minors but Lucretia P. married A.L. Carson in latter part of 1850.

May Term 1853

(127) William Carter died in Monroe Co. 26 Mar 1851 intestate and without issue, leaving widow Elizabeth and the following brothers and sisters: Robert and Fleming B. Carter, Jane C. Rowan formerly Carter wife of Samuel J. Rowan, and John A. Debrill, a minor and only heir of Mary E. Debrill formerly Carter, who had married Montgomery C. Debrill and died before her brother the said William Carter, all residents of Monroe Co. except John A. Debrill who lives in White Co; (136) the marriage of widow Elizabeth with William Neil is admitted.

(139) In 1848 John Brown brings suit against James H. Alexander, James Hickman, Joseph Marshall, Isaac C. Marshall, and E.A. Moore, Execs. of Willet W. Marshall, dec'd, to collect $500 which Brown claims he gave to Willet W. Marshall in City of Vera Cruz to deliver to Madisonville in Monroe Co.; Summons executed on Joseph Marshall in Campbell Co., on E.A. Moore (Inn Keeper) in Davidson Co., on James Hickman and Isaac C. Marshall in Jefferson Co.

September Term 1853

(208) William H. Montgomery of Knox Co. sues John Fine of Monroe Co. for fees for medical services.

(223) 12 Apr 1851, Drury Norman died intestate in Monroe Co. Feb 1851, leaving widow Elizabeth and children, Huldah Ann, Isaac B., Rhoda, and Amanda M. Norman, all minors of Monroe Co. (15 Jan 1852) Isaac Weaver, Adm., has died since last term of Court held Sep 1851, and Milton Morrison has been appointed Adm.

(234) Petition of John McClain of Blount Co., Adm. of Samuel Douthet, dec'd, to sell slaves; Samuel Douthet died intestate in 1852 in Monroe Co. where he had been a citizen for a great many years, leaving a large number of children and about ten grand-children whose parents are dead.

(238) Petition of heirs of Jacob Baker who died 6 Oct 1852 intestate in Monroe Co.

(242) James Lillard died in Monroe Co. Jul 1830, and James A. Haire and Samuel McCroskey were appointed Adms.; one of Adms. is dead and the other has not had anything to do with estate for twenty years. James Lillard died leaving widow Elizabeth of Monroe Co. and the following children, Lucy Jane wife of Isam Watson, William W., John B., and James A. Lillard all of Monroe Co., Rachel Ann wife of James Forsythe of Georgia, and Amanda C. wife of Wade L. Hampton. Amanda C. is now dead leaving Sarah E. and Mary Hampton her only children, who live in Miss. with their father and Gdn.

(245) Jacob Sheets died testate 18 Feb 1853; widow Margaret, a citizen of Monroe Co., dissented from said Will; Jacob left the following heirs: John and Henry Sheets, Polly Gaston formerly Sheets wife of James Gaston, Catharine Bogart formerly Sheets wife of John Bogart, Martha Mosier formerly Sheets wife of John Mosier, Margaret Shields formerly Sheets wife of Joseph Shields, all of age and all of Monroe Co.

January Term 1854

(248) John Norman, of Monroe Co., died 7 Apr 1851 leaving six children living, all of age of twenty-one, to wit, Allen Norman, Martha wife of Preston G.B. Melton, Susannah wife of Robert Sharp, Minerva wife of Richard Hicks, Milly wife of James W. Taylor, and John N. Norman; he also left seven or eight children of Elizabeth White, dec'd., and children of Matilda White, dec'd, to wit, Malen P. White about 19 years old, Isaac Jackson White about 16, and William M. White about 13; he also left the children of Drury Norman, dec'd, to wit Huldah Ann about 10 years old, Isaac Bartly about 7, Rhoda about 4, and Manda Margaret about 10 months old. Elizabeth the widow of John Norman dec'd is to have a child's part.

(260) Parker Hood of Monroe Co. died Jul 1851 testate; the Exec. named in Will refused to serve; Parker Hood died leaving widow Amanda and three minor children, John A., William H., and Sydney Caroline.

(269) Petition to sell land filed 6 Sep 1852; James Humphreys died about 26 Oct 1835 intestate leaving widow Nancy and children William C. and Adaline who are now of age and Van Buren and Sophira who are minors; on 28 Dec 1853 it is reported to the Court that William C. Humphreys is now dead leaving a widow and one child.

(276) Petition filed 12 Sep 1853 to sell land; William C. Humphreys died Jun 1853 intestate leaving widow Leona and son James.

May Term 1854 on page 304

September Term 1865 on page 305

(305) 11 Sep 1865, Pleas at the Masonic Hall in Madisonville, the court house being burned down or destroyed by fire; present and presiding the Hon. Elijah T. Hall, Judge.

(307-482) pages blank.

These abstracts are taken from nine books marked "Circuit Court
Minutes Record" as follows:

> November 1827-November 1834
> May 1835-May 1839
> January 1843-January 1847
> May 1847-January 1851
> May 1851-May 1856
> September 1856-January 1860
> May 1860-September 1866
> September 1866-January 1868
> May 1868-May 1870

November 1827

(1) Circuit Court of Law and Equity; first Monday of November
1827; present the Hon. Edward Scott, Judge.

(2) Michael Corbett VS C.M. McCoy and others; death of Cummings
McCoy is suggested.

(5) Death of Moses Humphries is suggested.

(17) John and Keziah Mize alias Keziah Vance not to be found in
Monroe Co.

(21) John J. Humphries appointed Gdn. pendente lite of Nathaniel,
David, Emaline, and Abraham Humphries, minor heirs of Moses
Humphries, dec'd.

May 1828

(27) Death of John Ogle is suggested.

(32) Death of Thomas Gregory is suggested.

November 1828

(58) Allen Christian, plaintiff in suit, is dead.

(78) Robert and John Gregory, Execs. of Thomas Gregory, dec'd.

(84) Death of John Clayton is suggested.

May 1829

(120) Silas Graves, Adm. of Stephen Graves, Sr., dec'd; Stephen
had gone on bond, May 1827.

(121) Mahala Gratton by next friend Thomas Johnson VS Thomas
Gratton, petition for divorce is dismissed by Court.

(123) Charlotte Shell was in actual possession of land in Monroe
Co. on 28 Nov 1826.

(124) John Wilson VS Caty Wilson, petition for divorce is dismissed by plaintiff.

November 1829

(133) John Sliger VS Letta Sliger, petition for divorce.

(133) Pension Application of Leonard W. Pace of McMinn /sic/ Co.;

aged 44 years; enlisted 1808 under Capt. Alexander Walker, Augusta
Co., Va., sent to Georgia and served five years there; in Nov 1813
enlisted in Charleston, S.C. under Lt. Thomas Elf in Second Reg.,
continued in service for five years; wounded in first enlistment
in 1815 as follows, he was driving a wagon for the army near
Norfolk when news of peace arrived, the soldiers firing their guns
caused the horses to run away and the wagon wheel ran over him; he
has wife and two children, one six and the other three; he continued in service until 1818.

(148) Jesse Melton and Edy Stow, Adms. of Able Stow, dec'd.

(152) Death of John Duff is suggested.

(152) Ann Hogshead, Execx. of William Hogshead, dec'd VS Walter
Carouth, Exec. of James Carouth, dec'd.

November 1830

(190) Power of Atty. from John Torbett and wife Nancy Jane acknowledged by makers.

(194) Death of Andrew Duncan is suggested.

(197) Death of James Logan is suggested and suit is revived in
name of Andrew Cowan, Exec.

(202) John O. Cannon appointed Gdn. pendente lite to James,
William, Margarett, Elizabeth, Martha, and Mary Blair, minor heirs
of W.S. Blair, dec'd.

May 1831

(225) Death of Andrew Henderson is suggested.

(242) Rebecca Duggan, Execx. of Solomon Copland, dec'd VS John
Duggan.

November 1831

(290) Patrick S. Peck VS Joseph R. Henderson, Exec. of Andrew
Henderson, dec'd, Polly Wilson, John Henderson, Nicholas S. Peck
and wife Nancy, Charles W. Norwood and wife Malinda, David Wear
and wife Betsy, Robert N. Henderson, Shadrack Inman and wife Sally.

May 1832

(310) E.B. Watkins, witness to bond, has died.

(315) Death of John Mise is suggested.

(361) Jeremiah Lillard VS Sarah Lillard; petition for divorce
dismissed by plaintiff.

(364) Wiggins and Mashburn, Adms. of William Mashburn, dec'd VS
Brown and Christian, Adms. of Allen Christian, dec'd.

November 1832

(408) William Wilson sentenced to six years in State penitentiary
for murder and John Morrison to two years for same.

(414) Michael A. Read granted divorce from Abigail Read; desertion.

May 1834

(541) Satisfactory evidence introduced to prove that Samuel Steel, Mary C. Steel, Robert Minis and Margaret G. Minnis who was Margaret Steel, William Steel, Sarah M. Steel, and Polly Steel widow of William Steel, dec'd, are the heirs and only heirs of William Steel, dec'd, who married Margaret Sister of Lieutenant Steel of the Navy who served in the war of the revolution that Lieutenant Steel died about the year 1801, 2, or 3, and that William Steel heir aforesaid died about the year 1829 intestate leaving the above named heirs.

(548) In 1833 execution against William Richmond endorsed by Sheriff of McMinn Co., as follows: "Not executed because the defendant was a licensed trader in the Cherokee Nation, transported as an Arkansas emigrant, and was not at any time after the writ came to my hands on the East side of the Hiwassee, but was during all that time within the limits of the Cherokee Nation East of the Mississippi, May 12, 1834."

(579) Death of James Henry suggested and cause revived in names of Samuel Henry and John R. Howard, Adms.

November 1834

(607) Jesse Lemons and wife and William Richmon and wife VS Amos Brimer, Exec. of George Hopkins, dec'd.

(608) Death of Toqua Will is suggested.

(620) Roddy May, Execx. of John May, dec'd.

(625) Death of John W. Stephens is suggested.

(636) Joseph Boyd VS Margaret Boyd; plaintiff suggests that defendant is a married woman and asks leave to amend warrant to read Margaret Graham and William Graham her husband.

(640) James Wilson and Ignatius Wilson for the use of Hiram K. Turk VS William Turk, exec. of Thomas Turk, dec'd; death of Ignatius Wilson is suggested.

(651) Richard M. Burk and John Gethern, Execs. of Allen Armstrong, dec'd.

(659) Alexander Rogers, Adm. of Joseph Rogers, dec'd.

(660) Benjamin Parker, Adm. of Elisha Spraggins, dec'd.

In this book, the following persons are qualified and admitted as attorneys in the Court, with year and page number noted:

1828

(27) Robert H. Hynds.

1830

(195) Samuel L. Childers and Wilson Duggan.

1832

(320) James A. Coffin and (330) William Lowry.

1834

(526) T. Nixon Vandyke, Samuel R. Rogers, (578) George W. Rowles, (580) Charles K. Gillespy, and (615) John R. Williams.

In this book, depositions were ordered to be taken of the following persons, with year and page number noted:

1827

(2) Edward A Lucy of Montgomery Co., with Jane Lucy as the plaintiff in the case. (3) Elizabeth Erby of Bledsoe Co. (16) Joseph
Philips by Jacob West, both of Cherokee Nation.

1828

(33) James Turk of Jackson Co., Ala. (59) John Montgomery and
James Houston of Blount Co. (61) Thompson Loftis of Georgia.

1829

(103) Elija Howell, Edward Maxey, and John Henson in Knox Co.;
Cyrus Turk in Monroe Co. (106) Henry and Isaac Tendle, Randle
Carter, and Martin M. McCoy, nonresidents of Monroe Co. (119)
Thomas Berry of Cherokee Nation. (127) A.B.S.D. Wilson of Hamil-
ton Co. (133) Manuel Smith of South Carolina. (142) Mc. McCray
of Huntsville, Ala.

1830

(202) Horatio G. Perry of Ala.

1831

(246) James Glasgo Williams of McMinn Co. (247) John Hardin,
Thomas Glenn, and William Brown of Burke Co., N.C.; Edward
Williams of Habersham Co., Ga. (255) John Hardin of Madison Co.,
Ala. (285) Michael Hildebran of Cherokee Nation.

1832

(320) Joseph Copeland of Overton Co. (336) John and Mary Taylor
of Bledsoe Co. (343) James McCully of Carroll Co., Ind. (345)
William G. Anderson of Buncombe Co., N.C. (350) John Gilliham of
Cherokee Nation; Joel Morrison of Creek Nation. (403) Jefferson
Dyer of McMinn Co.; Leonard Kean of Morgan Co., Ala.

1833

(432-439) William Montgomery of Creek Nation; Thomas Pruit of
Mecklenberg Co., N.C.; Jacob Pruit of Benton Co., Ala.; John
Rogers and John Curtis of Cherokee Nation; John Scrimsher, John
Hannah, James Chism, and Samuel Childay, all of McMinn Co.;
Isaac Johnston and Thomas Taylor of Roane Co. (467) Eskel Pealer
and Richard G. Dunlap of Lumpkin Co., Ga. (471) Matilda Martin
and Samuel Downy of Blount Co.

1834

(539) James Donohoo of Murry Co., Ga. (551) Benjamin Tinker of
Marion Co. (560) Hugh Montgomery of McMinn Co.; Robert Armstrong
of Knox Co. (586) William Montgomery of Ala. (615) Green C.
McSpadden of Carroll Co., Ga. (621) William Jarrett of West
Tenn. (623) James Young of St. Clair Co., Ala. (626) Daniel
Crutchfield of Anderson Co.; John Morrison of Ga.

MINUTES RECORD 1835-1839

May 1835

(16) William Burris, Adm. of Thomas Spradling, dec'd, VS Lewis Smith.

(23) Justice Steed surviving partner of firm of Joseph Callaway & Justice Steed for the use of Thomas H. Callaway, Arthur H. Henley, and John Callaway, Execs. of Joseph Callaway, dec'd, VS William Lockard.

(33) Alexander Stoal, Adm. of Jacob Thorp, dec'd.

(34) William Upton and Nathan Harris, former Gdns. of children of Absolem Smith, dec'd, for the use of Few Gregory and Stephen Blankenship, present Gdns.

(38) Jesse Lemons and wife, William Richmond and wife VS Amos Brimer, Exec. of George Hopkins, dec'd. Pltfs. dismiss appeal and Clerk to transmit to Clerk of County Court the Will with a copy of record.

(40) Received of John B. Tipton, Clerk of Circuit Court by his deputy Erskine H. Wear, his return from 1 Oct 1833 to 1 Oct 1834 certified by Commissioners of county; signed, John O. Cannon, Wm. M. Stakely, Wm. Grant, John F. Henderson, Comm. for Building the Court House.

November 1835

(74) John W. Stephens VS Allen H. Mathis; Cause is revived in name of Richard Stephens, adm. of John W. Stephens, dec'd.

(89) Charles T. McCray VS Thomas L. Twomey, Chairman School Commission Island Creek.

(97) Harden Carter granted divorce from wife Susannah.

(97) James S. Raper granted divorce from wife Rhoda.

May 1836

(100) Petition of George Selvidge to legitimatize his two illegitimate sons, Pryor and Green K. Oaks, make them joint heirs of his estate equal with his other children, and change names from Oaks to Selvidge; said sons being the children of petitioner and his present wife born before their intermarriage and they reside in his family; petition granted.

(101) Samuel Frazier appointed Atty. Gen. for third solicitorial district.

(101) Thomas J. Russell, Coroner of Monroe Co., certifies to election of Erskin H. Wear as Clerk of Circuit Court. Wear takes oath more effectually to suppress dueling, to support Constitutions of United States and of State of Tenn., also oath of office.

(134) William H. Montgomery and James Gamble VS William, Adaline, and Laura Price, minor heirs of Isaac W. Price, dec'd.

(136) William Bayless and Martina Hunt, Adm. and Adminx. of Thomas

Hunt, dec'd VS Anderson P.H. Jordan; Jury finds that said Thomas Hunt did not accept and receive the said fifty-one reams of paper mentioned in defendants plea; (136) same for fifty-three reams; (137) same for 250 reams.

(142) Elizabeth Norvell by her next friend and father Douglas Barksdale granted divorce from Alexander Norvell; abandonment.

August 1836

(157) Death of Toqua Will has heretofore been suggested and cause revived in names of Nedee or Ned, Anne or Ann, Archy or Archibald, Toqua Sal or Sal of Toqua.

(157) Death of Matthew W. McGhee is suggested.

(175) Charles Kelsoe and Bradley Kimbrough, Adms. of Isaac W. Price, dec'd.

September 1836

(199) William Yarborough dismisses his petition for divorce from wife Elizabeth.

(206) Moses Chambers granted divorce from wife Drotha.

December 1836

(224) William Roberts, Adm. of Elizabeth Millard, dec'd, for the use of Alexander Westmoreland VS William Roberts.

(232) Mary Reasoner, by her next friend Nathaniel T. Smallen, granted divorce from Nicholas Reasoner; abandonment.

April 1837

(265) Robert Gregory, William E. McClure, and Eve Lane, Adms. of Samuel Lane, dec'd.

(267) Polly Woodfin, by next friend Elijah Lee, dismisses her petition for divorce from husband Delin Woodfin.

(270) Petition of Michael Carroll for naturalization granted by Court; resident of Monroe Co. born in 1786 in Ireland, Kill Kenny Co., remained there until 1807 when he emigrated to New York, where he remained about three years, removed to New Jersey where he lived five or six years, thence to Virginia where he resided seven years, and then removed to Monroe Co. where he has resided for the last thirteen years.

May 1837

(300) Ibby Hicks formerly Ibby Miller, Almira Payton formerly Almira Miller, Lucinda Adair formerly Lucinda Miller and Andrew Miller, Lessee VS Charles Donohoo.

September 1837

(334) William Grant, Assignee, VS Samuel, John B., Henson, Emily, Nancy, Daniel B., and Sarah Hunt, James H. Rogers and wife Sina Rogers formerly Sina Hunt, heirs of Thomas Hunt, dec'd.

(338) Daniel Mosier granted divorce from wife Louisa; adultery.

December 1837

(349) Death of Azariah Shelton is suggested.

September 1838

(408) Jacob Kile granted divorce from wife Fanny; adultery.

(411) John Duggan granted divorce from wife Polly; abandonment.

January 1839

(436) Death of James White is suggested.

(446) Death of George C. Graves is suggested.

(446) Lucy Lawson, by her mother and next friend Martha Hood, granted divorce from Hinton Lawson; abandonment and adultery.

(466) Death of James R. Kirk is suggested.

May 1839

(483) Death of James White suggested at last term of Court, and now at this term the record of County Court of Washington Co., Va. appointing James and Eliza White as Adms. of James White, dec'd, having been produced to the Court and also the death of James White the co-administrator having been suggested, it is ordered that suit be revived in name of Eliza White, Adminx.

(487) D. & M. Shields VS William Upton and William A. Upton; death of David Shields is suggested.

(487) Henry Mesimore and Jacob Bible, Execs. of Henry M. Bible, dec'd.

(493) Mahala Duff, by her next friend Thomas Henderson, dismisses her petition for divorce from Nelson Duff.

In this book the following attorneys were qualified and admitted to practice in the Court, with year and page number noted:

1836

(104) William P. Dudley, (155) Napoleon B. Baird, (160) William Williams, (217) Hamilton L. Jarnagin, Robert Reynolds, Thomas N. Frazier, and (218) Samuel H. Copeland.

1837

(259) Thomas J. Campbell and Alexander E. Cannon.

1839

(436) John C. Gantt and (459) John C. Turnly.

In this book, depositions were ordered to be taken of the following persons, with year and page number noted:

1835

(51) John L. Richarson, James Black, and Sampson Black of Habersham Co., Ga.; (65) Amos Carter and Benjamin Carter of Union Co.,
Ga.; (74) Robert Small of Kingston, Roane Co.; (75) Baxter Brown
of Rhea Co.

1836

(105) Lewis Smith, John Grant, and Jacob Keller of Blount Co.;
Eostal Bealer of Campbell Co. in cause in which Armstread Bealer
is defendant; (117) Samuel Henderson of Talladega Co., Ala., in
cause in which John F. Henderson is plaintiff; (133) Isaac Carter
of Benton Co., Ala.; Isaac Murry of Washington Co.; Susannah Ruth
of Knox Co. in cause in which Edward Ruth is plaintiff; (164)
Benjamin Carter of McMinn Co.; (182) John Lowry of Talladega Co.,
Ala.; (213) John N. Shadden of Jefferson Co.; (216) Woods McReynolds of North Carolina; Caswell Hall of Walker Co., Ga.; Hugh
Leeper, James Wiley, and Betsey Scruggs of Blount Co.; Rebecca
Sherrald of Bledsoe Co.; (218) Mary Carter of Benton Co., Ala.

1837

(247) Levi and Peggy Carter of Bradley Co., in cause in which John
W. Carter is defendant; (261) Polly Carter of Benton Co., Ala;
(264-265) Mary Harris of Hamilton Co., Thomas Turk, Ann Turk, and
Robert M. Harris of McMinn Co., Robert Rhea of Blount Co., all in
the cause of Hiram K. Turk VS William Turk, Exec. of Thomas Turk,
dec'd; (270) David W. McReynolds of North Carolina; Joseph Duncan,
and Berry Abernathy of Blount Co.; Martha Miller of Roane Co.;
(279) Joel Hulsey, John Ross, Wiley Hulsey, Harvey Hulsey, James
R. Price, and Isaac G. West of Walker Co., Ga.; Solomon Stow,
Clinton Norvell, Joseph B. Car, and Julius W. Blackwell of McMinn
Co.; (299) Henry Lyon of Habersham Co., Ga.; (303) Robert Austin
of Jackson Co., Ala.; (325) Margaret Ramsey of Knox Co.; (337)
James Sevier of Washington Co.; (345) James H. Cowan of Knox Co.;
(347) Samuel Henry of Blount Co.; Joseph Donohoo of Bradley Co.;
Archibald Turk of McMinn Co.; Thomas J. Caldwell of North Carolina;
John Lowry at the Agency, Bradley Co.; (350 and 356) Caswell Hall,
Mary Ann Hall, and Marville Duncan of Walker Co., Ga. in the cause
of Adms. of James Hall, dec'd VS John and Margaret Hall.

1838

(371) John Malcom of Blount Co.; (415) Richard Martin and John W.
Blackwell of Ala.

1839

(460) Hiram Bayles of Adams Co., Ill. and Austin Gregory of Ark.;
(465) John Lowry of Cherokee Co., Ala.; William Ream of Macon Co.,
N.C.; Thomas W. Wilson, John Kennedy, and James Little in McMinn
Co.; (466) Hugh Cook of Greene Co.; (487) Jane T. Avery, Adolphus
Erwin, William Murphrey, Samuel McDowell, Dc. L. Tate, Robert C.
Ransom, Samuel Greenlee, and James H. Greenlee, of Burke Co.,
N.C.; John Kenady of Bradley Co.

MINUTES RECORD 1843-1847

January 1843

(20 and 118) Polasky W. Norwood, Adm. of Joseph R. Henderson, dec'd, for the use of John Henderson, Adm.

(36) David Bell and W. Martin, Adms. of J. Martin, dec'd.

(53) Richard Norris, of William.

(67) Wade Swann convicted of murder; appealed to Supreme Court.

May 1843

(117) Susannah Bradberry, Adminx. of Milton Bradberry, dec'd.

(120) Abraham Lillard, Adm. of James Ainsworth, dec'd, VS William Ainsworth.

(125) Margaret Morgan alias Margaret Walker VS John McGhee.

(125) N.J. Spillman, surviving partner of Thomas Glenn, dec'd.

September 1843

(147) State VS G.W. Morgan, Feloniously killing; Nolle prosqui.

(177) Mary E. Garner granted divorce from Vincent Garner, abandonment.

January 1844

(185) Commissioners appointed to take acknowledgement of Eliza Rodgers, wife of Berry Rogers, to a deed from the Rogers to Charles C. Henderson of North Carolina for an undivided 1/3 of land in Catawba Co., N.C., being Lot No. 14 of real estate of Devault Hansicker, dec'd.

(211) Tribute of respect by the Grand Jurors to express appreciation to the Hon. Edward Scott for his services as Circuit Court Judge for the last thirty years, upon his retirement.

May 1844

(213) Court holden by Hon. Ebenezer Alexander, Judge.

(214) E.E. Griffith elected Circuit Court Clerk.

(270) Abraham Dyer elected Sheriff.

(277) Benjamin Howard, Adm. of Nancy Howard, dec'd.

(280) Hon. Robert M. Anderson, Judge.

(292 and 320) George Snider, Adm. of Wilson Hagler, dec'd.

(300) Petition for naturalization of William Bowman, aged 31 years, a citizen and subject of Ludovia, King of Bavaria, one of the provinces of the German Empire; declaration filed 8 Oct 1838 in Essex Co., N.J. Court; thereupon came Alexander D. Keyes, William Hall, and James Vaughn, three citizens born in the United States and state that William Bowman has resided in Bradley and Monroe Counties for more than two years.

(309) Margaret Morgan VS John McGhee; Jury finds that plaintiff is a married woman and was at beginning of the suit and still is

the wife of Gideon Morgan who is still living; writ quashed.

(310) William J. Swaggerty petitions to be restored to citizenship which he forfeited by conviction of a felony.

(316) William Ainsworth granted divorce from wife Mary formerly Mary Raper who deserted him about 1 Feb 1842; married 6 Aug 1841.

(317) William T. Ghormly VS Mary Ghormley; death of petitioner is suggested.

(318) John Gossage granted divorce from wife Lucinda, adultery.

January 1845

(326) James and Charles Donohoo, Adms. of Charles Donohoo, dec'd.

(330) Few H. Gregory VS George and Richard Gregory; death of Richard Gregory is suggested.

(346) George Davis granted divorce from wife Perditta, abandonment.

May 1845

(368) List of voters in 16th section of Township Third and Range first East of Meridian, the major part of which lies in Monroe Co; election to decide on sale of school lands; 80 names.

(382) List of voters in Township 2 Range 2 East of Meridian; 105 names.

(399) Death of William M. Huson is suggested.

September 1845

(432) Petition of James M. Weir for divorce from wife Emily W. is denied by the Court.

January 1846

(469) Court held by Hon. Seth J.W. Lucky.

(504) Nancy Gentry granted divorce from Allen D. Gentry, adultery.

May 1846

(519) Court held by Hon. William C. Dunlap, Judge.

(523) List of voters in Township 2 Range 1 East of Meridian; 69 names.

(546) Wyatt Langford granted divorce from wife Rachel; abandonment and adultery.

September 1846

(576) List of voters in Township first District third East of Meridian, Monroe Co.; 136 names.

(602) Petition of William Stephens, Adm. of John Stephens, to sell slaves.

(603) T.C. and E.G. Smalling, Adms. of Jonathan Smalling, dec'd.

(625) David M. Scott granted divorce from Mary Ann Scott, abandonment.

January 1847

(640) List of voters of second fractional township Third Range East of Meridian; 49 names.

(642) List of voters in 1st Township Range East of Meridian; 151 names.

(644) William M. Stakely and G.C. Torbett, Execs. of John Torbett.

(650) Robert Pendergrass restored to citizenship which had been denied him when he was sent to prison in 1841 for larceny.

(656) Nimrod Lunceford granted divorce from wife Adaline Lunceford, adultery.

(673) Sarah G. Shields, Adminx. of William Hale, dec'd; a note signed by Sarah G. Hale, Adminx. of William Hale, dec'd. /This entry has been marked through, as if in error./

(687) Eli Hudgings granted divorce from wife Elizabeth, abandonment.

In this book, the following persons are qualified and admitted to practice law in the Court, with year and page number noted:

1843

(13) Granville C. Torbett and George Brown.

1844

(188) Joseph B. Heiskell, (231) Charles F. Keith, (274) John E. Toole and J.R. Love.

1845

(331) James R. Buchanan, (363) James B. Cook, Thomas J. Campbell, (442) W.W. Wallace, who received license in Alabama, (453) William F. Keith, and (459) **David W. Ballew**

1846

(519) Isaac N. Baker, (532) John R.C. Henderson, Elisha C. Harris, William D. McGinly, and (585) Thomas J. Taylor.

In this book, depositions were ordered to be taken of the follow-persons, with year and page number noted:

1843

(85) Daniel Hartly of Greene Co.

1844

(197) Joseph Wilhite of Bradley Co.; (206) David L. Knox of Polk Co.; John C. Kennedy of Maury Co., Ga.; (208) Augustus W. Elder of Kentucky; (233) Thomas Beavers of McMinn Co.; (243) Lorena Rogers of Walker Co., Ga.; (288) John and Richard McAndrew of Jefferson

Co.; Joseph McAndrew, Sr., Joseph McAndrew, Jr., William McAndrew, and Stephen McAslin of Bradley Co.; (319) Washington Nations, William Wilson, and Newton Bonds, all of Georgia.

1846

(473) William Freeman and Harrison Riley of Lumpkin Co., Ga.; (475) Michael Ghormley of Cherokee Co., N.C.; (503) John J. Humphries of DeKalb Co., Ala.; (515) Rutherford Witt and Josiah Childress of Polk Co.; (546) Robert Dearmon of Bradley Co.; (551) Peter B. Harralson of Georgia; (637) William Feazel of Greene Co.

MINUTES RECORD 1847-1851

May 1847

(1) David H. Cummings the Atty. Gen. being absent, Joseph B. Heiskell is appointed Atty. Gen. pro tem; "And now as a mark of respect to the memory of the citizen soldiers of Tennessee, and of the union who fell in the recent battle of Cerro Gordo the court adjourned....".

(10) List of voters in 5th Civil District; 110 names.

(13) List of voters in 4th District; 119 names.

(27) James M. Sharp and Samuel Pride, Execs. of John Sharp.

September 1847

(52) Petition of William Stephens, Adm. of Jehu Stephens, dec'd, to sell slaves.

(57) Jacob Graves granted divorce from wife Evaline, abandonment; married about Jul 1844.

(58) Frances Dayton granted divorce from Alonzo B. Dayton; desertion.

(86) James Jarvis VS Elizabeth Thomas and Job McKeehan, Adms. of Joseph Thomas, dec'd.

January 1848

(122) James Torbett died leaving Mahala Torbett now Mahala Cannon, Teressa Torbett, James Torbett, and Margaret Torbett his heirs.

May 1848

(131) James Torbett died leaving Caswell Torbett and Marcena Torbett as heirs in addition to other heirs named.

(140) List of voters in 13th Civil District; 140 names.

(142) List of voters in 18th Civil District; 39 names.

(143) Sarah Graves, spinster, indicted for perjury in swearing that Ebenezer Johnston was the father of her bastard child born 15 Dec 1847, when in truth she knew he was not.

(154) List of voters in 19th Civil District; 36 names.

(158) Jury finds Sarah Graves not guilty of perjury and (159) finds her guilty of keeping disorderly house.

(166) Mary Dyer, Adminx. of John F. Dyer, dec'd.

(173) Petition of Jacob Clemmer and Hannah Clemmer, Adms. of John Clemmer, dec'd, Ex Parte; in Jan 1841 Hannah filed petition for sale of slaves.

September 1848

(207) Philip Cole granted divorce from wife Eliza; abandonment.

(210) Houston Vinsant et al VS James Knox et al; William Heiskell appointed Gdn. ad litem of Lorenzo and William Vinsant.

(213) Petition to sell land: George W., James, Houston, Howel, and Jefferson Vinsant, heirs of Hiram Vincent, dec'd, VS Susan, Orphy, and Mary Vinsant, minor heirs of said Hiram Vinsant, dec'd.

(221) State VS Hugh Goins; Polygamy; Hugh Goins, late of Monroe Co., laborer, on 1 Apr 1820 in Rutherford Co., N.C. married one Elizabeth Goins, spinster, and remained so married when on 5 Jul 1848 in Monroe Co. he married Peggy Taylor, his wife Elizabeth being alive.

May 1849

(278) Indictment: William McCarroll and John M. Cantrell late of McMinn Co., yeoman, on 31 Jan 1849, did steal a marriage bond signed with name William Carroll and the said John M. Cantrell whereby they were bound to Gov. of Tenn. bearing date aforesaid to be void if no lawful cause should prevent a marriage from being solemnized between William Carroll and Margaret Long.... did steal with intent to injure one Margaret Longlee /sic7.

(282) Petition of George Montgomery, Gdn. of Mary Susan and Nancy Adaline Grubb, minor heirs of Franklin Grubb, dec'd, to sell land.

(282) Solen McCroskey VS Samuel McCroskey, Petition to sell land; David Lowry appointed Gdn. ad litem for Samuel a minor.

(290) List of voters in 14th District; 158 names.

(293) Charles M. McGhee and Hugh A.M. White, Adms. of Andrew R. Humes, dec'd, VS Elisha, Ebenezer, and Mortimer F. Johnson.

(303) List of voters in 7th Civil District; 168 names.

(309) John S. Allen and Mariline his wife.

(310) Douthit Hicks granted divorce from Hannah Hicks, adultery.

September 1849

(318) Julia A. Adkins granted divorce from Matthew Adkins, abandonment.

(319) William R. Benson granted divorce from wife Catharine, adultery.

(320) John T. Mitchell dismisses his petition for divorce from Louisa Mitchell.

(352) Daniel Givens of Monroe Co. indicted for shooting and mortally wounding, on 11 Aug 1849, Henry Newton who died of his wounds on 12 Aug 1849; Charles Newton is prosecutor.

(357) Petition of John D. Steel, by his next friend William Steel, to sell town lots and apply proceeds to his education.

(357) Petition of Grizzy L. Mayo for dower in lands of Blackmore H. Mayo dec'd.

(362) A suit is revived in name of George Brown, Adm. of Young L. Bicknell, dec'd.

January 1850

(368) List of voters in first fractional township North, third Range, East of the base line Ocoee District; 26 names.

(392) Death of Ebenezer Johnson is admitted.

(401) Mary Esmon granted divorce from John Esmon, adultery.

(407) Thomas G. Blythe VS Pamelia Blythe; Petition for divorce; no steps taken in this cause for twelve months and cause is stricken from docket.

(407) S.B. McMillan VS Rutha McMillan, Petition for divorce; no steps taken in this cause for twelve months and it is stricken from docket.

May 1850

(426) John Den Lessee of A.R., Enos H., James L., Elizabeth C., Richard J., and Mary C. White VS Daniel Stephens and John Isbell.

(430) Joseph Walker, Adm. of Polly Walker, dec'd, David P. Walker, John A. Rowan and wife Mary, James H. Johnson and wife Nancy, Jehu Cunningham and wife Sarah, heirs of Polly Walker; petition to sell slaves.

(436) Samuel Blair granted divorce from wife Cynthia, abandonment.

(436) John Esmon indicted for biting off a part of Samuel Ervin's ear.

(444-448) Constitution of the Eromathesian Society is spread of record.

September 1850

(498) Lucinda Gordan granted divorce from William Gordan, abandonment.

(521) Heirs of Micajah Carter, dec'd, are Elizabeth Carter, Lewis and Julia F. Parker, J.M. and Phelesia Brown, and James Clibourn, Gdn. of C.P. Carter.

January 1851

(569) John Alexander granted divorce from wife Matilda, abandonment.

(569) List of voters in 16th Civil District; 73 names.

In this book, the following attorneys were admitted to practice law in the Court, with year and page number noted:

1847

(4) Jesse G. Wallace and (22) Albert G. Welker.

1848

(116) William M. Bradford.

1849

(317) J.H. Parsons and J.W. Lemons.

1850

(374) R.M. Edwards, (417) John L. Hopkins, William L. Eakin, David M. Key, and Josiah I. Wright.

In this book, depositions were ordered to be taken of the following persons, with year and page number noted:

1847

(5) Andrew Agnew of Carroll Co., Ga. (12) Jacob Feazel of Greene Co. (24) James and Mary Dotson of McMinn Co. (50) Sarah Bayless of Monroe Co. to be read de bene esse, Phebe Crismon of Bradley Co., and John Bayless of Washington Co., all in cause of Parker Hood VS Smith Bayless.

1848

(102) John Mize of McMinn Co. (139) Archibald Evans of Ga. (213) Felix Axely of Cherokee Co., N.C.

1849

(266) Thomas B. Wilson of Bradley Co. (299) Charles Drake, Joseph T. and William Ellitson, and Samuel R. Anderson of Davidson Co. (341) R.W. Young of Ga. (356) Abraham Hester, William and A.H. Land of Polk Co.

1850

(412) John C. Vaughn of California.

(415) William Rider of Iowa in cause in which Alexander Rider is plaintiff. (416) James H. Galleher and Elizabeth McCain of Hamilton Co.; John Wright and Alexander Dodson of Roane Co. (435) James S. Bain of Ga. (449) John White, Thomas Dugan, James H. Witt, Robert McConnell, John P. Cooper, and Elisha Clayton all of Polk Co.; Abraham Hester of either McMinn or Rhea Co. (488) Berry and Sarah Ann Dodd, Larkin Rutherford, Samuel Firestone, Robert M. Newman, David Cobb, William Dodson, Thomas Dugan, all of McMinn Co.; James C. Carlock, Archibald Childress, Josiah Childress, Josiah Hughes, Albert Hughes, Harrison Hughes, John W. Pearson, William Morgan, Hugh Duggan, James Roberts, John Shamblin, H.C. Coone, Calvin M. Jordan, William Shamblin, John Gee, John Fagan,

Moses Parris, David Bradford, James Denton, Robert Hood, Henry
Ellis, and Andrew Witt, all of Polk Co. (489) Willis Wright of
McMinn Co. (507 and 557) John Moody of Maury Co., Ga. (511)
Lewis Burress of Roane Co.

1851

(558) John N. Griffith and Thomas Marshall of Ga. (559) William
Knox of Ark.; Joseph Alexander of Polk Co.; Nancy and Sarah M.W.
Peck of Jefferson Co.; James Park, William Swann, Sr., and Samuel
Rodgers of Knox Co. (566) John Shuler of Ga. (573) Tabitha Witt
of Polk Co.

MINUTES RECORD 1851-1856

May 1851

(56) Petition of Alexander Medway for naturalization; resident of
Monroe Co. and native of Hungary and subject of his majesty
Ferdinand 5th; is free white person age twenty-two.

(57) Samuel P. Hall, Gdn. of A.J. and Benjamin F.L. Wyly, minor
heirs of J.L. Wyly, dec'd; defendant is Arte Wiley.

(62) James M. Wear granted divorce from Emily J. Wear alias Emily
J. Duggan; abandonment and adultery; she has married William
Duggan since her abandonment.

(65) Hampton Kirkland granted divorce from wife Betsy, abandonment.

(69, 71, 81) Jordan Carden VS Joseph Upton, Adm.; paper purporting
to be last Will of Anderson North, dec'd, was brought before County
Court for probation; Jordan Carden contested; case was certified to
Circuit Court. Will: to wife Delila; to daughter Nancy Jane
Cardin; to grandsons Anderson, John, and William Hance; exec.
31 Jan 1851; wit: James Hamilton, Robert Cunningham. Delila North
fails to appear as a witness. Jury finds that paper is the last
Will and certifies it to County Court for probate.

(77) Richard, Valentine, John Q.A., and Del____ Cannon VS Thomas
L. Upton.

September 1851

(115) Petition of John Todd for naturalization; subject of
Victoria, Queen of England; born in Ayr, Scotland, 11 Sep 1814;
came to United States on 24 Sep 1848 and to Monroe Co. about
1 Oct 1848.

(127) Rebecca Starrett dismisses her petition for divorce from
Preston Starrett.

(128) Moses A. Redmon granted divorce from wife Sarah, abandonment
and adultery; she left him about 1840, going to Ga.

(132) David Rader granted divorce from wife Isabella, abandonment
and adultery.

January 1852

(139) List of voters in first fractional township, Range fourth,
East of basis line Ocoee District; 33 names.

(142) Petition of John Haugh for naturalization; citizen of Great Britain, born in Cumberland Co., Great Britain, now about age of 35 years; came to United States about 24 Sep 1849 and to Monroe Co. about Oct 1849.

(173) Margaret J. Sims granted divorce from James I. Sims; adultery.

(173) Mary Duling granted divorce from husband John R. Duling, abandonment about 1 Apr 1846; Mary to have control of their two minor children, John and Rebecca Duling.

September 1852

(237) Willis Cagle VS William Bain, Sr., Debt; Subpeona issued to Fereby Cagle now Fereby Bain to answer complaint of Willis Cagle on a plea of debt for services rendered in a suit as witness in Greene Co. in the cause, Cagle VS George Wells at Jul Term 1849; this 13 Dec 1851. Willis Cagle VS Fereby Cagle now Bain; "since commencement of the suit of Fereby Cagle VS George Wells, the said Fereby Cagle who was then a femme sole has intermarried with Wm. Bain (Mathew Cagle and Willis Cagle did bring suit against her for attending as witness in said suit) I therefore command you to summon the said William Bain to appear... this the 24 Jun 1852".

(239) Matthew Cagle VS William Bain, Sr.; same as above except witness in Sevier Co.

(241) Abraham Hicks and wife Mary are defendants.

January 1853

(262) John Stanfield, Adm. of Stephen Parshly, dec'd.

(262) Declaration of Lawrence E. Fernandez for naturalization; citizen of Republic of Mexico; born in Jalappa, Mexico on 12 Apr 1831; came to United States 17 Jul 1847 and to Monroe Co. about Aug 1847.

(266) Jacob H. Patton, Mary C. Gouldy and husband William Gouldy, Margaret A. Patton, and Francis A.R. Patton, heirs of William Patton, dec'd, VS William P. Wilson; Ejectment and Trespass.

(276) Cornelius L. Howard, Adm. with Will annexed of Samuel Douthit, dec'd, VS William H. Rodgers and others, heirs and distributees; the Will and all papers were sent from County Court to determine legality of said Will; Will of Samuel Douthet of Monroe Co.: to legal heirs; advancements have been made to some of children of larger amounts than others and all children to be made equal; Elvira's and Teressa's children to inherit their parent's share, but each of said daughters has received in her lifetime; Mary McClure has since received; son Isaac has had control of farms in Blount Co.; land in Blount Co. to be sold or rented out, reserving one acre where my people are buried; to son Samuel, my medical instruments and medical books and the telescope which was given me by my beloved wife formerly Jincy Turk shortly after our marriage; in spite of disapprobation of some of my heirs.... lands in Notchy Creek in Monroe Co. not to be sold but to remain as they are for the benefit of my blacks and of their

increase forever and to be under control of some discreet person of good, industrious, moral habits.... not any of heirs... but appointed by County Court... to occupy house in which I now reside... and prefer he should be of no or at least a small family; to Asbery Howard, the drum that formerly belonged to Asbery Douthet; saddle and bridle to little grandson Samuel Howard; executed 19 Oct 1852; Witnesses: William N. and Charlotte E.M. Marshall. /In this long Will, Samuel Douthet seemingly tries to make all arrangements so that his slaves will continue in the good treatment and care with which he has provided them./ Jury finds that paper is not the Will of Samuel Douthet, dec'd.

(281) List of voters in 2nd fractional township, Range four East of meridian, Hiwassee District; 103 names.

May 1853

(307) Declaration of John Stephens for naturalization; citizen of Great Britain, born in _____ County, Ireland on 12 Aug 1833, came to United States about 27 Mar 1852 and to Monroe Co. 6 May 1852.

(310) Samuel Douthet, Elizabeth and Cornelius L. Howard, Mary S. and Nancy A. Grubb by their Gdn. George C. Montgomery, Mary and Jefferson Waddle, Elizabeth and Joseph L. McClure by their Gdn. Joseph McClure, Mary Ann and William H. Rogers VS Francis A. McClure, Samuel D. McClure, Halbert McClure, Narcissa Tennessee McMillan, Malizza Alabama McMillan, Dialtha Donohoo and her husband Charles Donohoo, and Isaac T. Douthet, all heirs of Samuel Douthet, dec'd, petition to sell land.

September 1853

(314) William G. McAdoo the regular Atty. Gen. being absent, Josiah I. Wright, Esq., Atty., is appointed Atty. Gen. pro tem.

(335) Petition of Isaac N. Baker and balance of heirs of Jacob Baker, dec'd, to sell land; part of money left on deposit for C.C. Herd and wife who are absent and reside in Miss.; land divested out of heirs, to wit, Ann, James M., Isaac N., and John Baker, C.C. Herd and wife Sarah J., Daniel Shrader and wife Louisa, and H.H. Stephens and wife Martha E. (343) William Heiskell, Gdn. of Louisa Shrader has resigned and Ann Baker has been appointed Gdn.; James A. Haire is Gdn. of John Baker.

(353 and 505) John Key, Adm. Vs Andrew Gunn and wife Mary, Archimedes, James C., Franklin A., John S., Madison H., and Elizabeth J. Rogers, heirs of John Rogers, dec'd; A.T. Hicks is appointed Gdn. ad litem of last four named, minor heirs. (505, May 1855) Death of John Key is admitted.

January 1854

(365) Elisha Kimbrough, Adm. of Isaac Weaver, dec'd, VS Harriet Isbell, William A., John, Nancy M., James, Bradley K., Mary E., Lorenzo T., and Charlotte J. Weaver, minors, and Martin Isbell, Gdn.

(391) James Laws has departed this life.

(398) Declaration of Isaac Lowensteen for naturalization; at present a citizen of State of Rhein Hessein in German Republic; born 19 Dec 1833, came to United States 19 Aug 1852 and to Monroe Co. 1 Aug 1853.

(399) Declaration of Carl Hugo Sprenger for naturalization; at present a citizen of Kingdom of Saxony; born 29 Mar 1824; came to United States 15 Mar 1851 and to Monroe Co. 23 Feb 1854.

January 1855

(417) Robert F. Cooke and John L. Hopkins, Execs. of Sarah Bayless, dec'd, VS Abby, Houston, Jim, and others; petition for transportation to Western Coasts of Africa; alias processes awarded to Sheriffs of Monroe, McMinn, and Greene Counties for various slaves.

(420) Ex Parte petition of Lewis Stephens, Exec. of Richard Stephens, dec'd, to sell slaves.

(420 and 490) Death of Dialtha Donohoo formerly Douthet, wife of Charles Donohoo is admitted and it is further suggested that she left as heirs, Joseph, Samuel, and Mary Donohoo, minors, who reside in Bradley Co.

(422) Angeline McCray granted divorce from Thomas H. McCray, abandonment in Aug 1850; married in Monroe Co. 11 Oct 1845; she is to have possession of their two infant children.

(428) Declaration of Lewis Miller for naturalization; citizen of Starhenberg, Germany; born in Darmstadt, Germany in County of Starhenberg 6 Dec 1827; came to United States in 1853 and to Tenn. in Oct 1853.

(437) Thomas Robinson and William C. Julian, Adms. of John Holston, dec'd, VS Heirs; since filing of bill, Washington L. Price married Mary Jane and James Harrison has married Ann E., two of the minor defendants; all title vested out of Washington L. Price and wife Mary Jane formerly Holston, James Harrison and wife Ann E. formerly Holston, Thomas, Judy Ann, and John Holston.

(443) Petition of John Wilson, Adm. of David Starrett, dec'd, VS Sarah, William, John, and Jane Starrett, to sell land; widow Sarah is entitled to dower.

(450) Joseph B. Williams, James A. Crowder and wife Sarah formerly Williams, Margaret and Mathew Williams, minors, heirs of John R. Williams, dec'd; petition to sell land; widow Nancy has released her rights to dower.

(453) Petition of John C. Vaughn, Adm. of John Ellis, to sell slave.

(459) Sarah Garrett alias Sarah Watts, late of Monroe Co., spinster, indicted for bigamy; on 3 Jan 1855 she married Charles Givins, having before that time been married to William Watts, who is still alive and still her husband. (569) Nolle prosqui entered.

(461) Lewis Stephens VS George I. Cunningham, William Denton and wife Faitha, and Nancy, Martha, and Barnet Watson, minor heirs of Elizabeth Watson, dec'd, by their next friend Isam Watson; petition to sell land and slaves; sale to be held at late residence of Nancy Stephens, dec'd.

(467) Petition of John Greer for naturalization; born in Ireland
and is now near age of 20 years; came to United States when he was
about five, and to Monroe Co. Jun 1853.

May 1855

(516) John Hammontree, Adm. of Sylvania Colston, dec'd.

(520) Few H. Gregory and Hugh Chestnutt, Adms. of James Chestnutt,
dec'd, VS Louisa Chestnutt, widow, John, Henry D., and Almyra
Chestnutt, William Reynolds and wife Mary, Elizabeth and Tabitha
Chestnutt, and Archabald Bacome, Mary J., and Albert G. Love; lot
in Philadelphia where intestate lived at time of his death.

(525) Joseph Ervin, N.J. Spillman and others VS Mary and Alexander
Ervin; Court appointed Gdn. for Alexander Ervin, minor heir of
Patrick Ervin, dec'd; widow Mary is entitled to dower; Clerk to
hear proof as to amount advanced to each of heirs by Patrick in
his lifetime and to father of said minor.

(527) Daniel Gadd granted divorce from Nancy J. Gadd, adultery.

September 1855

(533) Chesley Hynds VS Charlotte Hynds, petition for divorce;
plaintiff fails to appear.

(556) "also the undivided interest that John H. Fetzer and Mason
Fetzer formerly Mathis, George W. Booker and Mary Booker formerly
Mathis, John Robinson and Nancy formerly Mathis, William Hunt and
Jane formerly Mathis".

January 1856

(581) Curtis Guild granted divorce from Eliza Guild, adultery.

(587) Rebecca McCarroll VS David McCarroll; petition for divorce
dismissed by Court.

(587 and 589) Robert M. Evans, Adm. of Robert Evans, dec'd, VS
Widow and Heirs; W.C. Morelock appointed Gdn. ad litem for minor
heirs of Demaris Cornelia Coltharp, dec'd, and of Mason K. Evans,
a lunatic.

(598) Charlotte Swaggerty dismissed her suit against John Swaggerty
for divorce.

May 1856

(603) Joseph E. Houston elected Circuit Court Clerk.

(604) The Surveyor General's original book of Hiwassee District
ordered to be deposited in Register's office in Monroe Co.

(604) Catherine Keys, Lewis Keys, Margaret Starr, Bluford W. Starr
VS Jackson B. and Benjamin F. Wylie, Samuel P. Hall, Jacob B.
Russell, Arty Wylie, and Elisha Cunningham.

(612) Certified copy of petition of Herman David for citizenship,
filed Coweta Co., Ga. 4 Apr 1853; born Hesse Darmstedt; is 21
years old, has blue eyes, brown hair, and fair complexion; subject
of Grand Duke of Hesse Darmstedt; emigrated from Havre in France,

landed at New York, and came directly to Coweta Co., Ga., about 1 Oct 1851, where he has resided since; came to Tenn. Aug. 1853.

(621) Death of Jesse Butler is suggested; Taylor Butler is Adm.

On loose paper in this book, undated, is written the following:
Heirs of Solomon Horton and his wife Nancy
    Sarah M. Chamley formerly Horton and husband Riley Shamlee
    Sophrona A. Nucom formerly Horton   John Nucom
    Mary M. Nucom formerly Horton   John Nucom
    Mathew Layfayette Horton age 21 years
      minors
    Nancy A. Horton
    Bersheba Horton
    Mahala Horton
    Louiza J. Horton
    Hastin T. Horton

In this book, the following persons were admitted to practice law in the Court, with year and page number noted:

1852

(224) William B. Reese, Jr.

1856

(568) W.J. Hicks and Andrew J. Vaught.

In this book, depositions were ordered to be taken of the following persons, with year and page number noted:

1851

(5) George W. Guin of Greene Co. in suit in which Peter R. Guin is plaintiff; Pike Bayless of McMinn Co. in suit in which Smith Bayless is defendant. (53) Matilda Witt of Polk Co. (54) David H. Hagler of Miss. (92) E.A. Moore of Sumner Co. (99) Andrew Taylor of Ark. (102) Nancy Black of Blount Co.

1852

(174) Robert B. Reynolds at Ft. Smith, Ark., or Knox Co., Tenn. (199) James Steel, Pinckney Stephens, and Robert Moore of Roane Co.; A.M. Cross, Frederick Smith, Sr., Bryant Honeycut, Stephen Thomas, Daniel Acres, Joel Chitwood, and Thomas Chambers of Scott Co. (201) William Ryan and Samuel D. Warren of DeKalb Co., Ala. (203) John Shamblin of Polk Co. and Hugh McD. McElrath of McMinn Co. (211) Martha Menefield of Roane Co.

1853

(320) James Willson, Sr., of McMinn Co. in case in which William P. Willson is plaintiff.

1854

(360) John Bean and Abijah Aikin in Washington Co., Ark. (375) Thomas K. Wyly of Humphreys Co. and James Wyly of Union Co., Ga.

MINUTES RECORD 1856-1860

September 1856

(6) Death of Hiram Lee is admitted.

(10 and 221) Benjamin F., Thomas A., and James W. Barksdale, Sarah
A. Willis and husband J.H. Willis, Fanny L. Willis, and L.B.
Willis, and Mary J., Louisa G., Nancy G., and Mary L. Barksdale
VS James H. Carmichael, Gdn. ad litem of Mary J., Louisa G., and
Nancy G. Barksdale, minor heirs of Nicholas G. Barksdale who died
in Monroe Co. 23 Oct 1855, leaving petitioners and defenders as
heirs.

(21) Petition of Isaac Guthman for citizenship; born at Grasgeren
in Hesse Darmstadt; is now age 21 and a subject of Louis III,
Grand Duke of Hesse Darmstadt; emigrated and landed in United
States at New York City 22 May 1855 and became a resident of
Tennessee 27 Nov 1855 where he has since resided.

(27) Mary K. McGhee, widow of Barclay McGhee, dec'd, VS Elizabeth
M., Ann E., Margaret W., John, Lavinia M., and Mary K. McGhee,
Jr., minor heirs of B. McGhee, dec'd, with C.M. McGhee as Gdn.;
contest of Will of Barclay McGhee; widow claims that paper is the
last Will and defendants claim that it is not; Will: to wife
Mary K. Henley; Jury finds that paper is the last Will.

(29) John Kirklan VS Widow and heirs of Thomas Giles, dec'd; alias
process awarded as to William Giles of Bledsoe Co.; it appearing
that Hugh Presley and wife Delilah are nonresidents. (95) John
Kirkland VS Christena Giles, petition to sell land; alias summons
issued to Polk Co. for Christopher Kirkland and wife Christina.
(504) Reuben Giles appointed Gdn. ad litem for Guilford, Rufus S.,
and John Giles, minor heirs of Thomas Giles, dec'd.

(38) Petition of Francis P. Gurtney for citizenship; native of
Germany; applied 12 Jun 1843 to Tuscareous Co., Ohio; free white
person; resided in Monroe Co. for twelve months before filing
petition.

(39) Christeny Clift granted divorce from B.D. Clift; abandonment.

January 1857

(52 and 199) Petition of heirs of Abraham Haun to sell land; heirs
are Jane Haun, widow, and Samuel M., N.W., and A.T. Haun, Joseph
Stakely and wife Mary E., E.S. Haun, Abraham Haun, Henry Wolf and
wife Jane, Minerva C. and Barbara R. Haun by their Gdn. William M.
Stakely.

(56) Petition of Herman David for citizenship. /Same information
as formerly copied, except that he is 31 years old./

(63) Petition of Emanuel Guthman for citizenship; now a resident
of Monroe Co.; born in Hesse Darmstedt and subject of Grand Duke
Lewis III; left that state 20 May 1855 and landed at New York 22
Jun 1855, came directly to Tennessee, arriving at Athens, McMinn
Co., 15 Aug 1855 and has remained in Tennessee since that time.

(65) David Kelso has died since last term of Court. (73) Charles
T.P. Davis, Adm. of David Kelso, dec'd, VS William S., Charles
A., Mary L., and Martha C., minor heirs, and Nancy Kelso, widow
of David Kelsoe, dec'd; Nancy Kelsoe, mother of said minors, is
appointed Gdn. at litem.

(78) Patrick McClung, Adm. of James Humphreys, dec'd, Nancy

Humphreys, widow, Van Buren Hunphreys, Ignitious Beard and wife
Sophronia, Leona Humphreys, and Anderson Humphreys by his Gdn.;
petition to sell slaves.

(81) James Hicks granted divorce from Mary Hicks; adultery.

(84, 137, 692, and 768) James and Calvin Denton VS Amanda Denton,
widow of William Denton, Martha, Isaac, Abraham, Thomas, and
Matilda Denton, minor children of William Denton, and their Gdn.
ad litem Lewis Stephens, Alvira and William Stephens, minor
children of Emily Stephens, dec'd, and their Gdn.

(86) Barbary Ann Shelton granted divorce from George A. Shelton,
abandonment; she is to have custody of their infant son, Albert
Cornelius Shelton, and her name is to be restored to her maiden
name of Etter.

May 1857

(91) 2 May 1857, William G. Swan of Knox Co. appointed as Judge of
second judicial circuit to fill the vacancy caused by the death
of the Hon. E. Alexander of Knox Co., who died 29 Apr 1857.

(96) George W. Morgan, Adm. with Will annexed of William H. Butler,
dec'd, and Martha K. Morgan VS T.L., William H., George W., Francis
C., and John Butler, and Jonathan Summett and wife Betsy; Plaintiff
produces paper purporting to be the last Will of William H. Butler,
dec'd, which is in words following: I, William H. Butler, Sr., of
Monroe Co.; to Martha K. Morgan wife of Capt. George W. Morgan, all
property of every kind, both real and personal; appoints William M.
Stakely and Joseph Johnston of Madisonville as Execs.; executed
25 Aug 1853; Witnesses: William Heiskell, H.H. Stephens; (219)
Jury finds that the paper is the last Will as to the real estate
and is not the last Will as to the personal property, and they
find the issue in favor of the plaintiffs as to the realty, and in
favor of the defendants as to the personalty.

(135) Citizenship granted to John Stephens who had filed his
petition more than three years earlier.

September 1857

(182) Joseph B. Gilbreath has died since last term of Court.

(185) State VS Sarah McEarly alias Sarah Henson of Monroe Co.

(196 and 672) Charles R. Hartsell and wife Amanda, Lewis Click,
William Click, Jeremiah Murr and wife Rachael, Alfred Denton
and wife Darcas, Hepsaby, Martha, and Mary Jane Click VS Hamilton
Lewis and wife Jane, Mary Ann, Emaline, Darcas, Andrew J., and
Henry Click, minor heirs of Henry Click, dec'd, by their Gdn.
ad litem S.S. Glenn; petition to sell land.

(220) Nancy C. Harrell granted divorce from Sampson Harrell,
abandonment and adultery; since abandoned, Nancy C. has given
birth to a child named James B. Harrell and she gains custody
of him.

(222) Nancy J. Brown granted divorce from John Brown, abandoned
about 1849; she gains custody of child, Martha Josephine Brown.

January 1858

(231) John T.M. Haire, Adm. of Sarah Hart, dec'd, VS Henry R.
Swisher and A.L. King; the plaintiff produced in Court a paper
purporting to be the last Will of Sarah Hart, dec'd; /copy of Will
is included7; plaintiff pleads that paper is the last Will. (315)
Jury finds for the plaintiff.

(243) Death of Joseph C. Stephens is admitted.

(265) Samuel Jameson of Monroe Co. indicted for bigamy; married on
1 Sep 1857 in Monroe Co. to Melvina Rodon, when he was previously
married to a female named Johnston whose christian name is unknown
to the jurors, and she is still alive. (574) Nolle prosqui
entered.

(287) Deposition to be taken of Michael Ghormly of Ark.

(288) Heirs of F.A. Patton, dec'd, are Amanda A. widow, and
Adaline Owens and husband Charles Owens, H.F. Patton by his Gdn.
Charles Owens, Sr., Francis T. Patton, Elizabeth Patton.

May 1858

(308) Washington Cannon, Adm. of R.W. Hix, dec'd, VS Mary A. Hicks
et al; Elisha Kimbrough appointed Gdn. for S.R., E.J., Sarah J.,
and G.W. Hicks, minor children of Robert W. Hicks, dec'd, J.C.,
G.R., Sarah J., and Harriet White, minor children of Mary White,
dec'd, formerly Mary Hicks, and who are defendants, as also J.H.
Hicks, minor child of Betsy J. Hicks, dec'd.

(345) Mary A. and Sarah Hicks have not answered summons. (349)
Mary A. Hicks is now Mary A. Henry; R.W. Hicks was owner of 6/8
interest in land. (745) all the interest of Mary A., T.R., E.J.,
Sarah L., and G.W. Hicks in 6/8 undivided land.

(310) State VS Owen Marion alias Maryman alias Kirby of Monroe Co.

(325) Declaration of Michael Stephens for citizenship; copy of
declaration filed 27 Oct 1852 in Roane Co.; native of Ireland;
came to United States 1841; a resident of Tennessee for more than
five years; petition granted.

(352) A.J. Mullins dismisses his petition for divorce from Mary J.
Mullins.

(358) C.W. Coffin, Treas. for the use of the Grand Division of the
Sons of Temperance of East Tenn. VS Joseph Upton.

September 1858

(474) Elizabeth Barnett granted divorce from Alexander Barnett,
abandonment and adultery; her maiden name of Estman is restored.

(488) William Duncan, Exec. of Jeremiah Duncan, dec'd, VS James
Taylor and wife; Contested Will; defendants withdraw contest and
Will certified back to County Court.

(508) Joseph Walker and Robert Cunningham, Adms. of Joseph Cunningham, dec'd, VS William Cunningham and others; deaths of William
Cunningham and Nancy Horton, two of the defendants, suggested.

May 1859

(554, 567, 654, and 747) Richard Hicks VS Widow and heirs of
Zachariah Hicks, dec'd; petition for dower and sale of land;
defendants and heirs are as follows: Celia Hicks widow of
Zachariah, J.H. Hicks minor heir of Elizabeth Hicks dec'd, J.C.,
G.R., and Mary J. White minor heirs of Mary White dec'd, and
Hariet White, S.R., E.J., Sarah L., and G.W. Hicks minor heirs of
R.W. Hicks dec'd, Catherine E., Lorinda, Rutha J., John S., and
Rebecca A. Hicks minor heirs of Isaac Hicks dec'd, James Hicks,
Elizabeth Osborne and husband whose christian name is unknown,
Sally and Benjamin Williams, Jane, John, and Mary A. Hicks (now
Mary A. Henry and husband Clifton Henry), Sally and John Kitchen,
Zacheus Hicks, Anna (Amy) and John Teffeteller, Martha (Matthew),
William, and Sarah Hicks, Zillah (Lilah) and Spencer Coleman,
Tabitha and Ozias Rhea, and H.B. Hicks; land includes 3½ acres
reserved to Hopewell Baptist Church and graveyard; land sold to
Richard Hicks.

(554, 658, and 746) Petition for dower and sale of land; James R.
Webb, Adm. VS widow and heirs of Larkin Webb, dec'd; heirs are
Sarah Webb, widow, and James R. Webb, Rhoda Webb, Nancy and John
Brannon, Polly Saffell, Barthena E. and Shade Cagle, Sarah E. and
Alex Bain, Meather (Nither) M. and Baptist Freedle, and C.A.,
Texanna, and James Monroe Divine, minors by their Gdn. Joseph
Divine.

(554) Joseph Walker and others VS Harden Cunningham and others;
deaths of Jehu Cunningham and Mary Hightower proven.

(559) Marshall Callaway of Monroe Co., laborer, indicted for
mortally wounding, with a knife, Benjamin Stafford on 10 Mar 1859,
from which wounds said Stafford died 12 Mar 1859; Ann Stafford is
prosecutor.

(571) Petition of Ulrich Heim for naturalization; emigrated to
United States in 1853 from Republic of Switzerland, being then age
16; has resided in Tenn. for more than five years; petition granted.

(578, 581, and 653) Elizabeth Barr, widow of Adam Barr, dec'd, VS
heirs Samuel W. Barr, James A. Barr, Irvin Brock (Birch) and wife
Nancy L., Henry W., Iselius D., Mary A., John L., Daniel E.,
Elizabeth L., and Isaac N. Barr, last two being minors.

(592) James E. Cole, Adm. of John Robertson, dec'd, VS William A.
and Phillip Robertson, Henry Sheets, and others, heirs.

(593) Granville B. Rogers dismisses his petition for divorce from
Nancy E. Rogers.

(593) Amanda Bane dismisses her petition for divorce from James
A. Bane.

(597) Sophrona Smith granted divorce from William M. Smith; abandoned her and her children.

September 1859

(630 and 756) G.W. Alexander VS Lawrence Henderson and others;
death of William Henderson, one of defendants, is admitted; suit
is revived in name of Amanda and Oliver C. Henderson.

(675) Joseph A. Walker et als VS Hardin Cunningham et als; in this
cause the deaths of Mary Hightower, Jehu Cunningham, George
Stephens and wife Nancy Stephens having been suggested.... cause
revived in names of E.C. Furgason and husband John Furgason, John
H., Joseph H., Mary H., Sarah M., Nancy J., Jehu M., Lodusca,
Mahala H., and Sarah Cunningham, heirs of Jehu Cunningham, dec'd,
Sampson and John C. Stephens, children of George A. and Nancy
Stephens, dec'd, Joseph and C.T. Hightower, Narcissa Harrell, and
Robert Harrell, Phoeba Hightower, Eliza Barker, Thomas Barker,
Mary Thomas and her husband Samuel Thomas, David Hightower,
children of Mary Hightower, dec'd, Anna J. and Sarah Cunningham,
/sic/ children of Mary Hightower /sic/, dec'd, and grandchildren
of Joseph Cunningham, dec'd, all heirs of Joseph Cunningham, dec'd.

(687) Mary A. Mullins granted divorce from A. Jackson Mullins,
adultery.

(688) Jane Skidmore granted divorce from John Skidmore; adultery
and abandonment.

(690) Joseph Walker and Robert Cunningham, Adms. of Joseph Cunning-
ham, dec'd, Haston Cunningham, John R. and Edith Orr, John, Joseph,
Caswell T., and David Hightower, Robert and Narcissa Harrell,
Phoebe, Eliza, Anne J., Sarah L., and James J. Hightower, Sampson
and John C. Stephens, John and E.C. Furgason, John H., Joseph H.,
Mary H., Sarah M., Nancy J., Jehu M., Lodusca C., Mahala H., and
Sarah Cunningham, and Sarah Cunningham widow of Jehu Cunningham
VS William and Harden Cunningham, Solomon, Nancy, Mathew L., Nancy
A., Barsheba, Mahala, Louisa J., and Hasten Horton, Rily and Sarah
M. Shamley, John, Sophia, John, /John listed twice/ and Mary
Newcomb, Joseph and Louisa Rogers, Hardin, Matthew, Equilla,
Leroy, Henry M., Elizabeth, James H., William, Sarah A., and
Mahala Cunningham, G.A. Gowan, Exec. of William Cunningham, dec'd,
Mahala C. and Matilda C. Brock, and Eliza Lawson; all except
Joseph Walker are heirs of Joseph Cunningham, dec'd; land and
slaves ordered to be sold for division.

January 1860

(724) William Seratt of Monroe Co. indicted for murder; mortally
wounded on 29 Sep 1859 Milton Lacky with a stone; said Lackey
lingered and died 20 Oct 1859 of the wound.

(727) Death of James Dyer is admitted.

(734) Calvin Ball alias Calvin Webb indicted for bigamy; on 21 Sep
1857 in Claiborne Co. married Eliza Parm otherwise called Parham,
and on 16 Jun 1859 in Monroe Co. married Malvina E. Swan while he
was still married to Eliza Parm; W.H.K. Swan is prosecutor.

(757) Emaline M. Givins granted divorce from Alex Givins; abandonment.

(769 and 775) Joseph Divine, Gdn. VS Jane Tallant, widow, and M.L.
(M.D.L.) and G.W. heirs and minor children of Thomas Tallent,
dec'd.

(770) James E. Cole, Adm. of John Robinson, dec'd, VS widow and
heirs; death of Glancy Curtis, one of respondents is proven and

cause is revived in name of minor child of said Glancy and the other respondents.

(772) Heirs of Joseph Cunningham, dec'd, listed again; interest in land and slaves vested out of them.

In this book, the following persons were admitted to practice law in the Court, with page number and year noted:

1857

(59) C.B. Neal, W.H. Briant, Frank S. Hale, (120) William McCampbell, and (172) William P. Jones.

1859

(427) J.S. Matthews, William P.H. McDermott, and (694) Henry G. Cook.

MINUTES RECORD 1860-1866

May 1860

(11) Deposition to be taken of Grimes A. Spellman of Mo.

(20) John A. Rowan, Adm. VS Sarah Cunningham and others; John H., Joseph, Mary H., Sarah, Nancy, Jehu, Mahala H., and Lodusky Cunningham are minor children of Jehu Cunningham, dec'd.

(24) Fugh H. Gregory and Hugh Chesnutt, Adms. of James Chesnutt, dec'd, VS Louisa, John, George, Henry D., and Almira Chesnutt, Mary Reynolds and husband William Reynolds, Elizabeth and Tabitha Chesnutt, Mary J. and Albert G. Love, and John Stanfield; Louisa the widow has dower in town lots in Philadelphia where James Chesnutt resided at his death.

(36 and 63) Cook and Hopkins, Execs. VS Abby, Jim, and others; In 1854 Sarah Bayless died in Monroe Co. having first made her Will, by which she bequeathed slaves their freedom; Court rules that the slaves, and their children born since the death of Testatrix, are free persons of color, on condition that they remove from State of Tennessee; sufficient money left to transport said negroes to western coasts of Africa and to provide for their support for six months thereafter; slaves Abby and George are not required to go because of age and disease; seven of the negroes have absconded and no order is made in reference to their freedom; negro slave Puss wife of John Mozley is daughter of slaves Jane and Roland Magill; defendants appeal to the Tenn. Supreme Court the decision of the Judge to remove them to Africa.

(43) John A. Rowan, Adm. of Jehu Cunningham, dec'd, VS Sarah Cunningham, widow, John H., Joseph, Mary H., Sarah, Nancy, Jehu Jr., Lodusky, and Mahala H. Cunningham, Catherine and John Furgason, and Robert Cunningham and Joseph Walker, Execs. of Joseph Cunningham; money coming from estate of Joseph Cunningham, dec'd father of Jehu, dec'd; all defendants are heirs of Jehu except Robert Cunningham and Joseph Walker; Sarah the widow is entitled to dower in the 1/13 part of lands of Joseph Cunningham, dec'd.

(46) Petition of Michael Maughan for naturalization; now a resident of Monroe Co.; born in Northumberland Co., England; in 1821; left

Great Britain 7 Jun 1849 and landed at Charleston, S.C. about 12
Aug 1849; came to Blount Co., thence to Monroe Co. about nine
years ago.

(47) Judgment rendered in favor of Tellico Mfg. Co. 14 Sep 1857
against Daniel Welch, William T. Harris, Lucien A. Harris, George
Welch, and John Caldwell and James H. Dobbins as sureties; George
Welch and Lucien A. Harris are now dead.

(54) Petition of Nashey Badrous for citizenship; a subject of
Republic of Mexico and a citizen of State of Puebla; about age
twenty-one; came to United States sometime in 1848 and has resided
in Tenn. since that time.

(79) G.W. Alexander VS Lawrence, O.C., and Samuel Henderson, and
Amanda and O.C. Henderson, Adms. of William Henderson, dec'd.

September 1860

(113) Death of Jonathan Millsaps is admitted.

(126) John W. Stratton and Asa Anderson VS Mary Humphreys, W.J.
Milligan and wife Eliza J., John Harrison and wife Sarah A., Moses
Humphreys, and Emeline E., Abraham J., John R., David W., Alfred
T., Joshua J., and Margaret R. Humphreys by their Gdn. Mary
Humphreys.

(133) Atless O. Crowder granted divorce from Sarah A. Crowder;
abandonment and adultery; he is to have custody of children Thomas
M., Mary Ann, William M., and Sarah J. Crowder.

(134) Rebecca E. Horn granted divorce from John Horn; adultery and
abandonment; she is to have custody of children Sarah A., Leonidas
C., and Louisa.

May 1861

(237) Amanda J. Davis granted divorce from Andrew S. Davis; abandonment; her maiden name of Russell is restored.

(240) James, Eli, Stephen, Nicholas, and Jeremiah McGuire VS
Michael and Josiah McGuire, Thomas and Julia A. Fortner, Matison
and Sarah McGuire, James and Mary Black; heirs of Josiah McGuire,
dec'd; widow Sarah entitled to dower.

September 1861

(282) James C. Hall VS Euphemia and Burton Howard; James C. Hall,
the purchaser of the lands, has paid into Court the 1/11 part of
the whole amount, which has been paid to Euphemia Howard; James
C. Hall is owner of 10/11 of said land, being the land owned by
James W. Hall at time of his death; subject to dower of widow
Rutha Hall.

January 1862

(307) Margaret E. Newman dismisses her petition for divorce from
L.C. Newman.

(308) J.M. Shaw dismisses his suit for divorce from Narcissa Shaw.

May 1862

(312) C.M. Alexander, the regular Atty. Gen. was absent; J.W. Hicks appointed Atty. Gen. pro tem.

September 1862

(324) No Judge being present...

March 1863

(327) Hon. George Brown, Judge.

(331) Death of John Boyd proven.

(331) Peter Rawlings, a free person of color, petitions to go into slavery to James C. Hall; Commissioners report that he is worth $1000.

(334) F.M. Philips granted divorce from Charlotte Philips.

(340) John Cunningham of Monroe Co., yeoman, indicted for murder on 1 Aug 1862 of Sampson E. Porter, by striking him on back of head with fence rail; James Porter, prosecutor.

(344) Clarissa Johnston widow of Josiah K. Johnston VS James A. Wright and wife Lettitia J. formerly Johnston, and E.C., C.J., and Esther S. Johnston, minor children of Josiah K. Johnston, and W.P. Snead, minor grandchild of said Josiah K. Johnston, dec'd; Clarissa avers that paper purporting to be the last Will of Josiah K. Johnston is the last Will. /Will is copied in book/ Defendants aver that paper is not Will; jury finds in favor of plaintiff.

(345) McGuire VS McGuire (see 240); "It appearing to the Court from a certified copy of the records of the Confederate Court at Knoxville, Tenn. that the shares owned by Michael & Josiah McGuire, Jr., two of the heirs of the said Josiah McGuire, dec'd, their interest in said estate, were sequestered by the act of Congress approved on 30th of August 1861 and by the said Confederate Court at its Nov Term 1862 and said Court decreed that all the right and title held by them in and to said estate be divested out of them and vested in the Confederate States of America."

(346) James E. Cole, Adm. VS William A. Robertson & others; death of Lathy J. Curtis, Fanny Sheets, and Philip Robinson, three of the legal heirs of John Robinson dec'd is proven in Court.

September 1863

(359) No Judge present; J.E. Houston, Clerk.

September 1864

(360) Hon. E.T. Hall presiding; John Crippin, Sheriff; William M. Smith produced a certificate of his election as Clerk on 5 Mar 1864; takes oath to support U.S. of America.

(372) State VS John Cunningham, murder; defendant is dead.

(374) State VS Margaret McCauley, Assault and Battery; Nolle prosqui entered and Joseph E. Houston, father of defendant is her security.

(377) Eliza J. Wilson dismisses her suit for divorce from William Wilson. Delilah B. Gann dismissed her suit for divorce from Robert M. Gann.

(384) "Testimonial - The undersigned grand jurors for the County of Monroe and State of Tennessee at the September term of the Court 1864, experience a high degree of joy and gratification at the restoration of order, Civil law and rightful authority after a reign of terror, anarchy, oppression, and usurpation.... It gives us pleasure to bear testimony to the able, impartial, and dignified manner in which the Hon. E.T. Hall has discharged the arduous & responsible duties of his Judicial position and to commend the clemency and moderation displayed in his Charge to us respecting our... misguided fellow countrymen who having been seduced into rebellion against their country have returned to their allegiance. We hereby most cordially tender him and D.K. Young our kind and affable atty. Gen. our sincere thanks for their courtesy...".

January 1865

(385) Circuit Court opened at the Court house; no Judge present.

May 1865

(385) Circuit Court opened at the Masonic Hall, Hon. Elijah T. Hall, Judge, presiding; the Court house having been burned.

(387) Deaths of William Elkins and Joseph Divine proven.

(390) Death of John W. Boyd and William Parker proven.

(391) Death of W.R. Pressnell proven.

(409) Death of W.H. Jones proven.

(419) Allen Freeman VS Elizabeth Freeman, divorce petition; Came the defendant by her atty. and plaintiff came not. Thomas K. Pittman dismisses his suit for divorce from Elizabeth Pittman.

(421) Death of A.F. Carson proven; Jefferson L. Carson is Adm.

(427) W.A. Birchfield indicted for murder on 15 Aug 1864 of Andrew Shaw, by shooting; Joseph Shaw prosecutor.

September 1865

(455) Court held at Masonic Hall.

(461) Deaths of J.C. Boyd and James M. Terry proven.

(485) Death of John Stratton proven.

(494) Jacob Eldridge, _____ Maddox (first name unknown), and Albert Stephens late of Monroe Co., yeomen, indicted for murder on 6 Sep 1864 of William Hampton.

(504) Thomas Weir of Monroe Co., yeoman, indicted for murder of James C.M. Edwards on 1 Mar 1865, by shooting; William Edwards prosecutor.

(516) Robert Burchfield granted divorce from Margaret A. Burchfield.

(516) William Henson granted divorce from Harriett A. Henson and granted custody of the minor child John P. Henson.

(528) Power of Atty., George C. Montgomery of Troup Co., Ga., late of Monroe Co., Tenn., to nephew James H. Montgomery.

(529) William M. Stakely, James A. Coffin, Execs. of James Smith, dec'd, for use of Martha A. Thornburg and husband J.M. Thornburg, heirs of James Smith, dec'd, VS George C. Montgomery.

January 1866

(533) Court held at Masonic Hall.

(534) Death of Thomas D.L. Trotter proven.

(535) Death of Thomas Arp proven.

(572) John and William Kirkland, Samuel Rodgers, Joseph Phillips, and Gale Roberts of Monroe Co., laborers, indicted for murder by shooting on 12 Mar 1865 of Anna Rodgers; Thomas Rodgers prosecutor.

(576) John H. Johnson VS Samuel Henderson and F.M. Johnson; a paper purporting to be the last Will of Joseph Henderson, dec'd, sent by County Court for reprobate upon an issue of devisarit vel non; paper with words as follows: Monroe Co., Tenn.... land to Sarah Caroline Pressley; money on hand to Matilda Henderson; $5 each to Nancy A. Landrum and John Henderson; balance to be divided with rest of heirs including Sarah Caroline Pressley as one of heirs, namely Samuel Henderson. Alexander Henderson, Esther Johnson, Rosannah Sands, and Sarah Caroline Pressly; the portion willed to Esther Johnson to be divided equally between her daughters Margaret Ann and Scynthia Johnson; signed 19 Aug 1865; witnesses: R.W. Hudson, Eli C. Johnson, W.F. Hudson; the defendants, Samuel Henderson and F.M. Johnson, two of the heirs of said Joseph Henderson, say writing is not last Will; Jury finds for defendants.

(582) Death of G.W. Morgan proven.

May 1866

(585) Court held at Masonic Hall.

(601) Death of G.C. Montgomery proven and suit revived against J.C. Montgomery, Adm. and Alpha Montgomery, Adminx.

(608) Jacob C. Boren of Monroe Co., laborer, indicted for murder with an axe on 10 Dec 1863 of Joseph Graves.

(616 and 632) State VS Albert Stephens, ____ Matox, and Jacob Ellege, murder of William Hampton; Jacob Ellege indicted under wrong name and indicted again as James Elidge.

(632) D.C. Simpson dismisses his petition for divorce from E.C. Simpson.

(636) John Hix of Monroe Co., laborer, indicted for murder by shooting on 10 Mar 1866 of Henry McSpadden, who died of the wounds on 11 Mar 1866.

(672) William Click, Jr., Charles and John Denton, and Pink Gentry, of Monroe Co., laborers, indicted for murder on 10 Apr 1864 of

Patrick Trotter by shooting; Mary Trotter is prosecutrix.

(707) James Schrimsher granted divorce from Susan Schrimsher.

(708) Nancy J. Parks granted divorce from David Parks and is awarded custody of the children, John L., Mary E., and Amanda M. Parks.

(718) Mary H. Ammons VS Joshua Ammons, petition for divorce dismissed by Court; no action taken on case for more than two terms.

(721) James McDonald granted divorce from Sarah McDonald and awarded custody of their infant children.

(725) Death of John Coppenger proven.

September 1866

(751) A.J. Cagle dismisses his petition for divorce from Matilda Cagle.

(753) A. Bacom VS Randolph Carter, Ejectment; leave is granted Elizabeth Carter, wife of defendant, to defend jointly with her husband.

(765) Thomas Jones of Monroe Co., laborer, indicted for murder on 26 May 1866 of Joseph Ivens by shooting; Ivens died 27 May 1866; Cynthia Ivens prosecutrix.

(774) State VS John Hix, murder; Change of venue to Roane Co., defendant could not get a fair trial owing to political feuds.

In this book, the following persons were admitted to practice law in the Court, with year and page number noted:

1864

(364) Mathew M. Young, W.H. Bryant, W.J. Hicks, and G.M. Hicks.

1865

(386) G.W. Lawrence, (474) J.M. Thornburg, and Theodore W. Birge.

1866

(538) T. Richmond, (598) E.C. Johnson, and (742) N.J. Temple.

MINUTES RECORD 1866-1868

September 1866

(32) John Duncan of Monroe Co. indicted for murder on 10 Nov 1863 of James Watson by shooting.

(73) John Minis, J.P. for Monroe Co., states that on 4 Jan 1865 the rebels made a raid in Madisonville, robbed his office, and put him under arrest.

(88) John T. Jones granted divorce from Celia Jones; desertion.

(92) Eliza A. Wilkins granted divorce from John M. Wilkins and awarded custody of their minor children.

January 1867

(126) Court at Masonic Hall.

(130) 30 Jul 1866, J.D. Jones, Jessee F. and R.R. Cleaveland, Execs. of Ely Cleaveland, dec'd, VS William D. Wilson and William Carter, Debt; Summons executed "as commanded except W.D. Wilson (Dead)", 31 Jul 1866.

(172) J.C. Martin VS Margaret Ann Harris and husband T.C. Harris, John H., Hugh E. Jr., Elizabeth, George W., and Susannah E. Martin; last five are minors.

(173) William Heartsell alias Bumgarner, Grief Ragsdale, and Jack Denton of Monroe Co., laborers, indicted for murder on 4 Jul 1864 of David B. Curtis by shooting.

(191) James F. and William R. Gregory and Susan Helton of Monroe Co. indicted for murder on 1 Dec 1866 of Edward Hankins by shooting; he died 3 Dec 1866; Julia Hankins prosecutrix.

(204) Alpheas M. Crowder and Mary Birchfield of Monroe Co. indicted for murder on 1 Aug 1864 of James F. Strickland by shooting; George Strickland prosecutor.

(212) Elisha Tallent dismisses his petition for divorce from Lucinda Tallent.

(213 and 468) Michael M. Rogers dismisses his petition for divorce from Frances U. Rogers.

May 1867

(341) Alexander Winder indicted for carrying an Arkansas Toothpick.

(385) Death of Allen G. Anderson proven.

(436) Wiley Ray granted divorce from Jane Ray. (542, Sep 1867) Wiley Ray dismisses his petition against Jane Ray.

(436) Elizabeth Goad granted divorce from James Goad, adultery.

(437) S.H. Caldwell granted his petition for divorce from S.V. Caldwell; abandonment and failure to care for their children, McPheason B., Charles Y., Samuel A., and Julia C. Caldwell.

September 1867

(439) Court held at Masonic Hall.

(486) S.H. Moore VS Elvira Moore, petition for divorce; plaintiff not appearing, Court dismisses case.

(515) J.L. Cline VS Nancy C. Cline, petition for divorce.

(532) State VS Elisha B. Simpson the Elder; Bigamy; on 10 Aug 1852 in Monroe Co. he married Caroline McCreary and whilst he was so married, on 26 Dec 1866, in Monroe Co. did marry Emma A. Abbott.

(562) Death of Frederick Dean suggested.

January 1868

(575) Court held at the Court House.

(654) Bartlett Fergeson granted divorce from Martha Ann Furgeson and awarded custody of their infant children.

In this book, the following persons were admitted to practice law in the Court, with page number and year noted:

1867

(163) John H. Payne and (289) H.A. Chambers.

MINUTES RECORD 1868-1873

May 1868

(77) Anna Waters granted divorce from Alston Waters.

(77) Equilla Jones granted divorce from Robert Jones.

January 1869

(176) Grand Jury indictment of George Pearce for mortally wounding, on 10 Nov 1867 in Monroe Co., A.L. Carson who died 20 Nov 1867.

May 1869

(280) Eunice J. Shelton granted divorce from J.K.P. Shelton; cruelty and abandonment; she is awarded custody of their two children.

January 1870

(322) Joseph Breakbill VS J.H. Kelso, Adm. of Frederick Dean, dec'd, and Elizabeth, Martha, Polly Anne, and Tennessee Dean, Eliza J. Axley formerly Dean and her husband S.D. Axley, G.D. Dean, the heirs of said Frederick Dean, and Elizabeth Dean the widow.

(323) Grand Jury indictment of William and James Hunt of Monroe Co. for murder by shooting, on 10 Nov 1869, of Caswell Hicks; Matthew Hicks prosecutor.

(340) State VS Joseph Rodgers, Bigamy; Grand Jury finds that Joseph Rodgers on 17 Nov 1865 in Monroe Co. married Laura Murphey and on 14 Sep 1867 in Monroe Co. married Roxey Ann Lockford.

May 1870

(407) Mary Ward granted divorce from M.T. Ward; desertion.

(The remainder of this Record Book is not within the scope of this Book.)

These abstracts are taken from four books in the office of the
Chancery Court Clerk and Master, as follows:

> Chancery Court Records 1843-1848
> Chancery Court Minutes Record 1848-1855
> Chancery Court Records 1856-1865
> Chancery Court Records 1865-1868

It should be remembered that from Sep 1845 until Feb 1848, the
Chancery Court in Madisonville held cases for McMinn County, as
well as Monroe Co.

March 1843

(1) Thomas L. Williams, Chancellor.

(4) John Key, Adm. of Alfred Pogue VS Creditors.

(33) John, Gavin R., and Benjamin Hambright VS Malissa Hambright,
widow, and Ann Eliza and John P. Hambright, infant children of
Amos Hambright; John and Gavin R. were appointed Adms. by Bradley
County Court.

(36) Franklin Yoakum, Adm. of George Yoakum VS Mary Yoakum, Gdn.
of minor heirs; widow has had dower set aside.

September 1843

(45) Robert Frazier, Adeline A. Blackwell, Execx. of Ann Blackwell,
dec'd, and John E.S. Blackwell VS Julius W. Blackwell and others;
Ann Blackwell died since original bill was filed.

(48) Margaret Simons granted divorce from William R. Simons;
married Jan 1834 and he deserted her in 1835.

(49, 228) James Walker, Adm. of Pleasant B. Taylor VS James, John,
Catharine, William, and Phoebe Taylor, minor children of Pleasant
B. Taylor; land in Blount Co. to be sold subject to dower of widow
Elizabeth.

(56) James M. Broyles was Clerk of County Court at time of his
death.

(59, 96) Elliott Peck, Adm. of Gilbert H. Peck, dec'd, VS Heirs;
the death of Elliott Peck is suggested and suit revived in name of
William F. Peck who was appointed Adm. by Hamilton County court;
paid to widow.

(63, 90, 149) Jared G. Dent and wife Mary Ann VS John J. Humphreys
and wife Sally, and others; March 1845: the death of Margaret
Donohoo is suggested.

March 1844

(71) Fine of $5 entered against Sheriff for not having Court house
in order.

(78) Gideon Morgan, Adm. of Betsy Walker, dec'd, VS John L.
McCarty, Exec. of John Walker, Jr., dec'd.

(92) Petition for dower; Elizabeth H. Thomson VS Heirs of Jesse
Thomson, dec'd; land in Blount Co. where Jesse lived at time of
his death.

(95) Land of John R. Davis, dec'd, vested out of heirs Lewis,
Susan and Peter Davis, Polly Kennedy and husband Robert Kennedy,
Martha and Elizabeth Smotherton and their husbands John and Joseph
Smotherton.

(98, 347) Guilford Cannon and James A. Coffin, Adms. of William
McConnell, dec'd, VS Alexander McConnell and others, heirs.

(101) Eliza C. Duggan VS heirs of John Duggan, dec'd; Eliza C.
dismisses her petition for dower.

September 1844

(118, 284) James Montgomery and Charles Owens, Adms. of John Duggan,
dec'd, VS Eliza C. Duggan widow, and Maria J., Margaret E.,
Adolphus M., James D., William C., Mary L. (Nancy L.), John L.,
and Eliza Angeline Duggan, minor heirs.

March 1845

(138, 233) Joseph and Joseph N. Willson, Adms. of John Willson,
dec'd, VS Heirs and Creditors; farm known as Caldwell farm bid
off by William Pugh; farm deeded by Samuel Johnston to John Henry
and John Willson bid off by William Wallace and interest in widow's
dower bid off by Joseph Willson.

(139) John Wilson, Gdn. ad litem for Elijah, John, Malinda, Elenor,
Rosannah, Sarah J., and Eliza Wilson, minor heirs of Charles
Wilson, dec'd, and Isaac, James, and Uriah Wilson, Joseph Winkle
and wife Mary, heirs of said Charles Wilson VS Heirs of Nathaniel
Smith and William Morgan; Smith sold land to Morgan who assigned
it to Wilson.

(148) Elisha Cooley VS Hamilton Stewart and wife Martha, and
Hamilton Stewart as Gdn. of Lydia Cooley; Clerk and Master to take
account of value of estate of John Cooley at time of his death and
what time the Stewarts boarded Elisha Cooley and his sister Lydia.

(150, 391) Mina J. Rudd VS William Rudd, Benjamin Ragsdale, and
others; the death of Benjamin Ragsdale is suggested; William Rudd
has received assets of $968.71½ to be distributed; owing to Mina
J. Rudd $148.45, to Parker Hood $26.90, to Alexander Hood, Bryan
Hood, Nancy Hayden, George Thompson and wife Sarah, each the same
amount, and to Solomon and Francis Kelly a similar amount, and
there remains due to heirs of Francis Kendrick, to wit, Betsy
Oneal, Tempy Huffy and husband John, Elender Kendrick, Thomas
Kendrick, and to William and Susan Clowder $28.06 in all, and that
Joseph and John Rudd who are entitled to $161.45 each, have
received same.

(152) David Walker and Samuel T. Bicknell, Adms. of Joseph J.
Walker VS Heirs and creditors.

(154) John McGhee VS A.H. Henly and others, Commissioners of Jones
County; it appears that the lines of the County of Jones as
designated in the act creating said county does approach within
less than twelve miles of Madisonville and Maryville the County
Towns in the Counties of Blount and Monroe and is therefore within
the prohibition of the constitution of Tennessee in that matter

and that the said Act of Legislature creating the said boundary
of Jones is unconstitutional and null and void... injunction be
made perpetual.

(159, 206, 394) Joanna Bond, widow, Robert P. Julian and wife
Rosannah, Rachel and Elizabeth Bond, heirs of Peter Bond, dec'd,
VS Amon Bond, Exec. of Peter Bond and Henry McGuire; Mar 1846:
the marriage of Rachel Bond and Montraville Reynolds is suggested;
Sep 1847: complainant Elizabeth Bond has married James West; Mar
1848: Peter Bond died testate /McMinn County/ and Amon and
Benjamin Bond were his Execs.; Benjamin Bond has died.

(162, 229, 311) Liggett Helms and wife Jane VS Goodwin Harris,
Exec. of Jacob Secrest; the share of complainant in estate of
Jacob Secrest.

(171) Alexander Hart, Adm. of William Price, dec'd, VS Gilford,
Caroline, and Mary Ann Price, minor children of William Price.

September 1845

(181) Susan Curd VS Richard Curd; death of defendant is suggested.

(188) Death of Henry Hannon is suggested.

(193) Samuel Ghormley, Adm. of Hugh Ghormley, dec'd, VS Heirs and
Creditors; Nancy Ghormley, widow.

(198) John J. Humphreys and wife Sally formerly Donohoo, and
Samuel, Henry, and Nancy Donohoo by their Gdn. Wm. P.H. McDermott
VS James and Charles Donohoo, Lewis Shepperd and wife Margaret
formerly Donohoo, Jarrot G. Dent and wife Mary Ann formerly
Donohoo, George W. Turk and wife Melinda formerly Donohoo, and
Margaret Donohoo widow of Charles Donohoo; Charles Donohoo, Sr.
died Aug 1842 in Monroe Co., leaving widow Margaret, who has died
since commencement of suit, and complainants and defendants as
his heirs.

March 1846

(213) Suits pending in Chancery Court at Athens lately abolished
by the General Assembly of State of Tennessee are transferred to
Chancery Court at Madisonville.

(226) John Avans, Adm. of Thomas Jourden, dec'd, VS Anderson and
Wily Jourden, Dialtha Wayne, William T. Jourden, Elizabeth and
Isaac Frits, heirs.

(229, 276, 318, 362) Sarah Ann Ragsdale and husband Sterling
Ragsdale VS George W. Carmichael, Exec., James H. Alexander, Gdn.
ad litem of Thomas E., Sarah Ann, Mary Jane, Margaret L., Eliza
K., and James Scott, minor heirs of Joseph Scott, dec'd; Mar 1846:
the marriage of Sarah Ann Scott to Sterling Ragsdale is suggested;
Joseph Scott, former husband of Sarah Ann Ragsdale, died Apr 1845
testate; Sarah Ann dissented to the Will; dower assigned.

(244) Harriet and Sarah Taliafero by W.C. Nelson, Gdn. VS Richard
H. Taliafero; defendant is a nonresident.

September 1846

(253) Heil Buttram, Adm. of Barton White VS Benton Keeton and widow and heirs of Barton White /Barton White was a resident of McMinn Co.7; title to land divested out of Benton Keeton and out of Emsly Wann and Polly Wann formerly Polly White, widow, and Susan, Nancy Ann, and Hannah Eliza White, children of Barton White.

(265, 278, 355) W.G. Bogle, Gdn. of minor heirs of E.H. Wear, dec'd, and E.L. Higdon and wife VS Robert Wear, Adm. of E.H. Wear; death of Robert Wear has been suggested and suit revived against his Adms., Stephen Decatur Wear and James Henry.

March 1847

(268) Death of Gincy Douthet is suggested.

(269) Syntha Stephens VS Daniel P., Mary J., Syntha E., and Margaret J. Stephens, minor heirs of John Stephens, by their Gdn. W.H. Plumlee; John Stephens died Oct 1845 intestate leaving widow Syntha and defendants his only children.

(272) Barbara Rogers granted divorce from Thomas Rogers; charge of adultery and driving complainant from his house and establishing Rebecca Sellers in her stead.

(286) Francis W. Lea and wife Rebecca C., Arthur H. Henley, Gdn. of Callaway Campbell, Pleasant J.G. Lea and wife Fanny Lucinda VS Thomas H. Callaway; Joseph Callaway made Will 20 May 1831 and died shortly after in Monroe Co., leaving children to wit Rebecca C. Lea, Fanny Lucinda Lea, Thomas H. Callaway, and Nancy Elvira Callaway who afterward married Charles Campbell, had issue son Callaway Campbell, and shortly died; in division of land, the said Rebecca C. and her then husband Joseph Donohoo, who has since died, received...; John Callaway, one of the Execs. of Joseph Callaway, has gone to Missouri.

September 1847

(326, 351) Pamela S. Bell, widow, and James P., John P., and William I. Bell, minor children of Ira Bell, dec'd, by their Gdn. Peter H. Bell; Ex parte case transferred from Chancery Court at Athens; land on Spring Creek in McMinn Co.; petitioners live in Virginia.

(332) Charles Hughs and wife VS M.H. Blackburn and Wesley Earnest and wife Nancy.

(335) John Caldwell VS Arthur H. Henley, Samuel Ghormley, John Best, Hugh McD. McElrath, Joseph S. Milligan, and John Grant, Commissioners of Jones County; no survey has been made by the Commissioners, as directed by the act passed 27 Jan 1844 entitled "An act to establish the county of Jones", of the counties of Blount and Monroe so as to ascertain that the said counties would not be reduced below 625 square miles each... that in the fraction proposed to be stricken off of Blount county there is a population of 270 qualified voters and in the fraction to be stricken off of Monroe County a population of 201 qualified voters... and that at an election, less than a majority had voted to establish the county of Jones; defendants perpetually enjoined from acting.

March 1848

(360) Death of Wilson Crowe is suggested.

(372) Ann Wilson VS Samuel Wilson, both of Monroe Co.; Ann on
14 Jan 1846 filed Bill of Complaint against her husband Samuel
Wilson, charging him with gross conduct and asking separate main-
tainance out of his estate; said Samuel filed his answer of denial
on 11 May 1846, charging that Ann had left without cause; arbitrators in the dispute declare that Samuel pay Ann $900.

(390) William R. Utter, Adm. of _____ (Ann, Nan, or Van) Lowry,
dec'd, VS William and David Lowry; complainant has leave to amend
bill by striking out all that part of bill having relation to the
making or suppression of the Will of John Wallace.

(393) Adms. of A.R. Humes, dec'd, VS John McGhee, Jr.; leave is
given complainants to amend their Bill by stating that the respondent is or was a citizen of Monroe Co. at the time he absconded.

(396) Douthet, Elizabeth, Talbert, Garrett, and George Hix, Ruth
Raper, and Mahala Cartwright, Marady, Isaac, and John B. Hix, heirs
of Shadrack Hix, dec'd, VS G. Cannon and John B. Hix; complainants
dismiss their Bill against the minor defendant, heir of George B.
Hix.

September 1848

(1, 31) Death of Abraham Haun is suggested; suit continued in name
of Newton W. Haun, Adm.

(8, 283) James Dyer VS Benjamin C. Jameson and the minor heirs of
Wilson Crow, dec'd, by their Gdn. Jonathan Shipley; order issued
to Sarah Ann, Abel, Martha, William, Wilson Jr., and Evalina Crow,
children and minor heirs of Wilson Crow. /McMinn County Case/

(8) Adms. of A.R. Humes, dec'd, VS John McGhee, Jr.; it is suggested that defendant had returned and is now residing within
jurisdiction of Court.

(9, 59, 91, 117) David P. Walker, Adm. of Thomas Harmon, dec'd,
Thomas H. Jones, James F. Jones and wife Louisa formerly Louisa
Harmon, Branch Tucker and wife Phebe formerly Phebe Jones, Enoch
Jones and wife Nancy formerly Nancy Harmon, David H. Jones, John
Marissa and wife Ellen formerly Ellen Jones, William Owens and
wife Jane formerly Jane Jones, Elijah Jones Jr., John Jones,
Athen B__ner and wife Mahala formerly Mahala Jones, P. Miller
Stacy and wife Lucinda formerly Lucinda Harmon, heirs of Thomas
Harmon, dec'd, VS James A. Jones, George Baily and wife Susannah
formerly Susannah Jones, Nelly Murphy formerly Nelly Harmon, John
Harmon, Susan Harmon, Alfred Baily and wife Catherine formerly
Catherine Harmon, Juda Smith formerly Harmon, William P.K. Barnett
or Barrett and wife Nancy formerly Nancy Harmon, and Lewis Carter
Gdn. of Catherine Harmon, heirs of Thomas Harmon, dec'd; it is
suggested that Catherine Harmon is an idiot and Gdn. is appointed;
Thomas Harmon died intestate in Monroe Co. Jul 1847 leaving widow
Rachel and heirs Catherine Harmon, the heirs of David Harmon, and
the heirs of Nancy Jones; land in Monroe and Hawkins counties.

(11, 208) Joseph Wilson and J.N. Wilson, Adms. of John Wilson VS

heirs and creditors; title to land in Blount Co. divested out of
Joseph N. Wilson, Margaret A. Hamil formerly Wilson, Nancy E.,
Malissa E., Silby C., and James M. Wilson, with exception of dower
of Mary, widow of John Wilson; George E. Hamil is the purchaser
of land.

(11, 47, 240) Joseph R. Douglass, Alexander Hogshead and wife
Harriet C. Hogshead VS Robert Sneed and John Stanfield, Adms. of
Jonathan Douglass, dec'd, DeWitt Clinton Douglass, Mary E., Oscar
E., and Theodore C. Douglass, minor heirs of said Jonathan
Douglass, by their Gdn. Elika A. Taylor, Jane C. Douglass and Mary
Douglass; Mary Douglass is a nonresident; Johnathan Douglass, now
deceased, on 10 Dec 1840 executed his Will which was duly proved
and recorded in County Court of Monroe Co., whereby said testator
devised a farm called Murray place to his wife, the farm he lived
on to his daughter Mary, and the balance of his lands to be equally
divided amongst his heirs, which has been done; he also directed
that all his personal property be sold to pay his debts and the
arrearages of Rail Road stock, and that his children, DeWitt
Clinton, Oscar E., and Theodore C. Douglass should get sum when
they arrive at age of 21; he also bequeathed money to defendant
Jane Douglass for the support of the father of said testator, and
said sum became a lapsed legacy by the death of testator's father
in the lifetime of testator; he also directed that each of his
children except Mary should receive $100 each from proceeds of
sale, and balance go to daughter Mary E. Douglass; he directed
that his Rail road stock should belong equally to his son Joseph
R. Douglass and his daughter Mary E. Douglass; it appearing to the
Court that said testator died intestate as to the following items:
the $500 bequeathed for support of father, the assets which came to
hands of Adms. in Missouri, and debts due estate at time of his
death; widow Jane C. dissented to Will, and Court rules that she
is entitled to year's support and dower in lands, and to a child's
part or 1/7 of personal estate; defendants except widow Jane appeal
to Tenn. Supreme Court.

(14, 30) Ann Lotspeich, widow of John Lotspeich VS Adms. and heirs;
petition for dower; answer of John Lotspeich for himself and as
Gdn. ad litem of Amanda M. and Charles W. Lotspeich; answer of
John J. Browder and wife Betsy Jane, and judgment pro confesso
against other defendants; widow has dissented to Will of John
Lotspeich.

(17, 66) Samuel N. Robinson and others VS William Robinson and
others; sale of land of Thomas Robinson, dec'd, in Ocoee District,
Bradley Co.

(21, 26) John H. Bright and Harvey S. Bright, Adms. of Merrit B.
Bright, dec'd, William, Ellison, and Mary Gay VS Elizabeth Bright,
widow, and Nancy Ann, William D., and Jesse E. Bright, heirs; John
H. and Merrit B. Bright were tenants in common to land.

(25, 36, 58, 98) George C. Harris and Henry Marshall and John
Griffith, Adms. of William Griffith, dec'd, VS Stephen D. Caldwell,
Jacob B. Russell, Sarah Caldwell, Alfred C. Humphreys and wife
Jane, and James Caldwell, and others; six months has elapsed since
death of David Caldwell, who died in Monroe Co., and no person has

as yet or will administer on his estate; John Wilson appointed
special Adm.

March 1849

(38) John H. and Samuel M. Johnston, Josiah Rowan and wife Esther,
Samuel Johnston and wife Margaret, Francis H., Josiah K., James H.,
Hamilton, and Samuel H. Johnston, James H. Jr., Sarah A., Esther,
Finly G., and Louisa J. Johnston, heirs of Samuel Johnston, dec'd,
and Nancy Johnston his widow; Ex parte petition to sell lands in
Bradley County and lands known as Starr's Reservation.

(44, 60, 235) John Wolfe VS Phillip Keller and wife, John, Francis,
Peter, Miller, and Jackson Moser, heirs of Peter Moser, dec'd, and
Samuel Edington Gdn. of Miller and Jackson Moser; the death of
Polly Moser, widow of Peter, is suggested.

(46, 141) Charles Hughes and wife Eliza VS Matthew H. Blackburn and
Wesley Earnest and wife; Thomas Blackburn bought land and had same
conveyed by deed dated 9 May 1814 from Eli Dixon to his two sons
Matthew H. and John A. Blackburn; John A. is now dead and was
living on land at time of his death and complainant Eliza is his
daughter.

September 1849

(60, 64) Richard, Joseph, Francis, Nancy S., James, and Rhoda
Kirby, and William Singleton Gdn. of Caroline Kirby, heirs and
legatees of James Kirby, dec'd; Land in Blount Co.; Richard Kirby
is Adm. with Will annexed.

(61, 115) Elizabeth Maxwell for herself and as next friend of
Margery Maxwell, her minor daughter, VS James and Archibald
Maxwell.

(65, 71, 99, 106, 227, 270) Wear VS Wear; residence of Robert Wear,
dec'd, in Blount Co.; Heirs of Robert Wear are John B. Tipton and
wife Louisiana; Thomas G. Harvey and wife Lucretia Adaline; Louisa
Caroline Dearmond and husband John W.; Elizabeth Jane Anders and
husband William Anders; Alexander Augustus, Lucretia Malvina,
Leonidas Haywood, Mary Emeline, and Mariah Louisa Girdner; Mary T.
Gallaher; Gilbert A. Wear; William Kerr and wife Letticia; Isaac
D. Wear; James W. Lea and wife Malvina; Samuel T. Wear; William
Singleton and wife Lucinda J.; Ferdinand M. Fulton; Lucretia P.
Wear; and Margaret E. Wear, last two minors. Samuel Thompson Wear,
one of children of Robert Wear, dec'd, is not living and had no
wife or issue and his 1/12 part to be paid to other eleven heirs,
upon their making bond in case he should prove hereafter to be
living.

(68, 88) William Ramsey Bogle, heir of Matthew H. Bogle by Guilford
Cannon, Gdn.; petition to sell slaves; Matthew H. died testate.

March 1850

(82, 139) Alfred M. and Margaret A. Lyle VS John E. and William M.
Lyle; William G. Lyle in his Will bequeathed land in Blount County
to John E. Lyle, a minor, who when reaching age of 21 was to pay
sums to complainants; Mar 1851: Alfred M. Lyle attained age of 21

on 25 Oct 1848 and Margaret A. Lyle now Margaret A. Roberts attained age of 21 in Mar 1845.

(94) Mary Parsons VS J.A.S., J.H., Sarah, and Modena Parsons, John and Elizabeth A. Rhea, heirs of Joshua Parsons; petition for dower; Joshua Parsons died possessed of a Turn pike road leading from mouth of Abraham's Creek in Blount Co. to the line between Tennessee and North Carolina on the Smoky Mountain.

September 1850

(121) James Johnson and wife Anna VS James Thompson, John Gamble, and John Hafely; complainants as heirs of Coonrod Hafely were entitled to interest in land in Blount Co.

March 1851

(128) Death of Thomas Henderson is suggested.

(131) E.W.P. Mayo and others VS Valentine Mayo; title divested out of heirs of B.H. Mayo, dec'd, viz, E.W.P. Mayo, Peyton Blankenship and wife Martha, William Gay and wife L.M. Gay, Ellison Gay and wife E.H. Gay, E.G.A. Mayo, Nancy Jane, M____ A., Cynthia K., Mary, Grizzy, and B.H. Mayo, and vested in A.B. Fletcher and Valentine Mayo.

(137, 266) David W. Harvey VS Thomas G., William Minor, and Charles M. Harvey; the death of William Minor Harvey is suggested; after the birth of David W. Harvey, an entry for land was made in name of complainant and defendants.

(144, 189) Trustees of Hiwassee College VS Trustees of Bolivar Academy; complainants enjoined from drawing any warrant from or receiving any money from the State, of the Bank Dividends belonging to County Academies, unless they first give bond to refund the same in the event the Chancellor shall decree that said complainants are not entitled to the same; Chancellor is of the opinion that the Act passed by the Legislature on 23 Jan 1850 incorporating Hiwassee College is unconstitutional so far as it authorized the transfer of the money and other evidences of debt belonging to Bolivar Academy and the annual appropriation of the Bank Dividends to the said Trustees of Hiwassee College.

(145, 179) Lucretia V. Pugh VS William Stephens, Josiah D. Pugh, Adm. of James Trice, Jr., dec'd, and the heirs of Hulda Pugh by their Gdn.; Clerk and Master ordered to take an account as to what money came into hands of Mary Trice, Execx., and James Trice Jr., Exec., of James Trice Sr., and what amount is due Lucretia V. Pugh, a daughter of James Trice Sr., and the minor heirs of Hulda Pugh as heirs of said James Trice Sr.; James Trice Sr. died about 1840 and Mary Trice and James Trice Jr. administrated on his estate in Blount Co. and held money to be distributed among eight distributees; they disbursed to each of the heirs except to Lucretia V. Pugh and the heirs of Hulda Pugh formerly Hulda Trice; James Trice Jr. died in 1848 and Josiah D. Pugh is his Adm.

(146) Hubbard Ragsdale fraudulently conveyed land to his son F.A.

(152, 301, 303, 306, 340) Samuel P. Hall, Gdn. of minor heirs of

James Wyley, dec'd, and others, Ex Parte; James Wiley, dec'd,
bequeathed home farm to John C. Wyly and to Mary Wyly for life
and in remainder to his daughter Mary M. Wyly and also devised
land to his daughter Ann A. Jackson; land and slaves divided,
after life estate of Mary Wiley, among Ann A. wife of John Jackson,
J.R., Benjamin F.L., Felix G., Mary M., and John C. Wyly, heirs.

September 1851

(163) Heirs of Ebenezer Johnson, a partner in Tellico Mfg. Co.,
are the widow Lucy E. Johnson, Mary wife of John C. Lord, Mariah
wife of Smith Ingleheart, Herbert L., Celia, Sarah, Charles
Ernest, and William Sherwood Johnson, last five being minors.

(181) James A. Coffin appointed Clerk and Master for six years.

(186, 325) John Key, Adm. of John H. Allen VS Eliza E., Margaret,
and William O. Allen, Nancy Marshall, Israel C. Smith, and William
Henry, Martha Jane, John Wesley, and Mary Caroline Marshall; John
W. Marshall issued bond for title to land on 7 Apr 1851 to John H.
Allen, and on 12 Apr 1851 said Allen executed his bond for title
to Margaret Allen for 1/3 of land together with the East end of
mansion house during her life; said Marshall and said Allen have
since died intestate.

(191, 271) Pugh VS Neiman; William Pugh, who died possessed of
lands in Blount Co. and slaves, had thirteen heirs, as follows:
Lucretia the widow; William and Glaphrey Bingham; James and Susan
May; the heirs of Jonathan Pugh dec'd; William and Martha E. Pate;
William J. Pugh; George and Amanda Cope of Missouri; Jacob and
Mary Neiman of Alabama; and five minors, Kerron H., Francis M.,
Lafayette, Samuel, and Josiah D. Pugh.

March 1852

(206) Title to lot in Philadelphia, Monroe Co., where Joseph
Scates resided at his death divested out of heirs Joseph C.,
George W., John W., Isabella, Jane, and Elizabeth Scates, the
widow and children.

(211) Death of John McGhee is suggested.

(213) John Weldon VS Lucinda, Matthew, and Joseph McSpadden, widow
and heirs of Samuel A. McSpadden; complainant sold land to
McSpadden Oct 1848 and McSpadden has died intestate.

(220) Death of James Smith, partner in firm of Stakely & Smith, is
suggested.

(220) Elizabeth Wilson, Gdn. of minor heirs of Charles Wilson,
dec'd, and Joseph Boyd VS minor heirs; title divested out of minor
heirs of Charles Wilson, namely, Malinda, Rosannah, Sarah J., and
Eliza Wilson, and out of minor heirs of Isaac Wilson, dec'd, viz,
Mary, Sarah, Isaac, and George Wilson.

(228) John Hammontree died in Blount Co. Aug 1840 testate,
bequeathing property to Philip and John Hamontree, Jr. upon
condition that they pay to Martha Henry a daughter of said John
Hammontree, dec'd.

March 1853

(253) George W. Givens granted divorce from Polly Ann Givens, fraud; at time of their marriage in Monroe Co. in 1850, Polly Ann was pregnant without the knowledge of complainant and about five months after the marriage gave birth to child.

(254) Land of Samuel Grimmett, dec'd, divested out of widow Fanny and heirs Hannah, Catharine, Patsey, William, and Caroline Grimmett.

(256) Title to land of George Yoakum, dec'd, divested out of his heirs, viz, Henderson Yoakum, M.L. Bayless and husband B.M. Bayless, Emily A. Stephens, Washington, Madison, Celia Ann M., Martha, and Polly Ann Yoakum.

(258, 310, 312) Shadden VS Edington; the marriage of Mary Jane Shadden, one of the respondents, with Allen Nipper of Monroe Co. is suggested; Mar 1854: the marriage of Margaret Shadden, one of the respondents, with John Helms is suggested; the heirs of John Edington, dec'd, are Leah Shadden wife of James W. Shadden; James Lesly and wife Ann; John W. and Philip C. Edington; Mary E. Smith and husband William R. Smith; James and William L. Edington; Mary Jane Nipper and husband Allen Nipper; Margaret A. Helms and husband John Helms; Cynthia J., John, Sarah, Elizabeth, and Penelope C. Shadden, minor children of Leah Shadden by their Gdn. Josiah I. Wright.

(261, 329, 359) Absalom White for himself and as Gdn. of John M. Cartwright VS Wilson Cartwright and wife Sarah, Thomas Symonds, and Benjamin White; Wilson Cartwright and wife failed to answer publication; Absalom White sold his interest to Symonds; Jun 1855: Absalom White has become non compas mentis.

(247, 267) Martha Parshley, widow of Stephen Parshley, assigned as dower the town lot in Philadelphia, Monroe Co., where said Parshley resided at his death.

(269, 308) Arthur H. Henley VS Ann E Henley Sr., Ann E. Henley Jr., and Samuel Henley, and their Gdn. C.W. Coffin, Elizabeth M. McGhee and Thomas Henley and their Gdn. Barclay McGhee, Barclay McGhee and wife Mary K., William A. (N.), David, and Alexander S. Henley; complainant's father, Arthur H. Henley Sr., died in Monroe Co. 15 Feb 1849 testate; Henley Sr. had placed son David Henley in possession of a farm in Blount Co. and in his Will provided that as soon as the balance of his sons should become 21, they should have land of equal value; complainant is now 21.

September 1853

(285, 365, 403) Louisa Shrader by her next friend and Gdn. Ann Baker VS Daniel T. Shrader and others; Daniel Shrader enjoined from receiving any property from estate of Jacob Baker in right of his wife; Dec 1855: Louisa Shrader granted divorce from Daniel Shrader, abandonment.

(286, 338, 351) John Stanfield, Adm. of James Taylor VS Paulina Taylor, widow, and heirs Jesse Taylor, Polly and Elijah Welch, Nancy and William Walker, William and Thomas Taylor, Susannah and Thomas Anderson, all of whom are over 21.

March 1854

(314, 334) George Selvidge died 1849 testate, having been married twice and having two sets of children; the older set, to wit, William Elkins husband of Eunice, James Sewell husband of Nancy, George V. and John Selvidge, took possession of land a year before the youngest set were made equal; widow Nancy supported the younger set for that year.

(315, 324, 353) Mary Ann Walker VS Pryor H. Walker; defendant has left his family and gone beyond jurisdiction of Court, leaving property and debts; Court appoints Elijah Cate, father of complainant, as Receiver; Dec 1854: Death of Pryor H. Walker is suggested, which is denied by complainant and proof required; Jan 1855: Death of Pryor H. Walker now proven.

December 1854

(323) Death of John Kirby is suggested.

(323) Death of M.D. Bearden is suggested.

(325) Death of W.P.H. McDermott suggested.

(342, 380, 397) James Clibourne, Adm. of Madison Clibourne, dec'd, and Malvina Clibourne VS Harbart T., Charlotte, Madison B., Scott, and Robert K. Clibourne, minor heirs of Madison Clibourne; land of Madison Clibourne in Monroe Co. and land in Knox Co., being the interest of Madison Clibourne, dec'd, in his own right and the one half of the interest of Robert Clibourne in the lands that Jubal Clibourne died possessed.

June 1855

(386) Robert Carter, Adm. of Garland Smith, dec'd, VS Margaret Elizabeth Smith widow, Polly Patterson, and Haseltine, Elizabeth, Martha, Mariah, Sidney, and Garland Smith, minor heirs of Garland Smith; widow assigned dower out of land on which she resides and on which Garland Smith resided at his death, being the same land owned by the late Absalom Smith at his death.

December 1855

(391) Death of Lewis Carter is suggested.

(393) Henry Sheets VS John and Margaret Sheets; death of Margaret Sheets is suggested; Jacob Sheets, dec'd, and complainant entered land 15 Nov 1824 and both lived on same until 1847.

(402) Elijah Cate, Adm. of P.H..Walker, dec'd, VS Mary Ann Walker in her own right and as Gdn. of G.A., Pryor, and Mary Walker, infant children of P.H. Walker, dec'd; David P. Walker is the grandfather of said minor children.

June 1856

(1, 120, 267, 343) Ann E. and David Henley, Execs. of A.H. Henley VS John Henderson, the heirs of John T. Wilson, W.P.H. McDermott, and others; Dec 1857: Death of Wm. P.H. McDermott is suggested and suit revived against the widow Jane and heirs, J.B. Cooke and

wife Penelope, W.P.H. McDermott Jr., and minor heirs Louisa,
Augustine, Alexander, John, Inez, and Julia McDermott. Dec 1859:
Death of David Henley is suggested. Dec 1860: Death of Ann E.
Henley is suggested.

(3) John W. Lotspeich VS Alfred Lotspeich and wife Susan, and John,
Henry, Nancy Ann, and Julia Mary Lotspeich, minor heirs of
Christopher M. Lotspeich, dec'd, and C.M. Lotspeich their Gdn. ad
litem; publication made as to Alfred and Susan Lotspeich;
Christopher M. Lotspeich in Apr 1850 sold to complainant his interest in estate of John Lotspeich, dec'd, and later died leaving
the aforesaid minor children and a widow the said Susan who has
since married Alfred Lotspeich.

(5, 85, 188, 226) James B. Craighead Jr., M. Craighead, and Thomas
D. Craighead by his Gdn. James B. Craighead Jr., James A. Haire as
Adm. of William B. Craighead VS Joseph Craighead, Pheby Craighead,
and John B., William, James, Charles D. and Jane Craighead, minor
children of John B. /sic/ Craighead, dec'd, and their Gdn. Pheby
Craighead, and Thomas B. Craighead and his Gdn. Matthew Craighead,
Tennessee, Virginia, Levinia, and James B. Craighead, Daniel C.
Preston and his Gdn. Thomas W. Preston, Robert Russell Gdn. ad
litem of David C. Preston, James B. Craighead, and others; land
of William B. Craighead sold to James B. Craighead, one of the
heirs; proceeds of sale to be paid to heirs or their Gdns., except amounts claimed by John B., William, James, Charles D., and
Jane Craighead, minor children of Joseph E. Craighead, dec'd,
Phereby Owen, and Thomas B. Craighead insane, which interests are
to be retained until further order of the Court; Phereby and
William E. Owens, Gdns. of minor children of Joseph E. Craighead,
dec'd, and Matthew Johnson is Gdn. of Thomas B. Craighead.

(6) Death of R.R. Young is suggested.

(11, 27, 111, 190) James W. Shelton and Lavinia Rogers VS Joab
Terry, Mary Shelton and children of David F. Shelton, dec'd; title
to land divested out of complainants and Mary Shelton widow, and
Martha Jane, Winnefert, Isabella, William, James, Frances, Sarah,
and Mary Lavenia Shelton, minor children of D.F. Shelton, dec'd.

(14) Petition of James and Euly Long, Catharine Cansler, Willis
and Polly Woody, Cornelius and Sally Welch, Adam and Barberry
Nichols, heirs of Conrad Cansler, dec'd; Conrad Cansler died in
Monroe Co. intestate in 1846; John Key, now dec'd, retained the
distributive share due the heirs of Willis Allen, dec'd, and wife
Betsy formerly Betsy Cansler; none of the heirs of Willis Allen
have been heard of for more than seven years. (287) Dec 1859:
it appears to the Court that the heirs of Willis Allen, dec'd,
who are grandchildren of Conrad Cansler, dec'd, are not dead.

(16, 36) Thomas C. Whitlock and wife Elizabeth, James and N.D.
Millsaps, Benjamin Davis and wife Mahala, William Marrs and wife
Gelina, James Gray and wife Polly VS Sarah Starrett, Barbara,
Samuel, and Polly Wright, Elizabeth Rhea and husband, John and
William Wright, minor heirs of William Wright, dec'd, by their
Gdn. ad litem John Wilson; sale of lands devised by Jonathan
Wright, dec'd, to his wife Sarah and his daughter Melizzia Wright,
now dec'd, and adjoining lands owned by David Starrett at his
death; title divested out of heirs of Melizzia Wright.

December 1856

(26) Death of David Kelsoe is admitted.

(26) Death of Susan Gentry is admitted.

(28, 62) Isaac Stephens, Gdn. of Rebecca A. Stephens VS Daniel and
W.H. Plumley and William Burris; Daniel Plumley resides in Bledsoe
Co. and as Adm. of John Stephens, dec'd, holds interest of Rebecca
Ann in estate.

(37, 72, 115, 198) Thomas Wallis, Adm. with Will annexed of William
Wallis VS William Wallis and others; William Wallis made Will 25
Jun 1851, and afterwards died in Monroe Co., in which he directed
that after death of widow Tempy his lands and slaves be sold and
money divided equally among all his children; Tempy has died; at
time Will was made William Wallis had the following living children,
to wit, Thomas, William, Gooden, Major L., and Charles Henderson
Wallis, Malinda Cadle formerly Wallis who has intermarried with
Mark Cadle, and Nancy English. Chancellor rules that only the
children living at time Will was made are entitled to proceeds of
sale, and that the descendants of John, James, and Preston Wallis
and Elizabeth Cardwell formerly Wallis, children of the testator,
but who had all died before Will was made, do not take any portion
of estate. In this Bill, defendants other than the children
named, are as follows: Houston or Hester, Thomas, and Lucinda
Wallis (later listed as Lucinda Sanders and husband Wiley Sanders),
heirs of John Wallis, dec'd, John Cardwell and his children, viz,
Obediah and William G. Cardwell, Sterling Wallis and Polly Hyden
and husband E.W. Hyden, Martha Cate and husband Oscar Cate, Neely
and Prior Wallace, children of James Wallis, dec'd, the last two
named minors by their Gdn., and the children of Preston Wallis
whose names are unknown; James H. Reagan was purchaser of the share
of the Cadles; widow Tempy died 1855.

(42, 101, 135, 227, 275) Ansel Gad, Exec. of William Gad VS Julian
Brannum and wife Polly, Leander Moses and wife Betsy Ann, William
Hicks and wife Jane, John Patterson and wife Martha, Daniel Gad,
and Mary Jane, Lewis, James, Elizabeth, Nancy Ann, William,
Caroline, Margaret, and Martha Brannum, minor children of William
and Elender Brannum, dec'd, Anderson Moses and wife Julia Ann,
William and Talitha Gad; complainant and defendants are heirs of
William Gad. Dec 1859: Talitha Gad is dead.

(50) Death of John Robinson is admitted.

January 1857

(53, 55) Mary Ann Spriggs granted divorce from Ezekiel Spriggs;
cruelty and desertion; Mary Ann asks for alimony; Ezekiel appears
to Tenn. Supreme Court.

June 1857

(57) Death of John Washburn is suggested.

(59, 204, 304) Heirs of Jacob Baker, dec'd; marriage of Louisa
Shrader with M.L. Benton is suggested; Jun 1860: death of John
M. Baker is proven.

(59, 153) Sampson Halcomb, Adm. of William Collaque VS Sally
Collaque widow, Benjamin Halcomb, Crawford Collaque and James W.
Kelso Gdn.; death of Benjamin Halcomb is suggested; Sally is the
widow and Crawford is the minor child of William Collaque, dec'd,
who had sold part of land to Benjamin Halcomb.

(59) James A. Coffin, Clerk & Master, appointed Caswell B. Neal as
deputy C & M.

(60, 166) Esther and Robert Cheynie VS Darthula Spears and husband
R.C. Spears, Elizabeth Williams and husband William Williams,
Sophronia Minnis, E.E. and Arm___ M. Cheynie, Jane A. Roy and her
husband James Roy, and Susan A., Sophronia, and T.N. Minnis, and
E. Cheynie, minors by their Gdn. ad litem John Minnis; dower
assigned to widow Esther out of land where Able R. Cheynie resided
at his death; parties to this suit are heirs of Able R. Cheynie;
share of money due the minor heirs of Margaret Minnis, dec'd,
turned over to their father John Minnis.

(65, 75) William Morris and wife Jane, Anna Caroline, Mary Matilda,
and Joseph Madison Wilhite, minor heirs of Reuben Wilhite, dec'd,
by their Gdn. Caswell L. Walker; Jane Morris is entitled to dower.

(81, 98, 156, 322, 373) Heirs of Isaac Wilson by Rebecca Wilson
their Gdn. VS E. Wilson widow of Charles Wilson and others; Charles
Wilson in his lifetime made advancements to his children, to wit,
Isaac the ancestor of complainants, James B. Wilson, and Polly
Winkle, and other advancements made by Elizabeth Wilson, widow of
Charles, to her minor children since the death of Charles.

September 1857

(96) Spriggs VS Spriggs; Ezekiel Spriggs has nine children; Court
gives 1/10 of his property to Mary Ann as alimony; appealed to
Tenn. Supreme Court.

December 1857

(104, 183) Henderson Hix and wife Catharine, Mary H. and Henry
Riggin VS John Mullendore, and others; Micaijah C. Rogers and
John Mullendore were the Adms. of Ignatius Riggin, dec'd, and
John Mullendore was afterwards appointed Gdn. to children of
Ignatius; complainants Catharine Hix and Mary H. and Henry Riggins
are now the only distributees to estate of Ignatius Riggin.

(110) Daniel Bain sold land to his son John S. Bain and made deed
of trust to one John R. Bain.

(114, 129) Adm. of A.D. Gentry VS Heirs and creditors; James R.
Gentry appointed Gdn. ad litem of Adaline, Margaret, and Nancy Ann
Gentry, minor defendants.

(122) John Baker by regular Gdn. James M. Baker; Ex parte petition
to sell his undivided 1/7 interest in the Baker Island Farm heretofore sold to H.H. Stephens who had failed to pay for same.

May 1858

(124) Hugh McReynolds VS Isaac D. and Robert McReynolds; the death
of Robert McReynolds is suggested and suit revived in name of widow

Nancy and heirs Margaret E. McCallie and husband Samuel McCallie, James McReynolds a nonresident, and the parties to this suit.

June 1858

(163) Josephine Young, by her next friend George P. Carmichael, is granted divorce from Thomas J. Young; adultery. She is restored to her maiden name of Carmichael.

December 1858

(171) Death of M.C. Parker is suggested.

(172, 403) Charles M. McGhee in his own right and as surviving Exec. of John McGhee, dec'd, VS J.W.J. Niles and wife Margaret W., and Mary K. McGhee widow of Barclay McGhee, and Betty, Ann E., Margaret W., John, Lavina, and Mary K. McGhee, minor heirs of Barclay McGhee, dec'd; sale of lands of John McGhee; Jun 1861: the marriage of Mary K. McGhee with William Parker is admitted and the death of Mary K. McGhee one of the infant defendants is admitted.

(177) Execs. of Sarah Bayless VS Thomas D. Belotte; title to lot divested out of Thomas D. Belotte.

(197) Elisha E. Griffith appointed deputy C & M.

June 1859

(203, 270, 330) Mark M. and Wesley J. Hicks VS Milton Hicks, Smith Bayless and wife, and others; the Clerk to determine what advancements were made by Charles Hicks in his lifetime to each of his children; widow's dower; advancements and distributive shares of Mark M., Charles R. dec'd, George Milton, and Wesley J. Hicks, Narcissa Bayless, and Eliza C. Joines being equalized; the 1/6 share of Charles R. Hicks, dec'd, to be distributed to the other five and the heirs of Albert G. Hicks, viz, Sarah E. and Cyrus M. Hicks, to take their father's part, namely 1/12 each; since Albert G. Hicks, dec'd, was advanced by his father Charles Hicks his full share, then his heirs to receive no distributive share except their share of estate of Charles R. Hicks, dec'd.

(211) Death of William Swan is suggested.

(212, 266) Mary Hudgeons VS Edward Hudgeons; Elizabeth J. Hudgeons is minor child of parties to suit; Bills dismissed by both parties.

(228) Cuson VS Galbraith; Clerk and Master to determine what amount of property John F. Galbraith received for G.M. Cuson and what length of time Galbraith kept the infant child of Cuson.

December 1859

(247) Minor heirs of Mary Ann Walker and Pryor Walker, dec'd, are Gustavus A., Pryor H., and Mary Ann Walker.

(253) Bain VS Stephenson; all the interest in land of their ancestor Joseph Stephenson, dec'd, divested out of William Bain, James and E.C. Clayton, James S. Bain, John and Jane A. Branner, Andrew R., Arthur C., Margaret S., and Martha D. Bain, William M.,

James, John, and Dialtha Stephenson, and vested in the purchaser
William M. Bain, also an heir.

(254, 292, 305, 333) David Lowry, Gdn. of James A. Lillard VS
Elizabeth Lillard and others; James A. Lillard has been declared a
person of unsound mind, and he has two infant children, Amanda T.
and Laura, and his wife is Mary A. Lillard; Jun 1860: Clerk and
Master to determine amount necessary for support of wife Mary Ann
and her infant child Amanda T. Lillard (Laura is not mentioned
here); F.M. Moses is father of Mary Ann Lillard.

(258) Andrew Allen VS Scates et al; all title in land of Joseph
Scates, dec'd, divested out of John Scates, Elizabeth Henderson
formerly Scates and husband Mastin Henderson, Mary Prater, widow,
and James, Hugh, and George Prater, minor heirs of William Prater.

(262, 454) Alfred Preston, Gdn. of David, John B., James B., Jane
P. Preston, and Thomas Craighead, minor children of Col. James B.
Craighead, dec'd, and Jane P. widow of said James B. Craighead VS
Lavinia Craighead, John B., William, James, Charles D., and Jane
Craighead, Phereby Owens and her husband William E. Owens, Gdns.
of minor heirs of John B. Craighead, dec'd, Thomas B. Craighead who
is insane, by his Gdn. Matthew Johnson; land of William B. Craighead, dec'd, sold to James B. Craighead; John B. Craighead was a
brother of William B. Craighead and was owner of ¼ part of said
land as an heir of William B. Craighead, but was dead at time land
was sold on 7 Mar 1857; lands vested out of widow and heirs of
John B. Craighead and vested in the five children of James B.
Craighead, dec'd, subject to dower of widow; John B. Craighead,
whose widow is Lavinia, had two children to wit Thomas B. Craighead
who is insane and Joseph E. Craighead who died before his father
and left the following children, minors, viz, John B., William,
James, Charles D., and Jane Craighead; Jun 1860: Col. James B.
Craighead late of Maringo Co., Ala. died intestate within last 12
or 18 months in said County, and he was a brother of William B.
Craighead; the five minors named at beginning of suit are his only
children, and Jane P. is his widow. Jun 1865: the death of
Joseph C. Boyd, one of the purchasers of the land, is proven and
suit is revived in names of his heirs, viz, Mary Ann Ross and hus-
band Randolph Ross, Elizabeth Jane Pettitt and husband B.C.
Pettitt, all of Monroe Co., Andrew L. Boyd, Nancy Ann Vaughn and
husband J.C. Vaughn, and Alvin Boyd, a minor, who are nonresidents,
Caroline Charles and husband James Charles who are residents of
McMinn Co., and Thomas G. Boyd, who is a nonresident.

(266, 357) Rebecca Keeble, by her next friend William Rhea, VS
Manly Keeble and E.E. Griffith; Rebecca is one of heirs of Jesse
Rhea, dec'd; her share to go to her and to her children free from
the marital rights of her husband Manly.

(272, 278, 315, 328) John B. and Quincy A. Tipton, Mary Ann Wear,
Edward W. Tipton, Lucretia A. Bradford, Lorenzo D. Tipton, Lavinia
M. Hall and husband Calvin M. Hall, Willie Blount Tipton, Johnathan
C. Tipton, Pleasant M. Wear and wife Tryphina, Pleasant M. Tipton,
Theopholus and Johnathan Wilkerson VS George P. Tipton, minor son
of E.G. Tipton, Joseph, Margaret, and Mary Ann Wilkerson, minor
children of Sarah Wilkerson; Suit to have Will construed; Margaret
Tipton is widow of Jonathan Tipton, dec'd.

(294) F.M. and Margaret A. Roberts VS John E. and William M. Lyle; Clerk to ascertain the number of heirs that Alfred M. Lyle left if dead and if any of them have transferred their interest to complainant Margaret.

June 1860

(303, 319, 371, 417) Mary Ann Spillman VS Fanny J., Margaret T., William T., Amelia A., Ella, and Newton J. Spillman, heirs of N.J. Spillman, Dec'd; Dec 1861: the marriage of complainant with Randolph Ross is suggested.

(308, 353, 355, 383) Alexander Dougherty, Brazeal Dougherty, Jeremiah Calfee, Execs. of John Dougherty, dec'd, VS Elizabeth Dougherty, and William, Jason, and Nancy Ann Dougherty by their Gdn., and Sarah C. and John Loftis, widow, children and heirs of John Dougherty; Jury finds that widow Elizabeth is of unsound mind; Judge construes Will; children Eliza Jane and Malinda have died since Will was made.

(310, 397) Mary E. Cotton granted divorce from John Cotton; his adultery with Rhoda Jane Pearce otherwise called Rhoda Jane Grove; Mary E. is restored to her maiden name of Mary Elizabeth Jones and she is allowed support for herself and child.

(312) Duff VS Duff; John Duff died intestate in Monroe Co. in 1829, leaving widow Sarah and seven children, among whom were Jacob N. and John C. Duff, and James H. Duff now dec'd, leaving widow Emeline and children, Washington, John, Willard, William, and Adaline Duff, minors.

December 1860

(347, 402) Joseph Johnston, Adm. VS C.T.P. Davis, Adm. of David Kelsoe, dec'd, Margaret J. Kelsoe, widow, and William, Charles A., Mary, and Martha Kelsoe, minor children of David Kelsoe. /Compare Circuit Court Records Jan 1857, page 65./

(351) Agreement; J.S., W.W., N.A., M.E., and D.A. Torbett VS Josiah and Elizabeth Malinda Atkinson, James M. Watson, Thomas and Mary Malone, Marion and Rebecca Jane McDaniel, William P., Robert, and Henry T. Watson, Edward and Nancy Coffman, Rebecca and George W. Watson; respondents are heirs of William Watson.

(360, 401, 418, 443) William and Catharine Lynn VS John Redmond and wife Elizabeth Redmond, et al; Frederick Weaver is appointed Adm. pendente lite of Edmond Van, dec'd.

(367) Amanda M. Griffith granted divorce from G.R. Griffith; abandonment; Amanda M. restored to her former name of Amanda M. Galbreath.

(370) William Wolf VS Joseph Wolf and W.M. Stakely; Stakely as Exec. of John Wolf, dec'd, holds share of complainant.

June 1861

(400) Death of Henry Doolittle is suggested and publication made as to his heirs whose names are unknown and who are nonresidents.

(407, 424, 459) Jacob Givens VS Esther Givens, William Ervin and wife and others; John Minnis appointed Gdn. ad litem for John and Martha Givens, minor heirs of Zachariah Givens, dec'd; Dec 1862: death of Martha Givens is suggested; the widow is willing to receive reasonable sum instead of dower.

(410) Mary E. Sneed granted divorce from Cyrus S. Snead, abandonment.

(411) Sarah E. Callaway granted divorce from Marshall C. Callaway, abandonment; her maiden name of Sarah E. Mayo is restored and Marshall is enjoined from interferring with her custody of their child, Ellen Mayo.

December 1862

(423) Death of Richard Hawkins is suggested.

(425) Death of Jane McDermott is suggested.

(426, 427) Petitions of Oliver and Nancy Bayless, free persons of color, to go into slavery to Bird P. Hankins, are granted, and a Commission is appointed to ascertain their cash value as slaves.

June 1863

(433) Death of John Strutton is suggested.

June 1865

(443) Death of George C. Harris is suggested.

(444) Death of J. Rufus Smith is suggested.

(444) Death of William B. Camp is suggested.

(472) Death of Daniel Ratledge is suggested.

(474) J.D. Jones et al, Execs. of Eli Cleveland, dec'd, VS Lodusky Walker et al, heirs of Joseph Walker, dec'd.

December 1865

(3, 496) Camp VS McDermott; Suit revived in names of Sarah F. Dugan and husband John F.L. Dugan, Mary Ann Dugan and husband Samuel Duggan, Julia Witt and husband William Witt, Martha McCormick and husband James McCormick, and William T.H. Camp, heirs of William B. Camp, dec'd.

(8) John Wright and Nathaniel Magill, Execs., and John C. Wright, Jr., and others, heirs of John A. Wright, dec'd, VS Thomas, Joseph A., and Andrew J. Wright, and Celia E. and Sarah J. Glass, minors; John A. Wright, dec'd, intended in his Will that Celia E. and Sarah Jane Glass, his grandchildren, (their mother being dead) share in his estate, as do the children of said John A. Wright, dec'd; Elizabeth Wright, Mary A. B___es, and Sarah, Madison G., Joseph A., and Andrew J. Wright, children of said John A. Wright, dec'd, have not received a horse.

(11, 167) James Allen VS William and Andrew Allen; Death of James Allen is suggested; Jun 1867: Death of William Allen is suggested.

(11) Death of J.R. Hays is suggested.

(12, 188, 306) Andrew Pickens VS Rutha J., Marius C., Jacob A., James L., and Hester L. Raper, minor heirs of Larkin W. Raper, dec'd.

(12, 44) Curtis VS Curtis; William R. Curtis, dec'd father of minors James and Joseph Curtis, and husband of Isabella Curtis, now his widow, and brother to John B. Curtis, dec'd, whose heirs are William and Isaac Curtis and widow Adaline.

(12) Isaac Elliott granted divorce from Ruth Elliott; adultery with Benjamin Johnston; Isaac to have custody of minor children.

(20, 22, 241, 315) Thomas Crowder VS Mary A. Cunningham and others; Michael Best of Blount Co. has been appointed Gdn. of Jackson, Jefferson D., Mary F., and Martha A. Cunningham, minor children of John Cunningham, dec'd, who are a portion of defendants; J.R. Robinson was appointed Gdn. of minor heirs of Clabourn Cunningham, dec'd.

(21, 22, 298, 442) Joseph Johnston and other creditors of John A. Rowan, dec'd, VS Mary A. Rowan, widow, and Mary H. and Joseph W. Rowan, heirs of said John A. Rowan, who died intestate about 13 Oct 1864.

(34, 121, 200) James H. Carmichael and John R. Henry Adms. VS Louisa Q. Carmichael, widow of Daniel L. Carmichael, and John B.F. Carmichael and one other, the two minor children; the reversionary interest in the dower of Mrs. Margaret Carmichael in the lands known as the John Carmichael farm in Roane Co., opposite town of Loudon.

(48) Elizabeth Simpson, Margaret Jane Prater and husband John Jefferson Prater, Mary Elizabeth Jackson and husband Dr. D.B. Jackson, B.G., Martha Teressa, James Crawford, David Fleming, Sarah Tennessee, and John Tate Simpson, and John Jefferson Prater the Gdn. of minor heirs of John Simpson, dec'd, VS Nancy Alexander and husband Joseph Alexander; 1927 acres owned by John Simpson, dec'd, divided into ten lots going to Mrs. Nancy C. Alexander, Mrs. Elizabeth Simpson the widow, James Crawford Simpson, Mrs. Margaret J. Prater, Mrs. Mary Elizabeth Jackson, Sarah Tennessee Simpson, John Tate Simpson, Martha Theresa Simpson, Bowman George Simpson, and David Fleming Simpson.

(65, 248) Henry S. Hensley and wife Dolly Jane VS John H. Milligan; Clerk to ascertain amount of money that has come into hands of Milligan as Gdn. of Dolly Jane from the estate of her grandfather, and the value of Dolly Jane's services while she lived with the Milligans.

(71) Elisha Johnson and E.M. Grant VS Benjamin Ratledge and M.F. Johnson, Adms. of the estate of Daniel and David Ratledge.

December 1866

(116) Death of Ben Johnson is suggested.

(127, 246) Jacob Sheets, Adm. of Samuel W. White, dec'd, VS James E. White; Isaac Burrelson and wife Mary J.; Nancy White widow; Isaac S., William N., Nancy A., and John W. White; Benjamin A., Lucinda M., Alfred T., and Samuel N. Clift; and Taylor Lankford

and wife Martha J.; Gdn. appointed for Lucinda M., **Alfred T.**, and
Samuel N. Clift, minor children of Emily C. Clift, dec'd, and of
Nancy A. and John W. White, minor children of William N. White,
dec'd, and of Isaac S. and William N. White, minor children of
Floyd S. White, dec'd; defendants are heirs of Samuel W. White.

(131, 196) Thomas Stephens, Adm. of Philip Stephens, dec'd, VS
Eliza W. Stephens, widow, and James M., Sarah C., William S.,
George M., John F., Rufus F.B., and Lewis P. Stephens, minor heirs
of Philip Stephens.

(132, 142, 226) A.L. Rodgers, Exec. of George W. Morgan, dec'd, VS
Martha K. Morgan widow, Mary S., Gideon, Frank, Elizabeth M.,
Wash, and Ella Morgan, minor heirs, and Olney Morgan, a nonresident, heir of G.W. Morgan; widow Martha K. dissented from the Will
and is allotted dower; George W. Morgan and A.L. Rodgers jointly
owned lands of Gideon Morgan.

(133, 158, 207) Polly Jackson and husband Josiah Jackson and
others VS Eliza Winton and husband Wesley Winton and others; James
Browder died testate in Meigs Co. in 185_ and was owner of farm in
Roane Co. which had been devised to said James by his brother Darius
Browder, subject to life estate of Ann D., widow of Darius, and
said widow has been dead for several years; Jackson, Mary A., and
Cassandria Browder, minor heirs of Jeptha Browder, dec'd, live in
Texas; in Codicil to Will, James Browder devised said farm in
Roane Co. to his brothers and sisters, viz, Jeptha Browder, Jane
Eldridge, Nancy Bowman, Juda Bussell, Polly Jackson, Eliza Winton,
and Fanny Edington; Jeptha Browder died since making of said Will;
Jonathan Woods and wife are defendants, but relationship, if any, is
not given.

(138) Robert Singleton and wife Catharine P., and James Taylor and
wife Mary Ann VS John E. Duncan; Complainants are heirs to land
known as the Jeremiah Duncan place.

(143, 253-270) Lavina W. and John O. Cannon and Thomas Henley VS
Sallie H. Williamson and others; Arthur H. Henley died in Monroe
Co. in 185_ testate and left the following children, Lavina W.
Cannon, Thomas and David H. Henley, Sallie H. Williamson, Arthur
H. Henley, Mary K. Parker, Alexander, William A., and Charles F.
Henley, and Ann E. Parshal; the said David H. and A.H. Henley,
Jr. have died without issue. The said testator, his widow being
dead, had one grandchild at time of his death, to wit, Bettie
McGhee, Jr., now married to Lafayette Johnston, daughter of Bettie
McGhee, Sr. formerly Bettie Henley, daughter of said testator, who
had died many years before her father; all heirs have agreed to
return their bequests of land and let them go in general fund;
pages 253 to 270 list division of lands into lots, with interesting
plats of same.

(148, 185) James L. and William Weathers, James R. Cunningham and
wife Sarah E., VS Erby, Sarah J., Millie C., John W., Samuel R.,
William, James, Robert, and Nancy Orr, and Joseph Sands Gdn., and
Hugh Goddard and wife Mary A., James F. Nichols and wife Julia
A., John and Henry J. Weathers. Under Will of Wilson Weathers,
dec'd, Henry J. Weathers takes no interest in estate and Court so
construes; Sarah Weathers, the widow, died before filing of Bill;

Complainants and defendants are heirs of Wilson Weathers.

(150, 430) J.T.M. Haire VS Joseph Johnston, Exec. of James A. Haire, dec'd, and others; Joseph Johnston and wife Caroline, and Joseph E. Houston and wife, and John T.M. Haire are legatees under Will. Martha J. Smith is due share as daughter of James A. Haire.

(169, 175, 277, 369) John R. Cole, John Robinson, Rhoda M. Peeler and husband George H. Peeler VS Rebecca Robinson, and Samuel, Joseph, and Sarah Robinson, minors by their Gdn. James Green, John Sheets and Sarah U. Sheets and Henry Sheets, Gdn.; Complainants and defendants own land; Henry Sheets Gdn. of minor heirs of Samuel Robinson, dec'd, and Gdn. of minor heirs of Fanny Sheets, dec'd.

(171, 281) Eusebius Summit, Adm. of Peter Moser VS Daniel and Joseph Moser, minors by Gdn. F.M. Phillips, Henry Moser, and F.M. Phillips and wife Elizabeth; land sold and title vested out of Daniel, Joseph, and Henry Moser, heirs, subject to dower of widow.

(172) Death of John Stratton was suggested and suit revived against heirs, viz, N.T. Stratton's heirs of Texas, R.D. Stratton's heirs of North Carolina, Sarah Ann, John W., and S.E. Stratton of Monroe Co., Joel Stratton's widow Elizabeth and son Joel H., Turner Glen and wife Caroline and children of Texas.

(173) Death of P.A. Newton is suggested.

(173) Death of Philip Roberts is suggested.

June 1867

(180, 316, 440) G.W. Alexander VS Evaline Temple and others; Subpoenas ordered to Blount Co. for Evaline Temple and Angeline Alexander and to Bradley Co. for Nannie A. Ragsdale and to Davidson Co. to James W. Alexander; Nannie Ragsdale not of Bradley Co. but of Virginia; Subpoenas to answer have been issued upon Alonzo A. Ragsdale, James W., Angeline, Evaline, W.B., George A., Caroline V., and John Alexander, all minors; subpoenas also served on defendants Evaline Temple and Matilda Alexander, and publication made as to Mary E. Temple and Nannie Ragsdale.

(195, 308, 350, 485) Samuel P. Hall VS Jonathan Thomas, Enos C. Hooper, Joseph B. Humphreys, Alfred Arp, Adm. of Thomas Arp, dec'd, Emeline, Lauricithia, Eunice, James, Tennessee, and Thomas Arp, minor children of Thomas Arp, dec'd, James McKelvey, Gdn. of said minors, and Guilford Cannon; Jonathan Thomas is a nonresident.

(202) David J. Marshall granted divorce from Nancy A. Marshall, a nonresident; abandonment; David granted custody of minor children.

(213) John Cotton VS Mary E. Cotton; the marriage of Mary E. Cotton with H.H. Porter is proven.

(275, 321) Joseph Hodgson VS John Carringer, Adm. of Andrew Millsaps, dec'd, and wife Rebecca Carringer, widow of Andrew Millsaps, and the heirs, Henry S., William, Joseph, Houston, Bartlett, and Andrew Millsaps, minors; Dec 1867: Complainant having died since last term of Court and suit revived in name of Thomas Sanderson and James Davis, Execs. of Will of Joseph Hodgson.

December 1867

(278, 341, 365, 436) J.L. Johnston and wife Bettie M. VS C.C. Jones and wife Margaret W. et als; C.C. Jones appointed Gdn. of his wife Margaret W., a minor, and W.J. Hicks appointed Gdn. for minor defendants John and Lavinia McGhee; Bettie M. Johnston, Margaret W. Jones, Ann E., John, and Lavinia McGhee are the only children of Barclay McGhee, dec'd.

(279, 412) James A. Wright, James W. Lackey and wife, Archibald Bacome and wife, et al; suit for division of lands of Josiah K. Johnston, dec'd.

(279, 372) Joseph Upton, Gdn., and others VS Mary A. Ross and husband Randolph Ross, E.M. Grant and wife Fannie J. Grant, William, Texie, Ella, and Amelia Spillman, last four being minors; defendants are heirs of Newton J. Spillman.

(279, 443) D.W. Latimore et al VS George Gurley and others, heirs of C.A. Gurley, dec'd; Gdn. appointed for George, Josaphine, Texana, Daniel, Charles, Sallie, and Calvin Gurley, minors.

(279) Stakely VS Amanda Strickland and others; Gdn. appointed for George and Charles Strickland, minors.

(280), 373) John F. Stephens and wife VS Elisha E. Griffith, and others; Gdn. appointed for Harvey and Hettie C. Rhea, and Pleasant, Mary C., Sarah F., John, Elizabeth, Jesse, Nancy J., and Evaline Lee, minors; Court to determine what assets came to hands of Griffith as Exec. of Jesse Rhea, dec'd.

(280, 358) Thomas A. Higdon, Adm. of Noah C. Higdon, dec'd, VS Martin Williams, Lydia A. Higdon, widow of Noah C. Higdon, and others; Gdn. appointed for Mary C., Caroline, and William T. Higdon, minors; defendants Calvin and M.C. Higdon, Mary A. and Robert Rivers; Rebecca M. and James Womack, William and Thomas Higdon, Nancy and George Miller, Thomas Barnard, William Lassater, and W.M. Dixon have failed to answer subpoenas or publication.

(282) Hicks VS Hicks; Cyrus M., Sarah E., W.J., G.M., and Mark M. Hicks, E.C. Joins, and Narcissa Bayless, heirs of Charles and Charles R. Hicks, are entitled to share of amount in hands of Court.

(286, 315, 459) John H. Johnston et al VS Elizabeth C. Russell et al; division and sale of lands of James H. Johnston, dec'd, into three farms, including the dower of the widow, now the wife of Ephraim Sawtell; Gdn. ad litem appointed for Sarah M., and Columbus M. Johnston; Joseph L. Abernathy, Gdn. of Nancy A. and Mary E. Abernathy, made a party respondent to Bill; Respondents Elizabeth C. Russell and Nancy C. Forkner are allowed to amend their answers.

(287) Louisa Shadden et al VS J.B. Cooke and others, heirs of W.P.H. McDermott; Louisa Shadden has married G.W. Payne.

(290) D.L. Stephens VS John Moore; Mary Ann and Elizabeth White, daughters of John Moore, pay his debt and get title to land.

(295, 479) Elihu J. Mumford, Adm. with Will annexed of Elisha Johnston VS Mary Ann Payne and others, heirs of John F. Payne;

Gdn. ad litem appointed for Loyd L., James W., Malinda A., and
Susan P. Payne, minors; Mary Ann, George W., John H., and Samuel
D. Payne, and Mary Jane Hamilton and husband Newton Hamilton have
failed to appear and make defense.

(315) Callaway VS John and J.N. Griffith; Edward Griffith has been
dead for more than six months and no Adm. has been appointed.

(342, 405, 499) Thomas F. Carter, Adm. of William Carter, dec'd,
VS Susan Carter, widow of William Carter, Nancy Wilson widow of
W.D. Wilson, dec'd, and others; E.C. Johnson appointed Gdn. ad
litem for Anderson, Thomas, Jane, and David Leonard, minor heirs
of Martha Leonard, dec'd, daughter of William Carter.

(363) Thomas J. Lewis granted divorce from Althea Lewis; she
refused to remove to this State with complainant and she has been
guilty of adultery.

(364, 366, 387) Anderson Hawkins and wife E.A. Hawkins, and David
B.S. Allen VS Henderson Allen and his Gdn. Samuel Haun, and John,
Mary A., Selias, Ann Eliza, and T.J.A. Bell; Samuel M. Haun
appointed Gdn. ad litem for Mary A., Selias, Ann Eliza, and T.J.A.
Bell, minor children of E.A. Bell, dec'd; defendant John Bell is a
nonresident; petition for sale of lands of Thomas J. Allen, dec'd,
subject to widow's dower.

(367) Richard F. Crowder granted divorce from Nancy Crowder, a
nonresident; abandonment and adultery.

June 1868

(409, 477) Edwin Hall, Adm. of Patrick T. Trotter, dec'd, VS F.D.
Blankenship and others heirs of P.T. Trotter, dec'd; Gdn. ad litem
appointed for John T. Moore and Isaac, Mary A., John Jr., Elizabeth, and Charles Trotter. F.D. Blankenship and wife Emily M.,
Mary Ann and Elizabeth Jane White, and Mahala A. and Thomas Moore
have been served with process; publication has been made as to
John Trotter, William H. Findley and wife Elizabeth, all defendants, and they have failed to answer.

(411) Tennessee Hospital for the Insane VS Martha E. Stephens,
and others; Gdn. ad litem appointed for Martha E., a lunatic.

(414) Elizabeth Clark, Execx. of Lewis Clark VS Caswell Hall; Court
dismisses suit because complainant is a foreign Execx; she appeals
to Tenn. Supreme Court.

(418) Elizabeth Taylor by her next friend Thomas D. Taylor VS
Elika A. Taylor; Elizabeth Taylor was the daughter of James Mayes
of Grainger County and married Elika A. Taylor about Mar 1830;
said Mayes died about 1842 leaving a noncupative Will; letters of
Adm. were granted by Monroe Co. Court to Henry Mayes, Elika A.
Taylor, and D.C. Carmichael, who filed Bill in Chancery Court in
Tazewell, Tenn. for sale of land for partition among the heirs; all
the adult children and heirs, including femes covert and minors,
were made parties to said Bill, except complainant, who was and is
a feme covert and the wife of said Elika A. Taylor; at time Will
was made Elizabeth and Elika were living on land of her father's
in Monroe and McMinn Counties, and all the parties before the Court

agreed that this land would not be sold, but would be her share of
her father's estate, but deed was made to Elika; plea to have land
vested in complainant; Elika agrees to said plea.

(432, 458) Charles W. Hicks, Adm. of Joseph F. Allison, dec'd, VS
James H. Scott et al; G.M. Hicks appointed Gdn. ad litem to
Elizabeth, Robert, and Franklin Allison, minor defendants; Joseph
F. Allison and James H. Scott were in partnership in lands.

(454) Tallent VS King; Henry Swisher and wife Elizabeth are
nonresidents and the residence of Rebecca Swisher and Jesse G.
Swisher is not in Bradley Co. but is unknown.

(475) Death of H.D. Chesnutt is suggested.

Compiled by Genealogical Forum of Portland, Oregon

Volumes 1 and 2 - Claims filed at Oregon City Land Office

No. 1376   Jack, Jeremiah; res: Marion Co., Ore.; b. 1787 Knox
Co., Tenn.; Arr. Ore. 2 Oct 1847; m. Susanna Aug. 1816 Tenn. Aff:
Mitchell Whitlock, Alfred Marquam.

No. 1381   Wilton, Joshua E.; res: Multnomah Co., Ore.; b. 1822
Monroe Co., Tenn.; Arr. Ore. 15 Sep 1852; m. Nancy 3 Dec 1847
Meigs Co., Tenn. Aff: Archon Kelly, Plympton Kelly.

No. 1600   Jack, Thomas P.; res: Marion Co., Ore.; b. 1824 Monroe
Co., Tenn.; Arr. Ore. 1 Nov 1847. Aff: Alfred Marquam, Mitchell
Whitlock.

No. 1969   Humphreys, Wm. I.; res: Marion Co., Ore.; Arr. Ore. 19
Sep 1853; b. 1828 Monroe Co., Tenn; m. Penelope Jane 21 Jul 1852
Monroe Co., Tenn. Aff: William Morley, James Parker, William L.
Patton.

No. 3424   McCully, John M.; res: Linn Co., Ore.; b. 1825 Monroe
Co., Tenn.; Arr. Ore. 19 Sep 1853; m. Clementine Elizabeth 8 Sep
1850 Monroe Co., Tenn. Aff: Lewis Ray, John P. Humphreys, Thos.
M. Humphrey, Jesse B. Irvine.

No. 3648   Hendrix, Harrison H.; res: Washington Co., Ore; b. 1823
Monroe Co., Tenn.; Arr. Ore. Sep 1852; m. Zerilda J. 15 Jun 1846
Wapello Co., Iowa. By 17 Apr 1869 Stephen Sell was owner of part
of this claim. Aff: John R. Porter, Benj. Q. Tucker, Edward A.
Pedigo, William McLin.

No. 3731   Humphrey, John P.; res: Linn Co., Ore.; b. 2 Jan 1832
Monroe Co., Tenn.; Arr. Ore. 19 Sep 1853; m. Margaret Clemtine
21/30 Jul 1852 Monroe Co., Tenn. Aff: Robt. A. Irvine, Washington
Crabtree, Francis Berry.

No. 4678   Haugh, John; Clackamas Co.; b. 1815 Cumberland Co.,
Eng.; Arr. Ore. 15 Sep 1853; Settled claim 30 Oct 1853; m.
Margaret 20 Jun 1846 Cumberland Co., Eng. Declared intention of
becoming citizen 21 Jan 1852 Madisonville, Monroe Co., Tenn. Aff:
John Todd, Henry F. Kayler, Chas. B. Dart, Robt. Hall.

No. 5056   Todd, John; Clackamas Co.; b. 11 Sep 1814 Ayrshire,
Scotland; Arr. Ore. 15 Sep 1853; settled claim 14 Oct 1853; m.
Esther 30 Apr 1845 Cumberland Co., Eng. Declared intention of
becoming citizen 8 Sep 1851, Circuit Court, Madisonville, Monroe
Co., Tenn., stating he was "now 37 yrs. of age". Arr. U.S. 24
Sep 1848 and to Monroe Co. 1 Oct 1848. W.W. Randall and Mrs. S.
Ann Broughton gave aff. that Todd went to Idaho gold mines and
there have been "no tidings from him since 1870, general belief
in the neighborhood is that he is dead". 15 Apr 1878 Esther Todd
gave aff: "lived with said John Todd as his wife from 30 Apr 1845
until year 1861 when he left for Elk City, Idaho and where he was
engaged in mining. I had letters from him frequently until 1870.
Since then I have not heard from him & believe he must be dead. I
have lived on claim from 14 Oct 1853 with my children, Margrette,
James R., Hartly & John T. Todd, up to present time". Aff: John
Haugh, Geo. W. Jackson, John Wilhoit.

No. 5260   Humphreys, Thos. M.; res: Linn Co., Ore.; b. last of Sep

or 1 Oct 1800 "do not recollect County", Tenn.; Arr. Ore. 19 Sep
1853; m. Jane 2 Jun 1825 Monroe Co., Tenn. By 15 Nov 1873 Jane
Humphreys was dec'd and Thos. M. Humphreys had sold his wife's
part of the claim to J.R. Thorp, who was also dec'd by 1873. J.T.
Thorp was adm. of J.R. Thorp estate. Aff: Wm. M. Gilcarist, Lewis
Rhea, Francis Berry, John McCullough, H. Bryant.

Vol. 3 - Claims filed at Roseburg Office

No. 106 Hill, Isaac; res: Jackson Co., Ore.; b. 1805 Claiborne
Co., Tenn.; Arr. Ore 5 Sep 1849; m. Elizabeth 26 Dec 1826 Monroe
Co., Tenn.

No. 716 Dillard, Wm. M.; res: Douglas Co.; b. 1833 Monroe Co.,
Tenn.; Arr. Ore. 18 Oct 1850.

No. 8383 Dillard, John; res: Douglas Co.; b. 1813 Knox Co., Ky.;
Arr. Ore. 15 Oct 1850; m. Jane 22 Jan 1832 Monroe Co., Tenn.

No. 888 Moore, Saml. C.; res: Douglas Co.; b. 1827 Monroe Co.,
Tenn.; Arr. Ore. 2 Jul 1853.

No. 2030 Dillard, Saml.; res: Lane Co. Ore.; b. 1811 Knox Co.,
Ky.; Arr. Ore. 16 Aug 1853; m. Elizabeth Julian 8 Dec 1831/32
/both dates given7 Monroe Co., Tenn.; they have three sons,
Stephen R., Rufus, and Wm. Dillard and two daughters, Ann Eliza
and Sarah E. Dillard. Aff: Robt. H. Renshaw, Wm. D. Renshaw,
Chas. Bennett, Wm. L. Greenwood, James C. Reed.

In an old trunk in the attic of the home of Mr. and Mrs. Earl
Black, Vonore, Monroe Co., Tennessee, there has recently come to
light a veritable treasury of letters and papers, dating from
1776. Mrs. Black is a descendant of Thomas White, who came to
Monroe Co. in the 1820's, and his wife Jane Young White.

Some of these papers belonged to Josiah I. Wright, an attorney of
Monroe County, and a son-in-law of Thomas White. Letters to and
from his clients and the Pension Office are sources of information
about many Monroe County citizens.

The most important paper found, historically, is the list of
soldiers who were sent from Washington County, Tenn. to "Charles
Town". From Tennessee History, we know that this was in 1776.

In the following abstracts, I have included the most interesting
of the papers and letters, omitting many of the White family
letters, which would not be of great interest to the general
public.

29 Oct 1857; Jacob Loyal to W.L. Eakin, Power of Atty. to draw
Jacob's pension money from the U.S. Government at Knoxville,
which will be due March and September 1858, and pay same to
Frank Henry, "I having sold the same to him".

Sep 1841; Letter from Richard L. White, Emory and Henry College,
Glade Springs, Va. to Thomas White, Monroe Co.; "Dear Parents";
has seen Grandmother and Uncle John White since they came in and
they are going to start in a few days; travel seems to agree with
Grandmother.

14 Sep 1843; Letter from Isaac Murray, Washington Co., Tenn. to
Thomas White, Madisonville; Mrs. Joseph Yong died a short time
ago; "Saw John Murray's wife who lives near your brother John
White & all are well".

4 Jun 1856; William Payne son of Thompson and Sarah Payne, formerly of Davidson Co., N.C. to J.I. Wright, Power of Atty. to sell
his undivided interest in land in what was Davidson Co., N.C.,
being the land willed to Sarah Payne by James or Jason Payne.

25 Oct 1881; Letter from Bettie Templeton, Corsicana, Texas, to
cousin Annie Cunningham; all of mother's brothers and sisters
have died except Aunt Bettie White; the writer is 24 years old,
the oldest of five children, the others being Loula 18, Allie
(brother) 14, Madie 5, and Hubert 3; brother Bird is living in
Waxahachie and has just been elected County Judge and has just
started today to Tennessee for the purpose of marrying; he expects
to go to Knoxville to see brother Jerome; brother Billie lives in
Fayetteville; Father expects to go to Nashville, Tenn. on some
Church business.

22 Dec 1849; Letter from John Wayman, Clay Co., Mo. to Miles
Cunningham, Monroe Co.; Wayman evidently has gone from Monroe
Co.

6 Dec 1857; Letter from A.T. Haun, Springfield, Mo. to J.I.
Wright, Monroe Co.; has not obtained a sale for Mrs. Kimbrough's

land because Circuit Court has not met for 18 months; Mother and family came here safely 15 Oct and are well pleased with new home; Newton has gone to Lawrence Co.

20 Mar 1854; Letter from Pension Office; papers of Adam Garren are returned in order that Dr. Young may make oath to his affidavit; Dr. Young states that applicant was a farmer before he went to Mexico, and describes his illnesses.

22 Apr 1835; Receipt from Thomas White to Joseph L. Burt for amount due to Rebecca Erwin and Heirs from Estate of Joseph Young, dec'd.

25 Nov 1868; Letter from Richard C. White, Elizabethton, Tenn. to Uncle Thomas White, Madisonville; oldest son lives where father died and oldest daughter who married a Smith lives near Fish Springs; has only five children, three sons and two daughters; youngest daughter will be 13 on 8 Apr 1869.

12 Aug 1853; Power of Atty. from Bartley Cash, Hamilton Co., to Benjamin W. Kiser, to receive from Jacob Tipton, Adm. of Joel Cash, dec'd, of Monroe Co., his share as heir.

5 Mar 1860; Letter from John A. Wimpy, Dahlonega, Ga. to Joseph I. Wright, Madisonville; is sorry he did not become a Mason in lodge in Madisonville.

24 Jul 1855; Letter from Pension Office to Eakin & Wright, Madisonville, in regard to case of claim of Elizabeth McCallister of Tenn.

27 Sep 1853; Letter from Pension Office to E.E. Griffith, Madisonville, stating that they do not find the case of H.H. Stephens in their files; that Warrants for Bounty Land were issued 7 Apr 1852 and 15 Jan 1853 to Sarah, widow of William Bayless, a private in Capt. Vance's Company, Tenn. Militia, War of 1812.

9 Mar 1853; Letter from Pension Office to Hon. A. Johnson, H. of R., enclosing pension certificate of Henry Click.

26 Sep 1854; Letter from Pension Office concerning case of Richard Allgood, who was a private of Co. C, 5th Regt. Tenn. Volunteers; Capt. Vaughn does not appear to have distinct recollection of the soldier's condition.

19 Mar 1857; Letter from Pension Office; Land Warrant, issued in name of Augustus Presswood 23 Oct 1855 was sent to Benton, Tenn.

4 Dec 1854; Monroe Co.; James Montgomery makes oath that Alexander Roddy was a private in a company of drafted men in the War of 1812-14, commanded by Capt. William Walker in 39 Regt. Inf. commanded by Col. John Williams; enlisted about 8 Jan 1813 at Knoxville and served for twelve months and was honorably discharged in Dec 1813 or Jan 1814; James Montgomery also makes oath that he himself was in said Company and was discharged in Sep 1813 on account of being wounded.

13 Feb 1857; Letter from E.B. Grayson, Washington, concerning pension for widow of Duke Kimbrough; encloses Land Warrants for William Bain, Capt. Thompson's Co., Boothe's Regt., Tenn. Militia, War of 1812, and for Jacob Hammontree of Capt. Gallespie's Co.,

Thornburg Regt., Tenn. Militia, War of 1812; also letter from
Pension Office in relation to claim of Sally Housely.

In this collection are several letters written to Thomas White,
Four Mile Branch, Monroe County, from his sons, Richard L., Ewing
Y., Oliver, and Charles, during 1846 and 1847, from E. T. University, Knoxville, now the University of Tennessee. It was "the
Hill" then, as now. Following are some excerpts from these letters: we have received the several articles...the color of the
pantaloons is presisely like the uniforms they have here...the
bare meat was the best meat I have ever eat...I have my resitations
with Mr. Garvin and Lea...I have never been marked as I know of but
one and that was for studying after ten o'clock... (16 Apr 1846)
Mr. Estabrook wife died a weak or two ago, on that ocasion the
exercives of the colege was suspended untill the burial was over,
in honor of the departed and respect to the president...the number
of students is greater than has ever been before, the number is
about a hundred and thirty...I hope that yew will excuse me for not
writeing before this time and excuse me also for the way I have
writtin this letter for this is the first time that I have attempted to write a letter...

24 Nov 18__; Letter from J.E. Cunningham, Camp near Mossy Creek,
to Capt. J.I. Wright; Dr. Heath was Killed instantly 22 Jul near
Newtons...was buried nearby; we got in the fight at Piedmont the
5th Jun. Hugh & King Heiskell was killed. Andy Millsaps was
killed. Or. Hall was mortally wounded. Lieut. T. McGuire,
William Henly and P.P. Mosier was captured. Nathan Davis was
wounded in the thigh on 2d Sep; We went to Va. with 14 men and returned to Tenn. with 5; Heartsell boys was captured at Morestown;
Bill Heartsell was wounded, the Yankees left him at Morestown; we
gave the Yankees a good chase...the boys got Yankee tricks. I
got Col. John Brownlow's hat. there is about 5 of the old Co. now
besides Hall he is always _____, T.C. Knight, William Clemmer,
N.H. Davis, William McGuire and myself is all that is left. Hugh
Fry is detailed in the ordinance department.

6 Oct 1871; County Court, White VS Cunningham; - Miles Cunningham
late of Monroe Co. died intestate several years ago; left following children and heirs, viz: Lincoln, Alfred, David, and John
Cunningham, Elizabeth White formerly Cunningham, wife of C.F.
White, Isabella Cunningham, Mahala Templeton formerly Cunningham.
Since the death of Miles Cunningham, his children David and John
have died without issue; his son Alfred died leaving widow Margaret
and minor children, Anna, James, and John, of Monroe Co.; his
daughter Mahala Templeton has died leaving William and Byrd
Templeton of Loudon Co. and Bettie Templeton of Bradley Co., also
under age; his son Lincoln has died without issue but made a Will
leaving his 1/5 interest in estate minus the 1/42 inherited from
David by Mrs. Templeton, David having died before him - In said
Will Lincoln gave all his interest to Alfred and John who were
then living and to Isabella - said Will has been lost and also the
record of probate if same had ever been probated; Jerome Templeton
of Loudon Co. is a Complainant also, but his relationship is not
stated.

Many family letters from Lawyer J.I. Wright and wife Susan who
move to Rome, Ga., after the Civil War.

23 Nov 1858; Letter from J.W. Carter, Daneville, Kemper Co., Miss. to Eakin & Wright, Madisonville: had expected to be in Texas before now but has been detained by wife's health.

28 Apr 1858; Letter from J.M. Hopper, Calhoun, Henry Co., Mo., to Joseph Wright, Jr.

18 Jan 1821; Receipt from Thomas and Jane White to Rebecca Irvin, Adm. of estate of Charles Young, dec'd, for $885 of "my father's estate".

16 Oct 1815; Receipt from Ewin Young to Rebekah Irvin, Adm. of Charles Young, dec'd, for $864 of "my father's estate".

8 Apr 1824; True copy of Will of Wilkins Young: my part of land to mother during her lifetime and then to sister Jane White and then to her children; all money to mother; to William Irven a sorrel mare for a debt I owe him; Exec: mother; Test: James W. Young, Eliza Boring, William W. Young.

17 Mar 1853; Letter from Ivy S. Reynolds, X Roads, Ill., to nephew J. Ivy Wright; requesting him or his brother to attend to business in N.C.; encloses a Power of Atty.; received a letter from brother James informing that he was Adm. of brother John's estate.

19 May 1860; Letter from A.T. Haun, Springfield, Mo. to J.I. Wright; ascertained that Thomas Marshall died in Lawrence Co. and that Adm. never paid the money into the County Treas. but died with it in his hands.

9 Apr 1860; Letter from Pension Office; the application of Susan Mashburn, widow of Levi Mashburn, for a renewal of a pension has been examined.

24 Mar 1861; Letter from John Cotton, Ossian, Wells Co., Ind., to Wright & Vaughn; concerns his divorce from Mary E. Cotton.

17 Mar 1852; Letter from E.B. Grayson, Washington, to J.I. Wright; has brought claim of Mrs. Bayless to a close; from testimony of the old lady now living in Abbeville Dist., who waited on Mrs. Bayless when she was married to Wm. Dickson, Wm. Dickson was never an officer and the marriage took place after Jan 1794; there were two or three Wm. Dicksons who served from S.C. in War of Revolution.

Scrap of paper: "On 13 of May 1826 my revered Father departed this life - Richard White - T. White."

Scrap of paper: "Rec'd of Joseph Young, executor of Robert Young, dec'd $70 - 15 Sep 1803. Signed Rebekah Irwin."

Sep 1799; Received of Mrs. Rebecka Young for examing the lines of the land which her husband died seized.

15 Feb 1859; Copy of Chancery Court Bill; Susan Davis of Monroe Co. VS Daniel Daily and wife Nancy, William Miller and wife Martha, her daughters and sons-in-law; Susan also has son whose residence is unknown.

31 Jul 1864; Letter from J.C. Vaughn, Martinsburg, Va. to "Dear Tom"; "Since I wrote you we have been in some ten fights - the first at Piedmont... that Battle ____ at the place was a blunder

of Genl. Jones; he ___ 10,000 men & only had about 4500 & nearly
all of them dismounted Cavalry with short range guns. The Genl.
was killed trying to rally the 60 Va. that give way first. I & my
horse was hit five times in attempting to do the same thing... ___
& S.H. Brett were Captains at Peadmont. I hope Alex. wife may see
him as she has been sent North. Also David Gilaspie's wife. Mrs.
Vandike & daughters & others. My wife & daughters are confined
under Gard... is it not horable to think of the condition of my
family. Old John McGaugha & others had better leave E. Tenn.
soon - do you know what place my family is at. a gard drew his
gun on my oldest daughter, threatened to shoot her... Send word
to Capt. J.I. Wright that his Broonlaw Dr. O.P. White was killed
leading a charge against Avrill's Brigade... Tom, I have the best
men in the Army... the true stock of E. Tenn.... Capt. Dick &
John both safe yet... Col. Carter 1st Tenn. wounded in neck not
dangerus... James Everheart of Dick's Co. wounded on the 29th in
Maysland he was a noble soldier. When Genl. Early advances on the
Enemy he puts my Brigade in front - when he falls back he places
us in the rear. So you see we are in a fight all the time... on
the 25th in a fight at this place I got my right ankle badly bruised
& mashed my horse ran against a stump. I think I can ride by the
2d or 3d I keep as near up as I can in an Ambulance... Col. Bradford... Col. Lillard... Tell Col. Rowan to get his Regt. together
at Bristol as soon as he can... Tell Sam Rowan that Carter is all
right he threw his horse away & went into the fights had his horse
killed from under him. Tell Maj. Stephens that he is exchanged &
that I need his Service amediately... Lieut. Tom Boyd & Capt Bob
Houston of my Staff are both in Ebbert Co. about Ebberton send
them word to report amediately to me. Tell Genl. Lain that his
son is safe & a gallant soldier. Tell Stearl Neal that Capt.
Neal & Shearman are all right... Tell Capt. McClendon of 31st
that Colbert his last man is mortally wounded. I fear will die.

This has been the grate Campaign of the War... I have no
Idea what Genl. Early will do. his Infantry is moving back today
towards Bunker Hill to watch the Enemys force at Harpers Ferry.
Said to be three Corps 6th 19th & one other at that point... We
have drove out of Maryland thousands of cattle & horses & much
valuable property. Q.M. & Some Big ones have stole anoughf to do
them during the war. this whole sale plunder I am opposed too...
Tell Andrew Stevens of Augusta that his son Frank is with me all
right he rec'd a letter from his Father yestardy. I still have
strong hopes that Hood will hold Atlanta - Richmond is safe - we
were before Washington (in Sight three miles off) nearly two days
Could have Capture the City when we first arrived Cause why not I
don't know... Genl. Ramsour with his devission meet with a defeat
at Winchester some two weeks ago... I charged the Enemy & Saved
his command from being nearly all Captured... Alf Caldwell is
with us fine health. Tell Col. Cook that I rec'd his letter...
Col. Brown 59th was badly hurt by fall of his horse a few days
ago... Capt. Hardy Capt. Jennings of 12th Tenn. Batallon are
wounded... I regret to say that Adjt. Reagan was wounded on our
last fight near Winchester on last Sabbath & had to have his leg
amputed 6 inches above the knee... Your true friend, J.C. Vaughn."

Feb 1859; Letter from Pension Office regarding application of Mrs.

Elizabeth Lillard, who had filed under Acts of 1850 and 1852 but not under Act of 1855.

1859-1860; Benjamin Ratledge and his two sons David and Daniel; Benjamin has mail contract in name of son Daniel; Copy of Chancery Court Bill.

Copy of Chancery Court Bill; Donald A. McKenzie VS E.P. Clark and son Willie; In 1839 John L. McKenzie, father of Donald, died in Monroe Co. intestate, leaving widow Mary A. and children, to wit, E.J., W.G., Nancy C., John R., Mary A., and Donald A. McKenzie; Nancy C. married E.P. Clark before 1856, but before bond for title was complied with, Nancy C. died leaving infant son, Willie.

30 Dec 1858; Letter from Pension Office regarding claim of William Bain.

8 Jan 1857; Letter from Richard L. White, Laggoon, Sacramento Co., Calif. to brother Ewing Y. White, Madisonville; "we think you can make some seven or eight hundred dollars a year here".

23 Mar 1860; Letter from R.B. Brabson, Washington, to Joshua Halcomb, regarding application for pension.

16 Jul 1852; Letter from Pension Office regarding Land Warrant for widow of James Glass.

27 Sep 1853; Letter from Pension Office regarding claim of Isam Queener for Bounty Land.

26 Aug 1839; Andon McLemore, dec'd, in a/c with Thos. White.

1858-1860; Copy of Chancery Bill, Blount Co.; Samuel Ghormley VS Stephens; About Feb 1846, Jehu Stephens of Monroe Co. died leaving widow Ann and children Henry, Hugh L., Albert, Cleveland, and Darthula, all minors at his death, but all now of age except last two, and all of Monroe Co. except Henry who lives in Blount Co. and Hugh who is perhaps of Arkansas.

15 Jul 1856; Letter from Pension Office regarding application of minor children of soldier Jacob Fisher, dec'd.

Copy Chancery Court Bill; William Brannum VS Mary A. Spillman, Adminx. of Newton J. Spillman; several years ago Brannum contracted with Spillman to obtain a Bounty Land Warrant for Brannum's alledged service in Capt. Jefferson Caldwell's Co. of Mounted men, as a volunteer, about year 1836-1837.

5 Jun 1841; Copy of Chancery Court Order; A.B. Clift, James and Luticia Redmon VS G.W. and Celia Crawford, Tilmon and Cintha Fry, Nancy Ann and Celia Levins; division of lands which Shelton Levins, now dec'd, and David Hammontree purchased jointly.

20 Mar 1867; Letter from R.C. Wilhite, Harmony Grove, Georgia.

7 Sep 1864; Letter from J.I. Wright, Macon, Georgia, to Thomas White; has had several letters written at Bristol, East Tenn. where Genl. Vaughn and his entire command were on the 25th Aug; Mrs. Dr. Parshall of Sweetwater and Mrs. Cook of same place with her children and Alfred Caldwell's wife of Athens, Tenn. had been sent out... Mrs. Parshall represents my wife and children are well... Genl. John H. Morgan was killed on the 4th Inst

at Greenville, E. Tenn.... was surprised - it is astonishing our
Generals will suffer themselves thus to be surprised...

29 Sep 1854; Letter from Bank of East Tenn., Knoxville, to Josiah
I. Wright, enclosing pensions for Elizabeth Witt, Adam Garren, and
A.J. Vaughn.

4 Nov 1859; Copy Chancery Court Bill; Jeptha Tallent of Monroe Co.
VS Richard McDaniel and James Tallent of Monroe Co., W. Russell
Tallent of Bradley Co., and Thomas McDaniel who has gone to parts
unknown; Jeptha is father of W. Russell Tallent who lived with him
in 1851; Jeptha paid for land with land warrant which he had
received for military services which he himself had rendered.

12 Jan 1856; Letter from Pension Office to Nathaniel Watson,
Madisonville; Claim of Nathaniel for bounty land as father of
Perrin Watson, dec'd, for services of said Perrin, as Lieut. Tenn.
Vols, in War with Mexico, is rejected.

15 Sep 1864; Letter from J.I. Wright, Macon, Ga., to Thomas White;
met up with L____ Hood from Madisonville, Tenn. When Wheeler went
in then he came out with him... he says before he left there some
Yankee Robbers went to your house and demanded wheat or meat &
that Lieu refused admittance they tried to force her away from the
door and shot her in the face inflicting a painful wound in the
face - no danger... It is known who shot Lieu... Mama and Pine
knew them... He says Dr. Bicknell, B. Kimbrough, & Dr. Cook are
the worst of union men there. Clicks and Dentons & Bill Burriss
boys are the worst tory bushwhackers - they killed old Pat Trotter
after having give him 250 lashes then shot him in the presence of
his Mother. When Wheeler went in there Bicknell, Cooke, Jones &
others set out for Ky. at a double quick... He says the Denton &
Click boys had killed Rily Curtis & Burt - He says that Jim
Henderson son of Sam who deserted our army and joined the Yankees
last fall was engaged a short time ago to Mary a daughter of Amos
Carson & on a day or so previous to the marriage on the road from
Carsons to Town he was shot dead... He says Mrs. Kimbrough has
been robed several times lately... Bicknell telegraphed S.M.
Henderson who was in Massachusetts with his wife about Jim's death
and also telegraphed him on no account to come back as he would
be killed too. Jim Henderson was aiding Joe Divine to raise a
regiment for the home defense of Blount Monroe & McMinn Counties...
Jack Peace to Miss Pettitt. Jack and her run away to Ill. Amos
Carson is dead - none of the county officers elect have entered
upon the execution of their office unless it is Ben Pettitt. Hood
says Pettitt has done all he could for all Southrens and that he
now stands fair with them more so than any other union man...

Copy of Chancery Court Bill; Noah Mosier bought land of Garland
Smith who died about 1853 leaving widow Margaret E. and children,
Haseltine, Elizabeth, Martha, Mariah, Sidny, and Garland Smith.

9 Sep 1864; Letter from J.I. Wright, Macon, Ga., to Thos. White,
Carnesville, Ga., in care of Col. Wm. A. Upton; thinking that
maybe I can change the monotony of your moments... have not heard
anything since I wrote you last from home or E.T., except that I
saw Joe Selvage the other day, he tells me that Nic Thomas was
just out from Monroe Co... the Yankees caught Thos. L. Upton

between Sweetwater & home & took him to Knoxville and thence to
Fort Delaware... There is no doubt but that Cook Sam Rowan Bob
Rowan & Joe Rowan are all in jail at Knoxville...

30 May 1864; Letter from J.I. Wright, Macon, Ga., to Thos. White;
it is hard to be thus exiled from home from wife and children and
parents... I saw Sam Rowan... /who/ says that the tories are
having a high time of it... John Minis is now a great man in
Monroe... Henderson Hicks was making up or trying to make a
company of Home guards to protect the place from Southern men.
Jack Peace had moved out & took possession of old Sammy Henderson
farm. Old Sammy had moved to young Sam's in McMinn County. Could
not live at home...

23 Jan 1843; Letter from Richard C. White, Daggins Ferry, C. Cty,
Ten. (envelope reads Taylorsville, Tenn) to uncle Thos. White,
Madisonville; my Father held a note on David Russell... bearing
interest from 19 Oct 1829... and I not long since heard of his
death... note unpaid... Rec'd a letter from John A. White dated
Novr. 24, 1842 in which he states that Grand Ma is living with him
and Aunt Isabella in one mile of him and also that he has been
honored with a seat in the legislature of Mo. from Platt County...
I have married since you was here and have two interesting children, boys. James Lawson and William Tell are living with my
Mother at the old place the ballance of the boys are all married...

20 Mar 1861; Letter from James A. Bare, Barry County, Missouri
(Envelope: Washburn Prairie, Mo.) to J.I. Wright, Madisonville;
concerns suit on note given by Bare to James Lowry, Sr. in Feb
1842 which was paid to Execs. of James Lowry, Sr. Oct. 1851;
witnesses in Mo. are Larkin A. Stapp and John H. Higgins who live
in Kings Point, Dade Co., Mo.; witnesses in Bradley Co., Tenn.
are Silas M. Wan, Guilford Gatlin, and Johnson Cruse; all know
that Bare was solvent and unencumbered; wishes to sell his interest
in father's land.

6 Aug 1860; Letter from E.E. Baldwin, Bonham, Fanin Co., Texas,
to Jo Wright, Madisonville, by William King; is sending a set of
gavels by King to present to the lodge in his name.

12 Mar 1852; Certificate that Sarah Bayless formerly widow of Wm.
Dickson who was a private of Cavalry & Infy. in the revolutionary
war, is inscribed on the pension list.

11 Apr 1864; Letter from J.I. Wright, Macon, Ga., to Dr. O.P.
White, Decatur, Ga.; Dear Bro.; Genl. J.C. Vaughn says that Capt.
Stephens, Jim Thomas, & Fox White are at Garbers near Jonesborough,
Tenn. and that they three said they were going to California -
that Jim Thomas had been to Richmond and bought gold with all their
money - Vaughn says he advised them to stay and fight it out...

Copy of Chancery Court Bill; William D. Swann of Arkansas, Samuel
E. and Ann V. Swan of Knox Co. VS Alexander Ish and wife Elizabeth
of Blount Co., Josiah H. Johnston and wife Clarissa of Monroe Co.,
D.D. Berry and wife Lutitia of Missouri, John Lee and wife Mary of
Knox Co., H.B. Leeper of Blount Co., and Thomas B. Odell of Knox
Co.; Alexander Swan died in Knox Co. in 1837 leaving William D.,
Samuel E., Ann V., and Robert T. Swan surviving him as his children;

the said Robert T. died in Arkansas in Spring of 1860 without wife
or children; the said /sic/ Harvy Swan since died; Benjamin Prater
died in Roane Co. in 1850 and Elizabeth Ish, Clarissa Johnston, and
Lutitia Berry are his children; the Execs. of Benjamin Prater were
Alexander Ish and William Prater, son of Benjamin; William Prater
has since died and his widow Mary (now Mary Lee, wife of John Lee)
and H.B. Leeper administered on his estate; suit concerns sale of
slaves to Benjamin Prater while Orators were still minors.

27 Jun 1803; Letter from John and Mary Gray to "honored mother,
Mrs. Isabel Young, Living in Washington Count on nob creak"; "we
are all in good health at preasent but iby and I doant think that
She will Liv"... your loving Son and Daughter.

1 Sep 1825; Letter from Ewing Young, Franklin, to mother Mrs.
Rebeckah Irvin;... after a long absence... I have just returned
from the spanish Country after a long and fetiugeing trip for
the last four years I have been in that country... a short time
before I left this Country I received a letter from my sister...
she informed me of her marriage... I am setting out on another
trip to n___ Mexico. I expect it will be probably one year before
I return if I am sucksessful in this trip I think I will be to
see you next fall or winter this will be my third trip to that
country in my first I was tolerable sucksessfull my last rath
unfortunate. I was Robed of a number of Mules and horses by the
indians. we pass through a wilderness of about eight hundred
miles... I am yet single... my best Respects to Mr. Irven & my
brother.

21 Feb 1822; Letter from Richard & Susanna White, Grove Springs,
Abingdon, Va., to "Dear Children &c in your Quarter"; addressed
to Thomas White, Esqr., Goshen, Monroe County, mail: the mouth of
Notchey Creek on Tellaco River, Tennessee; Chota p.o. 18½; We
Rec'd Two letters Last week... one from Eleanor to her mother
date The 12 January last... we are in hopes she will safely
Recover. All Relation here are well. I have not heard from Lawson
for some time Claborne is here from Kentucky... I shall be down
come in the spring to see You all and Bring Eleanor home. Your
mother wants much to see Eleanor but knows that she's well used by
Both familys Yours & Mr. Russell's... your Sisters & Bros. here
Joins in Love to you all... Your loving Father & mother... N.B.
You spell the name of your place rong not Gotion but Goshen.

20 Nov 1794; Territory South of the River Ohio and County of
Washington; Personally came Robert Cashady and made oath that he
had a Note of hand on Charles Young for the sum of thirteen pounds
Virginia Dated August the 20th 1792... lost or Mislaid... Received
full satisfaction... (signed) Joseph Young, J.P.

9 Sep 1797; State of Tennessee, Washington County; this day came
Jas. and Mary Young be me one of the Justices for sd County and
made oath that the estate of Charles Young Deceased Stand Justly
indebted to the estate of Thomas Young Deceased one dollar and
Seventy five Cents. (Signed) John Tipton. (On reverse side:
Mary Young's acct)

10 Nov 1849; Letter from James W. Bicknell, San Francisco, C A,
to E.E. Griffith, Esq., Madisonville;... Doct. White & Dick

Requested me to drop you a line from this place to let you know
that they had landed safe & sound in California. I left Doct.
White Dick Nels Cannon & Hu Heiskell at Weaver Town in what is
called in this country the dry diggins. It is about 50 miles
Northeast from Sacramento City or Suter's Fort. they remained
there for the purpose of selecting a place to dig & to get timber
to build us a cabin to winter in. Tyler John Brown Anderson
Humphreys & myself came on to Sacramento City to buy our winter
provisions & make arrangements to dispose of our Cattle &
waggons... Sent me to this place to get our Letters & papers...

The Athens Post, Vol. 2, Number 72, Friday Feb 8, 1850: This
paper contains a long letter from Tyler D. Heiskell, Sacramento
City, to his father Col. Wm. Heiskell, 5 Nov 1849, and gives news
of the following persons: Col. Bicknell, Brown, Humphreys, Oliver
and Dick White, Nelson Cannon, Hugh Heiskell, Mr. Howard, Dr. R.A.
Paine "my old College mate", John M. Barnes formerly from Blount
county who now lives in Oregon, Frank Smith, Cornelius Howard.
Note of Editor: Later dates bring intelligence of the death of
Hugh B. Heiskell and Nelson Cannon.

The Athens Post, Vol. 2, Number 72, Friday Feb 8, 1850: Married on
Wed 30 ult by Rev. H.F. Taylor, James B. Cooke, Esq. of this place
to Miss Penelope, daughter of Col. Wm. P.H. McDermott of Tellico
Plains.

The Athens Post, Vol. 2, Number 72, Friday Feb 8, 1850: Died at
Weaversville, in Sacramento valley, Calif., on 16 Nov last, Mr.
Hugh Brown Heiskell, son of Maj. F.S. & Eliza Heiskell, of this
vicinity, in the 24th year of his age.

19 Dec 1859; Letter from C.C. Webb, "Mary County, Georgia,
Connasagga post office" to J.I. Wright. Envelope: Connysogga,
Bradley Co., Tenn.

Will of Rebecca Irwin, Washington County, Tennessee, executed 20
Feb 1834; to daughter Jane wife of Thos. White, half of money that
son Wilkins Young left me; the other half to grandchildren, the
heirs of Thos. & Jane White; to son Ewing Young one dollar if he
ever returns; appoint Joseph L. Burts & James W. Young as Execs.;
Witnesses: Benj. Drain, John C. Harris. A True Copy from the
Original (Signed) James Sevier, Clk. by Saml. Greer, D.C.

The Athens Post, Vol. 2, No. 68, Friday, Jan 11, 1850: Married on
Thurs 3d inst by Rev. Austen Gunn, Mr. Saml. M. Henderson to Miss
Louesa P. Boldman, all of Monroe Co.; Married on Thurs 3d inst by
Rev. Wm. Jones, Mr. Jefferson Jones to Miss ____ Jones, daughter
of Allen D. Jones, all of Monroe Co.; Died in Monroe Co. on 13
Dec last, Mrs. Nancy Johnson, aged 74 years, 11 months and 25 days.

13 Jan 1828; Article of agreement between Samuel McAdoo, school
teacher, and Subscribers; school to be taught at house on Thomas
White's farm; subscribers to pay one dollar per month per scholar;
Subscribers and No. of Pupils: Isaac Hagler½; David Russell 2;
Thos. White 5; W.A. Upton 5; Miles Cunningham 5; William Upton by
order of his wife 2; Cornelius Howard 1; William Isbill 1; George
Snider _; Philip Robinson 1; Saml. McCluer by order in the presents
of Wm. Isbell ½; Jno. Robinson ½; John R. Woody ½; John M. Isbel ½;

Wm. Snider 1. /Note: there is no explanation for the ½7.

12 Mar 1858; Letter from T.J. Young, Blairsville, Ga., to J.I.
Wright; complains that after he left to visit Texas, many untrue
things were told about him, but "that which wounds me the most is
Carmichael the man I have done so much for has done everything in
his power to keep Josie from coming back to me... she is willing
to come if her folks were willing..."

Letter from C.W. Beatie to his cousin Charles Fox White, no date;
"to inform you of the death of my Dear old Mother who departed
this life may the 1st 1866".

Obituary in torn section of the "Southern Christian Advocate":
Elizabeth Stillwell was born in Mecklenburg Co., N.C., Nov 3d 1773
and died in Spalding Co., Ga., Dec 14th 1871...daughter of William
and Margaret Houston...married Elijah Stillwell 17 Jan 1793, who
died 6 Sep 1846...she remembered many incidents of the revolutionary war, her father being an earnest Whig...much of his time in
the army.

Letter 2 Nov 1853 from Joe I. Wright, Madisonville, to Miss Susan
White, Four Mile Branch, written on eve of their wedding on the
morrow.

Copy of Chancery Bill, undated: In Jan 1839 John Stephens was
appointed Gdn. of Rebecca J. Stephens, then a minor child of
Jethro Stephens, dec'd; in 1846 said John Stephens died intestate
leaving widow Cynthia and children Daniel, Jane, Eliza, and
Margaret Stephens, all of age unless it be the youngest Margaret;
widow Cynthia died over a year ago; Daniel Plumley, one of Adms.
of John Stephens, has long since removed from Monroe Co.

Letter 13 Nov 1852, from R.L. White, Indian diggings, Calif., to
father Thomas White, Madisonville: you will probably hear of the
death of Uncle John White...he had started across the plains with
his family this season and died of colera the third of Jun and his
family returned to Mo. Wes McLemore killed a man two or three
weeks ago and has escaped...he had the small pox when he got away.

Letter 9 Sep 1866, from Chattanooga, Tenn., signature gone, to
Thomas White; I have learned that your son Newton has returned
from California. Will you please ask him if he knows anything
of my son Marion McCrary, as I have not heard from him since the
breaking out of the war.

Scrap of paper: Charles Fox White was borned in 1825 Apr 10.

25 Jun 1840; Elizabeth Blanton, a single woman, declares on oath
before Thomas White, J.P., that Joseph B. Gilbreath is the father
of the bastard child of which she was delivered on 19 Mar 1840.

Scrap of paper: "1st service Isaac Hartsell, Wm. McLin, volun-
teers; 2d service Jno. Hampton, Henry McCray, Barron, Drafs;
Col. Ellison, creek service; Jerry Boyd, Jno. Hall, Sr., Jesse
Whitson from Carter Co."

Scrap of paper: "Margaret Caroline White departed this life on
the 26 day October 1840. I have strong reasons to believe she
rests in heaven & never will be forgotten by me. Jane White".

Letter 8 Oct 1848 from O.P. White, Lexington, to parents (Thomas White, Monroe Co.); he and his horse stood the trip well; he is attending lectures.

Letter 1 Oct 1858 from Pension Office concerning application for an invalid pension for John Moore.

Letter 8 Aug 1864 from Thomas A. Cleage, Bank of Tennessee Athens, Augusta, Ga., to J.I. Wright; a letter from Gen. Vaughn dated 31 Jul at Martinsburg, Va., stating "that your brother in law Dr. White was killed whilst leading a Charge against Averill's Brigade"; this letter is enclosed with one to Thomas White, Carnesville, Ga., telling him of Oliver's death.

Letter 19 Jun 1903 from P.L. Griffith, Hopewell Springs, to J.I. Wright, Fort Worth, Texas; "Dear Brother; I have no record of my fore parents, but will tell you what I know. Isaac White was my great grandfather..." /The information given in this letter from Paulina White Griffith is condensed below.7

Isaac White married a Lawson and had 13 children, all boys, 11 of them killed in Revolutionary War and Raleigh who died in Ky., and Richard White (my grandfather) who married 1st a Lawson, his cousin, and had 10 children: Anna married a Wright; Eliza married a Wright; Mary married David Russell; Theodosia married Thomas Finley; Lawson married a Baity; Richard married a Baity; Claburn married Leonidas Hogue /no other names given7.

Richard White (my grandfather) married 2nd Susan Henry who was widow of William Henry who was son of Patrick Henry, and they had 10 children: Thomas (my father) married Jane Young; John married Margaret Adkins; Paulina married Robert Baity; Ellen married Josiah Baity; Rachel married a Trig; Rebecca married 1st Sidney Hogue who died and married 2nd Josiah Baity, widower of sister Ellen; Rhoda married a Whitten, and the others died young.

Joseph Young (my great grandfather) married Jane Dillard and had five children: James; Joseph; Ruth who married three or four times and whose last husband was a Henry; Mary Jane married Robert Taylor; and Charles Young (my grandfather) who married Rebecca Wilkins and had three children: Wilkins died single; Ewing died single in Oregon (was jailed in Mexico and received sum for false imprisonment); and Jane Young (my mother).

Rebecca Wilkins was the daughter "I think", of Charles and his wife Jane Hazard. Jane Hazard married a Wilkins and had Rebecca (my grandmother) and Margaret who died single. Jane Hazard married 2nd Robert McCaby or Mcleaby and had one child Robert.

Letter from J.I. Wright to his son Tom Young Wright, no date, and
this is evidently a copy. Information in this letter is condensed
below:

> Elisha Reynolds lived in Wilkesboro, N.C., was Revolution-
> ary soldier, married Judith Patton, and had children:
> John; Wesley; Bowen; Ivy; James; Sarah S. who married
> William Griffith, parents of Elisha Griffith; and Nancy
> A. Reynolds Wright.
>
> _____ Wright married and had Josiah; Sally who married
> a Hoots and lived Coles Co., Ind.; and Ann who married
> Timothy Holland and lives or did live in Salem, N. C.
> These three children were left orphans and raised by an
> aunt named Spoonhoward at Salem, N.C.
>
> Susan Henry was Susan Walker (wife of Richard White).
> Ewing Young, of whom mention is made in life of Kit
> Carson, died in Wallamette Valley, Oregon Territory,
> in 1844 and left a large estate which has never yet
> been sued for or recovered. Richard Lawson White,
> your mother's brother, died in California some years
> ago.

The next paper deserves special attention. The faded paper has
no date and only the top half remains, but from the context, it
is clear that this is a list of soldiers who went to Charles Town,
South Carolina, in 1776 from Washington County, North Carolina,
now Tennessee. Judge Samuel Williams, in his writings on
Tennessee history, tells of this event.

A list of soldiers Drafted from the Washing Ridgment
of Militia on the States service to Charles Town

from John McKnabbs Company 1st Captain in the Regment

1.	David Hickey	)		William Clark Esqr. 6th Capt.			
2.	Wm. Brown	)			)		
3.	Alexr. Greer	)			)		
4.	John Nave	)	Soldiers	Moundsain	)	Special	
5.	Charles Young	)			)		
6.	Matthew Talbert Jr.	)		Mulliply	)	Soldiers	

George Russell Esqr. 2d Captain

Mark Mitchel
Richard Fletcher
  thomas brown
Andrew Fagan
Hall Massingill
Edmond Sinkness
Samuel Phane

Adam Wilson Esqr. 7th Capt.

1. Joseph Gist
2. Alexr. Morrow
3. Wm. Fain
4. Alexr. Campble
5. Wm. Chambers
6. John McVeigh
     John McVeigh
7. Andrew Eng____
     Thomas Woodward

Joseph Wilson Esqr. 3d Capt.
1. John Morrison

Josiah Hoskins Esqr. 8th Capt.

The following is written across the lower right hand corner:

Patrick Hockshaw takes the place of John McVeigh in this Comp.

The names Andrew Fagan, Hall <u>Massingill</u>, the first John McVeigh
and Andrew Eng____ have been marked through, as if in error.

On the reverse side of paper:

The Foregoing or within Mentioned Soldiers was taken
from the several Captains Companies therein Mentioned
According to their Divissions in there Respective
App___tments.

To which Robert Sevier Acts as Captain &
Christopher Cuningham Junr. Lieutenant
certified by

This list of names is taken from the lists of jurors, officials,
and plaintiffs and defendants who are expressly listed as citizens
of said county, in three Circuit Court Record Books, as follows:
Circuit Court Civil Cases 1820-1829, Circuit Court State Cases
1820-1830, and Circuit Court Minutes Record 1827-1834.

1820

Airhart, Nicholas
Anderson, James
Bane, William
Black, John
Blair, William S.
Brown, John G.
Carouth, James
Coil, Jacob
Cordial, John
Edington, John
Foute, Daniel D.
Grisham, Thompson
Hammontree, John
Hargis, John
Hart, Josiah
Hathaway, Samuel
Henry, William
McCaffery, John
McCroskey, John, Sr.
McCuiston, James
Martin, John
Morrison, Thomas
Parks, Samuel
Perry, Silas
Richmond, George
Simpson, Thomas
Taylor, Andrew
Taylor, Campbell
Taylor, David
Taylor, Isaac
Tipton, John B.
Torbet, John
Upshaw, Elizabeth
Upshaw, Peter
Warren, Thomas B.
Waugh, John
Wear, John
Wilson, Joseph
Wright, Jonathan

1821

Anderson, James
Beard, Welcome
Beaty, John
Black, John
Blair, William S.

1821

Bowman, George
Boyd, Erby
Breeden, William
Bright, William
Brown, Jesse
Caldwell, David
Cary, Alexander
Carson, Samuel
Carter, Allen
Carter, John
Castal, John
Chapman, John O.
Chapman, Joshua H.
Chesnut, Henry
Clark, Benjamin
Cline, William
Comstock, W.
Copeland, William
Croft, Thomas
Cunningham, William
Curry, Anderson
Davis, George
Davis, Samuel
Dillard, John
Dixon, William
Doherty, John
Dooly, John M.
Douglass, Jonathan
Duggan, Daniel
Duggan, John
Duncan, Joseph
Edington, John
Farmer, Lewis
Faw, Jonathan
Fine, John
Flanigan, William
Foute, Daniel D.
Gaines, Joshua
Gamblet, James
Gilbreath, Samuel
Goddard, Thornton C.
Golliher, Harris B.
Gregory, Robert
Griffin, Jones
Grigsby, James
Grigsby, John
Grimes, John

1821

Grimmet, Jacob
Grimmet, John
Gunter, David
Hall, James
Hard, Isaac
Harman, Stephen
Harris, George C.
Harvey, Thomas
Hicks, Charles
Hicks, John
Hill, John
Holeman, Daniel
Hollaway, Minter
Howell, Stephen
Hulson /Hutson?/, Robert
Hunter, David M.
Inman, John
Johnson, Archer
Johnson, Samuel
Kelso, Charles
Kelso, Hugh
Kimbrough, William
Koil, George
Laine, Samuel
Lea, Alfred
Lea, Hiram
Low, Stephen
Luker, Joseph
McAffrey, John
McCaul, John
McCuiston, David
McCuiston, James
McCuiston, Thomas
McCroskey, Samuel
McDaniel, James
McGuire, Nicholas
McKnabb, William
McReynolds, Robert
McSpadden, Joseph
McSpadden, Mathew
McSpadden, Moses
Manes, Jacob
Martin, Alfred
Martin, William
Melton, Jesse
Murray, Isaac
Murray, William
Murray, William B.
Neel, Benjamin
Nicholson, James
Orr, Azariah
Orr, William
Patterson, James

1821

Patterson, Samuel
Patton, William
Pennington, William
Perry, Silas
Phillips, Joseph
Price, Josiah
Ramsey, John
Read, Jeremiah
Reagan, Ahimas
Richardson, John
Richmond, Charles W.
Richmond, George
Richmond, William
Rider, Austin
Robertson, Thomas
Robertson, Williamson
Routh, Jeremiah
Samples, Charles
Scrimshire, David
Scrimshire, James
Selvige, William
Shaw, Robert
Shipley, Christopher
Simpson, Thomas
Smallen, Nathaniel
Smith, John
Smith, Philip
Snider, John
Starrett, Preston
Stephens, Henry
Taylor, David
Tipton, Jonathan
Torbet, John
Trim, Anderson
Utter, Abraham
Waugh, John
Wells, Jesse
White, Richard
White, Thomas
Whitenbarger, Henry
Williams, John
Wilson, Samuel, Jr.
Wofford, Nathaniel
Wolf, Jeremiah
Woods, Isaac
Woody, Amon (Naamon)
Wright, Jonathan

1822

Adams, William
Alexander, James
Bane, William

1822

Blair, Thomas
Brannum, Edward
Brown, John G.
Bryant, Elias
Burris, William
Callaway, Joseph
Carruth, James
Carter, Jabash
Carter, Joseph
Carter, Micajah
Chandler, James
Clark, Thomas
Clayton, John
Clayton, Robert
Cook, Jacob
Croft, Thomas
Crossland, William
Davis, Jonathan
Dillard, John
Dillard, William
Earhart, Nicholas
Eldredge, Thomas
Flannagon, William
Gantt, Samuel M.
Gilbreth, John
Gray, James
Griffith, Edward
Griffith, John
Hackney, Joseph
Harmon, Stephen
Harp, Rolly
Henderson, John F.
Henderson, Thomas
Hickman, John
Higdon, John
Hollaway, Minter
Humphreys, John
Hutchison, Furney
Hutson, Robert
Isbell, Miller
Johnston, Samuel
Julian, Isaac
Kennard, William
Lane, Samuel
Lea, William
McCalester, James G.
McDaniel, Bryant
McGuire, Henry
McGuire, Nicholas
McGuire, Thomas
Melton, Carter
Mise, John, Jr.
Mise, John, Sr.

1822

Mitchell, James
Mitchell, John
Murray, Isaac
Peck, Nicholas S.
Philips, Beaty
Philips, Joseph
Rider, Alexander
Robertson, Samuel
Robertson, William
Routh, Jeremiah
Routh, Joseph
Russell, John
Russell, Martin
Snider, Michael
Stephens, Henry
Stephens, Peter
Taylor, Andrew
Taylor, William
Tomey, Thomas L.
Trim, Anderson
Upton, William
Waugh, John
Wear, Abraham B.
Wear, Berry
Webb, Martin
Weir, Samuel
Wilson, Alexander
Wilson, Robert
Wilson, Samuel
Wolf, Jeremiah
Wright, Iredell D.

1823

Adams, Elijah
Alexander, James
Baker, James
Bane, William
Beck, Absalem
Beard, Welcome
Best, Daniel
Biggs, Alexander
Blair, Thomas
Blair, William S.
Boyd, John
Britton, Joseph
Broghill, James
Burton, Thomas
Caldwell, John
Callaway, Joseph
Carder, Susan
Cardin, Larkin
Carouth, James

1823

Carter, Lewis
Cary, John
Cary, Thomas
Cathcart, David
Chaldwick, Thomas
Chandler, James
Clayton, Elijah
Colquitt, Samuel
Coppoch, John
Curtis, James
Davis, James
Davis, William
Denton, Adonijah
Dicus, George
Donohoo, Charles
Duggan, John
Duggan, Samuel
Edmonds, George
Edmonds, Mathew
Eldridge, Thomas
Ensley, James
Farmer, Lewis
Ghormley, James
Graves, William
Griffith, John
Griffith, William
Haire, James A.
Hale, Isaac
Hall, Michael C.A.
Hamilton, Elijah
Harris, George C.
Henderson, Andrew L.
Henderson, Thomas
Henry, William
Herlson, James
Hicks, Charles
Hicks, George
Higdon, John
Houk, Michael
Humphries, John
Irvin, Patrick
Isble, Miller
Jack, Jeremiah
James, William
Johnston, Samuel
Knox, John
Lawson, Mor___
Lotspeich, John
Love, John
McAffrey, John
McCroskey, John
McCroskey, Samuel
McCullock, William

1823

McFall, John
McFarland, Robert
McGhee, John
McHenry, Robert
McRhea, William
Martial, Joseph
Mayo, Blackmore H.
Mize, John
Moreland, George
Morrison, Thomas
Mosier, John
Neal, Benjamin
Nicholson, James
Nicholson, William
Noblet, William
Parker, Evan
Patterson, Lewis
Peck, Nicholas S.
Pearson, Jacob
Price, Josiah
Ragan, Peter
Ragan, William
Ramsey, John
Reagan, James
Renfro, John
Rider, Alexander
Rider, Austin
Roach, Aron
Robertson, William
Roper, John
Rowan, Josiah
Scrimsher, James
Selvidge, William
Shamblin, George
Shook, Isaac
Simpson, Thomas
Smalling, Jonathan
Smalling, Robert
Smalling, Samuel
Smith, Jason
Smith, John
Smith, John N.
Smith, Lewis
Smith, Russell V.
Snider, John
Snider, Michael
Stephens, Henry
Stephens, John B.
Stephenson, Joseph
Stephenson, William
Tate, Robert
Tipton, John B.
Tipton, Will

1823

Todd, James
Tomey, Thomas L.
Trim, Henderson
Tucker, Henry
Tucker, Kincher
Upton, William
Vines, Benjamin
Watterberg, Peter
Waugh, John
Wear, John
Webb, John
Webb, William
Wells, Jesse
White, Nathaniel
White, Thomas
White, William
White, William, Jr.
Williams, Benajah
Williams, David
Williams, Godfrey
Wilson, William
Wiseman, Albert G.
Wright, Iredell D.
Young, Mathew M.

1824

Adams, John
Ainsworth, William, Sr.
Airhart, Nicholas
Anderson, Isaac
Anderson, Stephen
Bain, Daniel
Baker, James
Baker, William
Banes, Adam
Barker, John
Barnes, Edward
Beck, Absalem
Bedwell, William
Biggs, Alexander
Blanton, James
Blanton, Vincent
Bowers, William
Bowles, Traverse
Boyd, John
Boyd, Joseph
Bradford, Hamilton
Brannon, Edward
Briden, William
Brittain, Joseph
Brown, John G.
Burnett, John

1824

Caldwell, David
Calloway, Joseph
Cannon, Bartlett
Carden, Larkin
Carter, David
Carter, Isaac
Carter, Jabes
Carter, Lewis
Cathcart, David
Cavit, John
Chadwick, Thomas
Chaney, A.R.
Chesnutt, Henry
Christian, Allen
Coppoch, John
Craighead, Thomas
Davis, John
Davis, William
Dean, John
Dell, George
Derossett, Daniel
Dikas, George
Dillard, William
Donohoo, Charles
Donohoo, Joseph
Doty, Thomas
Edmonds, George
Eldredge, Thomas
Fowler, Philo
Frazier, Thomas
Friddle, John
Gibson, James
Gibson, William
Gladden, John
Gray, James
Griffin, Jones
Griffith, John
Griffith, William
Hail, John W.
Hall, James
Harmon, Stephen
Harris, George C.
Henderson, John F.
Hickman, John
Hicks, Charles
Hicks, John
Hoge, John
Holeman, Daniel
Hunt, Thomas
Hunt, Uriah
Irvin, Patrick
Isble, Miller
James, William

<u>1824</u>

Johnston, Samuel
Johnston, William E.
Julian, Isaac
Knox, Joseph J.
Land, Stephen
Lea, Hiram
Lillard, John
Little, Isam
Litton, Esram
Lowry, John
Lowry, Thomas K.
Lusk, Samuel
Lyle, William G.
McAllister, James G.
McBryant, Spencer
McCray, William
McCroskey, John
McCuiston, Thomas
McGill, Robert
McManes, Eli
McNabb, William
Mayo, Valentine
Medlock, Jasent
Montgomery, James
Morelock, Jacob
Mosier, Peter
Nicholson, James
Nimer, Jacob
Orr, Azemiah
Parker, Aaron
Parker, Benjamin
Parker, Evan
Patterson, Lewis
Patton, James
Perry, James
Perry, Silas
Person, Jacob
Phillips, Joseph
Price, William
Ragan, Daniel
Ragan, Peter
Ragan, William P.
Rider, Alexander
Rider, Austin
Roberson, William
Rogers, William
Routh, Joseph
Scrimsher, James
Scrimsher, Robert
Seahorn, Luvici
Selvage, George
Shamblain, George
Sharp, Edward

<u>1824</u>

Sheets, Henry
Shook, Isaac
Smith, Charles G.
Smith, John N.
Smith, Joshua
Smoke, Jacob
Snider, John
Spriggens, Thomas
Starrett, Preston
Step, Akilles
Stephenson, Joseph
Stuart, Walter
Sutton, James
Taylor, John H.
Taylor, Leroy
Thompson, William
Tipton, John B.
Tipton, Jonathan
Tipton, Willie B.
Torbet, James
Tormey, William
Trim, Carter
Tucker, Willey
Vaughn, Foly
Vernon, Thomas
Waugh, John
Wear, John
Webb, Martin
Welcher, Martin
West, John
Westmoreland, Alexander
White, Samuel
White, Thomas
Wilkerson, Jefferson
Wilkerson, Perry
Williams, David
Wilson, Charles
Wilson, John
Wilson, William
Wimpy, Aider
Wolf, Jeremiah
Woods, Joseph B.
Worden, Thomas
Wright, William
Yearwood, William

<u>1825</u>

Adams, John
Anderson, Isaac
Bacomb, James
Bain, William
Baker, Jacob

1825

Blair, John
Blankenship, Ashford
Blankenship, Stephen
Bowers, William
Boyd, Erby
Bradley, James
Branum, Edward
Brown, Jesse N.
Broyles, John C.
Burris, John A.
Callaway, Joseph
Carter, Allen
Carter, Isaac
Carter, Jesse
Carter, Micajah
Carter, Robert
Cathcart, David
Chayne, Abel R.
Chesnutt, Henry
Christian, Allen
Cochrane, Alexander
Coffman, John
Cumpstock, Jasper W.
Cunningham, William
Davis, William
Dell, George
Dillard, William
Duff, John
Dugan, Daniel
Eldredge, Thomas
Ensley, James
Fender, Michael
Foute, George W.
Gallehorn, H.B.
Gentry, Allen D.
Glass, Jessee
Glass, Willie B.
    and wife Mary
Gratton, Thomas
Gray, Robert
Griffin, Jones
Griffith, Edward
Griffith, John
Griffith, William
Hare, James A.
Harris, George C.
Henderson, John F.
Henderson, Thomas
Hendrix, Nathan
Henly, Arthur H.
Hensley, Felix
Hickmon, John
Houck, Enoch

1825

Hughs, Francis
Hunt, Thomas
Hunt, Uriah
Hyler, James
Ingram, Aaron
Jamerson, Samuel
James, Blackburn
James, William
Jamison, Benjamin C.
Jobe, John
Johnson, Samuel
Johnson, Samuel, Sr.
Johnston, Samuel M.
Kirkland, Nathan
Knox, Joseph J.
Lane, Street
Laughmiller, Samuel
Lay, David
Lemons, Samuel
Likens, Thomas M.
Love, Robartis
Lyle, William G.
Lyons, Edmund
McAllister, Athiel
McAllister, Jesse
McAllister, Wesley
McCray, William
McGhee, John
McKinsey, Andrew
McSpadden, Joseph
Mason, James
Michael, William
Miller, Jesse
Montgomery, George
Montgomery, James
Morrison, John T.
Murry, William
Nichols, John
Norton, Sampson
Owens, Daniel
Parsons, Joshua
Patterson, John
Patterson, Lewis
Peck, Nicholas S.
Peck, Thomas P.K.
Perry, Silas
Phillips, Beaty
Ragan, Daniel
Rhea, Singleton
Richardson, James
Richmond, William
Rider, Austin
Roach, John

1825

Roach, Joshua
Roach, Littleberry
Roberson, Lindsey
Roberts, Bazzel
Samples, Jesse
Samples, John
Scrimsher, James
Scrimsher, Robert
Scruggs, William
Selvage, George
Smith, Lewis
Starrett, Preston
Stephens, Henry
Stephenson, Joseph
Stover, Orrie
Tate, Robert
Thacker, Valentine
Thompson, John C.
Tipton, John B.
Tipton, Will
Torbett, James
Vaughn, Foly
Vernon, Thomas
Watson, Nathaniel
Waugh, John
Webb, John R. or K.
Whisenhent, John
White, William
Wilson, Charles
Wilson, John
Wilson, Joseph
Wolf, Jeremiah
Yoakum, George

1826

Adams, John
Adams, William
Ainsworth, William
Alexander, John
Anderson, Isaac
Arp, James
Bacom, James
Baker, Andrew
Baker, James
Baker, William
Bane, Arthur
Barker, Solomon
Bass, Alexander
Bayles, Abraham
Bayles, Samuel
Bayles, William
Bell, William

1826

Bicknell, Samuel
Bird, James
Blackburn, Samuel
Blair, Thomas
Blankenship, Stephen
Boyd, Erby
Boyd, Hugh
Boyd, Joseph
Bradford, Hamilton
Brown, Robert
Broyles, Cain
Burnett, John C.
Butler, Jesse
Callaway, Joseph
Campbell, Daniel
Cannon, Barthell
Cantrell, Moses
Carter, Allen
Carter, Caleb
Carter, David
Carter, Isaac
Carter, Jabash
Carter, James
Carter, Jesse
Carter, John
Carter, Lewis
Carter, Micajah
Cary, Thomas
Casteel, Edward
Cathcart, David
Chayne, A.R.
Christian, Allen
Christian, Thomas
Clayton, Elijah
Cobbs, Richard
Cook, George
Corhorn, Alexander
Cornelison, William
Cotrell, John
Couch, Jacob
Crews, William B.
Daniel, Robert
Davenport, Runell M.
Davis, George
Davis, Nathan
Davis, Peter P.
Dicus, George
Dillard, John
Dodson, Elijah
Donohoo, Charles
Donohoo, James or Joseph
Duff, John
Dunlap, Richard D.

1826

Dya, John
Edington, James
Edington, John
Edmonds, George
Eldridge, Thomas
Farme, Lewis
Flanigan, William
Friddle, John
Foute, George W.
Fowler, Philo
Garner, William
Gentry, Allen D.
Gilbreath, Joseph B.
Gilbreath, Samuel
Girdner, Michael
Glass, John G.
Glass, Wilie B.
Gratton, Thomas
Graves, Silas
Graves, Stephen, Jr.
Graves, Stephen, Sr.
Greenlea, Lewis
Gregory, John
Griffin, Jones
Griffith, Edward
Griffith, John
Grisham, Michael
Harmon, John B.
Harle, John
Harris, George C.
Harris, Robert
Hart, Alexander
Hawkins, Joseph G.
Henderson, George
Henderson, Thomas
Henderson, William
Hendrix, Nathan
Henley, Arthur H.
Hicks, John
Hightower, John
Hix, George
Holloway, Minter
Hughs, Francis
Hull, Abraham
Hunt, Levi B.
Hunt, Thomas
Hunt, Uriah
James, William
Johnson, Samuel
Johnston, Samuel M.
Jones, Thomas
Jordan, Anderson P.H.
Kelly, John D.

1826

Kerr, James
Key, John
Kimbrough, William
Knox, Joseph J.
Lea, John
Lillard, William
Litton, Esram
Lomax, Theophilus
Lowry, William
Lusk, Samuel
McAlister, Athiel
McAlister, Jesse
McAlister, Wesley
McCaslen, John
McDowell, Eliazer
McFarland, James
McGhee, John
McIntire, Richard
McKee___, Landon C.
McKenzie, Samuel A.
McPherson, Jesse
McRea, Hugh
  and wife Mary
McSpadden, Mathew
McSpadden, Thomas
Mar, Joseph
Marshall, Henry
Marshall, John
Mason, James
Mathis, Elijah
Mayberry, Yrepts
Meek, James W.
Mize, Keziah
Montgomery, James
Morrison, Thomas
Morrow, William I.I.
Mosier, James
Mosier, John
Mosier, Peter
Murry, Isaac
Newton, Henry
Nichols, John
Nicholson, James
Nieman, Jacob
Nolin, Thomas
Orr, Arthur
Orr, Finley
Owen, Charles
Parker, Caleb J.
Parsons, Joshua
Pasely, Hezekiah
Patterson, William
Peck, N.S.

1826

Pettigrew, Bennett
Pettigrew, Ebenezer
Price, Josiah
Prock, William
Proctor, James
Ragan, Daniel
Ragan, William
Ramsey, John
Richmond, William
Rhea, Robert
Rhea, Warren
Roach, Aaron
Roach, John
Roach, Littleberry
Robeson, John
Roberson, Linsey
Roberson, William
Rogers, William
Rose, James
Routh, Joseph
Samples, John
Samples, Thomas
Seitzer, Moses
Shamblin, George
Shoemaker, John
Smalling, Jonathan
Smith, Benjamin
Smith, David
Smith, Jasent
Smith, John N.
Smith, Joseph
Smith, Lewis
Snider, Joseph
Spradlin, John
Starrett, Preston
Stephens, Henry
Stephenson, Joseph
Sutton, William S.
Swanson, Westley
Tatum, Hardy C.
Taylor, John H.
Taylor, Leroy
Taylor, Shadrac
Tennsworth, Thomas
Thompson, John C.
Tindall, Henry
Tipton, John B.
Tipton, Wyley B.
Tomey, Thomas L.
Torbet, James
Trim, Carter
Trim, Henderson
Trotter, Philip

1826

Turk, Hiram K.
Upton, William
Utter, William B.
Vance, Keziah
Vaughn, William
Vaught, Jacob
Vernon, Thomas
Vestal, James
Vinsant, Hiram
Wadkins, E.B.
Warren, Jacob
Watson, Josiah
Waugh, John
Wayman, Edward
Wear, Abraham B
Wear, David D.
Webb, Larkin
Westmoreland, Alexander
Westmoreland, Edward
White, John L.
White, William
Whitson, Charles
Wilburn, Isaac
Williams, James
Wilson, John
Wimpy, A.
Wolf, Jeremiah
Wright, Jonathan
Wright, Josiah

1827

Adams, John
Ainsworth, William
Alexander, James
Anderson, Isaac
Anderson, John
Ayers, Alpha
Baker, Jacob
Baker, James
Bane, Daniel
Baxter, Levi
Bayles, Samuel
Bayles, William
Bicknell, Samuel
Blair, John
Blair, Thomas
Blankenship, Spencer
Boyd, Erby
Boyd, Levi
Britton, Joseph
Brotherton, Thomas
Brown, Jacob

Brown, Samuel
Buck, Abram
Bunyard, Ephraim
Burris, John A.
Burris, William
Caldwell, David
Callaway, Joseph F.
Callaway, Thomas F.M.
Campbell, Daniel
Cannon, John O.
Cantrell, James
Cantrell, John
Cantrell, Minter
Carden, John
Carney, Eli
Carson, David
Carson, Samuel
Carson, William
Carter, Amos
Carter, Caleb
Carter, Isaac
Carter, Jabes
Carter, Jesse
Carter, John W.
Carter, Lewis
Carter, Robert
Cary, Thomas
Case, Jesse
Cavet, Manuel
Chesnutt, Henry
Christian, Allen
Clift, Benjamin D.
Clifton, Elias
Colles, Richard
Coltharp, John
Cook, George
Cornelison, William
Cotrell, John
Craighead, William B.
Cumstock, J.W.
Cunningham, Will
Curtis, James
Davis, John
Davis, Jonathan
Douglass, Thomas
Duff, John
Duggan, John
Duggan, Samuel W.
Duggan, Sarah
Dunsworth, Thomas
Edgar, George D.
Edington, David
Edington, James

Ervin, Patrick
Ferguson, John
Ferguson, Robert
Ferguson, Thomas
Fine, John
Forsythe, James
Foute, G.W.
Fowler, Filo
Frazier, John
Gentry, Allen D.
Ghormley, Michael
Gilbreath, John
Gilbreath, Joseph B.
Givins, John
Graham, Samuel
Grant, William
Gray, John
Gray, William
Greenfield, Peter
Gregory, William
Griffith, John
Hacket, Oliver
Haire, James A.
Hampton, Thomas
Hankins, Joseph
Hankins, Thomas
Harle, John
Harp, James
Harrison, William
Hart, Edward
Haydock (Haddox), John
   and wife Mary
Henderson, Andrew L.
Henderson, George
Henderson, John
Henderson, John F.
Hendrix, Nathan
Hensley, Christian
Hisaw, Joseph
Hix, Charles
Hix, George
Hix, James
Holloway, Jacob
Holloway, Minter
Houston, John
Houston, Thomas
Hoyt, Edward
Hughs, George
Hull, Abraham
Humble, Samuel
Hunt, Thomas
Hutson, Robert
Hyler, Abraham

<u>1827</u>

Isbell, William
Jamerson, Benjamin C.
James, William
Jamison, Samuel
Johnston, James
Johnston, Samuel M.
Johnston, Samuel, Sr.
Jones, Thomas
Jordan, A.P.H.
Kelsoe, Charles
Key, John
Key, Peter
Knox, Joseph J.
Lawson, John
Lawson, Russell
Lea, James
Lowry, Samuel
Loyd, James
Lusk, Robert M.
McAllister, Athiel
McAllister, Jesse
McAllister, Westly
McCleary, Joseph
McCray, Thomas
McCray, William
McCroskey, John
McCulock, Henry F.
McFarland, Joseph
McGhee, John
McGhee, Mathew W.
McGill, Robert
McKenzie, Samuel A.
McNabb, Baptis
McNabb, Lon___
McSpadden, Joseph
McSpadden, Moses
McSpadden, Stuart
McSpadden, Thomas
Malone, Jesse
Mangus, Henry
Marr, Benjamin
Marr, Joseph
Marshall, Henry
Marshall, Joseph
Marshall, Richard
Mashburn, William
Matlock Jason
Meek, James W.
Melton, Carter
Melton, Elisha
Melton, Jesse
Melton, N___d
Michael, James

<u>1827</u>

Michael, Peter
Mitchell, John
Montgomery, George W.
Montgomery, William
Mosier, Peter
Mowrey, John
Murry, Ephraim
Murry, Isaac
Newton, Henry
Nichols, John
Nicholson, Thomas
Nolen, Thomas
Orr, Finley
Parker, Benjamin
Parker, Evan
Parsons, Joshua
Pearson, Jacob
Peck, Nicholas, S.
Province, William
Ragan, Peter
Reveley, James
Rhea, Warren
Richmond, Alexander
Richmond, James
Richmond, William
Riley, Charles
Roberts, Lewis
Roberts, Samuel
Robertson, John
Rose, James
Ross, John
Routh, Joseph
Russell, David
Selvage, George
Selvage, William
Shadden, Flora
Shadden, James W.
Shadden, John
Shadden, John H.
Shook, Isaac
Smith, Joseph
Smith, Lewis
Snodgrass, Robert
Spriggins, Thomas
Starrett, Preston
Stephens, Henry
Stephens, Levi
Stephens, Richard
Stephenson, Joseph
Summey, Solomon
Sutton, William
Tabor, John H.
Taylor, John H.

<u>1827</u>

Taylor, Leroy
Taylor, S.W.
Taylor, Shadrac
Thompson, James R.
Thompson, John C.
Tipton, John B.
Tipton, Jonathan
Tolbert, Jacob C.
Tomey, William B.
Torbet, John
Townbey, William
Trim, Carter
Turk, Hiram K.
Twomey, Thomas L.
Upton, William
Utter, William R.
Vaughn, Abel
Vaughn, James
Vernon, Thomas
Vinsant, Hiram
Walker, David P.
Watkins, E.B.
Watterbarger, Peter
Waugh, John
Wear, Abraham B.
Wear, Hugh
Wear, John
White, David
White, John L.
White, Richard
White, Thomas
White, William (Govr)
White, William (Miller)
Whitson, Jesse
Wilburn, Isaac
Williams, Benaja
Williams, Godfrey
Wilson, Harvey N.
Wilson, William
Wolf, John
Woods, Joseph
Wright, Iredell D.
Wright, Jonathan
Yoakum, George

<u>1828</u>

Adams, Moses H.
Ainsworth, William
Alexander, John
Anderson, John
Anderson, Stephen
  and wife Susan

<u>1828</u>

Bayles, Samuel
Bayles, William
Biggs, Abel
Biggs, Alexander
Blackburn, Enoch
Blackburn, Samuel
Blair, John
Blair, Thomas
Blair, William S.
Borrin, John D.
Bowman, James A.
Boyd, Erby
Boyd, Levi
Bromley, Isaac
Brotherton, Thomas
Brown, Benjamin
Brown, Jacob C.
Brown, James
Brown, Jesse C.
Brown, John G.
Brown, Thomas
Burnett, John C.
Burris, John A.
Burris, William
Callaway, Joseph
Cannon, John O.
Cantrell, Minter
Cardin, John
Carroll, Michael
Carson, John
Carter, Allen
Carter, Caleb
Carter, David
Carter, Isaac
Carter, Jesse
Carter, John B.
Carter, Robert B.
Case, Jesse
Casky, John
Caves, William
Chaney, Abel R.
Christian, Allen
Coltharp, John
Cook, William
Cooper, Jonathan
Cooper, Robert
Cornelison, William
Cox, John
Crage, James
Craighead, William
Crisp, Joel
  and wife Rhoda
Cunningham, Robert

1828

Cunningham, William
Curtis, Samuel
  and wife Fanny
Cuson, Rebecca
Dean, John
Denton, Reuben
Dicus, George
Donohoo, Joseph
Duff, John
Duffy, John
Duggan, John
Duggan, Samuel W.
Duggan, Sarah L.
Dyer, Abraham
Dyer, James O.
Edgar, George D.
Edington, David
Edington, Samuel
Eli, David
Erwin, Thomas
Felton, Gary
Forsythe, James
Foute, G.W.
Gentry, Allen D.
Ghormly, Hugh
Ghormly, Turpin
Gilbreath, Joseph B.
Givens, Zach
Glass, Jesse
Goad, Ayres
Gold, John
Gold, Samuel
Gollaher, Asa K.
Gollaher, Mary
Gollihon, Clary
Grant, William
Griffith, Edward
Griffith, William
Grimmett, Jacob
Grimmett, John
Grubb, Washington
Hacket, Oliver
Hackney, George
Hackney, Joseph, Jr.
Hagler, Isaac
Hair, James A.
Hammontree, William
Hampton, Thomas, shoemaker
Harmon, Joseph
Harrell, John
Harris, Alford
Harris, George C.
Harrison, James

1828

Hart, Andrew
Hart, Edward
Hawkins, Richard
Headrick, John
  and wife Mary
Heiskell, David
Henderson, John
Henderson, Robert
Henderson, Stephen
Henderson, Thomas
Hendrix, Nathan
Hickey, Joseph
Hix, Charles
Hix, George
Hix, John
Hix, Tolbert
Hughs, Francis
Humble, Isaac
Humphreys, James
Humphreys, John J.
Humphreys, Thomas M.
Hunn, Richard D.
Hunt, Thomas
Hunt, Uriah
Isbell, Miller
Isbell, William
Jack, Jeremiah
Jacobs, Lewis, tailor
Jamerson, Samuel
Johnston, James
Johnston, John
  and wife Tempy
Johnston, John H.
Johnston, Samuel
Johnston, Zachariah
Jones, Thomas
Jordan, Anderson P.H.
Kelly, John D.
Kelly, Samuel
Kelso, Charles
Key, John
Knox, John
Lakesly, Richard
Ledford, James
Lemons, John
Likens, John
Lucus, Joel
Lyle, William G.
Lyons, Edward
McAlister, Athiel
McAlister, Wesley
McAlister, William
McCoy, Joseph

1828

McCrosky, John
McGhee, John
McGinnis, Noble
McGonigal, Floyd
McKeehan, Landon C.
McKenny, James
McKey, Charles T.
McRay, Mc.
McSpadden, Joseph
McSpadden, Moses
Mansfield, Thomas
    house carpenter
Marshall, John
Marshall, Joseph
Mashburn, David
Mason, James
Mason, William
Meek, James W.
    house carpenter
Melton, Jesse
Miller, John
Milligan, Joseph S.
Mills, Barrett
Mills, William
Mitchell, James
Montgomery, James
Montgomery, William
Moody, Sally
Morrow, Armstrong
Morrow, John
Moses, James
Murry, Isaac
Norman, John
Orr, Finley
Padgett, John
Paine, Jacob
Parker, Benjamin
Parsons, Joshua
Pearson, Jacob
Peck, Nicholas S.
Price, William
Ragan, N.
Ragan, Peter
Ragsdale, Edward
Raper, William
Ray, John
Rhea, Warren
Richmond, Alexander
Richmond, John
Richmond, William
Rider, Austin
Riley, Charles
Roach, Aaron

1828

Roach, David
Robertson, John
Rush, John
Russell, James
Russell, John L.
Sandler (Shandler), George
Scruggs, William
Sloan, Alexander
Sloan, Archibald
Smalling, Nathaniel
Smith, Benjamin
Smith, Joseph
Sneed, Robert
Snodgrass, Robert
Spraggins, Elisha
Starrett, Preston
Stead, Justice
Step, Achilles
Stephens, Henry
Stephens, Joshua
Stephens, Richard
Stephenson, Joseph
Stephenson, William
Strictlin, James
Summey, Solomon
Suton, William
Syl___, Edward
Tabor, John H.
Tankersly, Richard
Taylor, Leroy
Taylor, S.M.
Taylor, Shadrac
Taylor, William
Tipton, Abraham
Tipton, John B.
Tipton, Jonathan
Tomey, William B.
Upton, William
Utter, Abraham
Utter, William R.
Vaughn, James
Ware, John
Ware, William
Watkins, E.B.
Waugh, David
Waugh, James
Waugh, John
Whitson, Jesse, Jr.
    and wife Elizabeth
Whitson, Jesse, Sr.
Wilkerson, Thomas
Williams, David
Williams, William

1828

Wilson, A.B.S.D.
Wilson, Charles
Wilson, Harvey N.
Wilson, Joseph
Wilson, Samuel
Woody, James
Wright, Jonathan
Wright, Willis
Yearwood, William
Young, Mathew M.

1829

Abels, Thomas
Adams, John, Jr.
Adams, John, Sr.
Ainsworth, William
Alexander, James H.
Anderson, George W.
Baily, John
Beesley, James
Bicknell, Samuel
Blackburn, Samuel
Blair, Thomas
Blair, William S.
Bonham, Samuel D.
Borrin, John D.
Bowman, George
Brown, James
Brown, Jesse
Burnett, John C.
Burris, John A.
Burris, William
Butler, Jesse
Cannon, John O.
Carden, John
Carter, Caleb
Carter, Isaac
Carter, Levi
Cary, Thomas
Case, Jesse
Clark, Fetherston
Clayton, Robert
Clift, Benjamin D.
Coltharp, John
Colvert, Stephen
Cunningham, Robert
Davis, Peter P.
Dean, John
Dillard, John
Douglass, Jonathan
Duff, Jacob N.
Duff, John

1829

Duffy, John
Dugan, David
Erwin, Patrick
Erwin, William
Fartheree, William
Felton, Gary
Ferguson, Thomas
Fine, John
Ford, Horatio
Forshee, Joseph
Friddle, David
Ghormly, Hugh
Gilbreath, Joseph B.
Gillespie, John F.
Gladen, John
Glen, Squire S.
Graham, William
Grant, William
Gray, Robert
Gregory, William
Griffith, John
Hackney, Hugh
Hackney, Joseph
Hall, James
Hare, James A.
Harris, Alfred
Harris, George C.
Harris, John A.
Harris, Robert
Harrison, James
Harrison, Thomas
Harrison, William
Hart, Andrew
Haston, Isaac
Haun, Abraham
Haynes, James
Henderson, George
Henderson, John F.
Henderson, Legrand
Henley, Arthur H.
Hix, James
Humphries, John J.
Huson, John
Isbell, Pendleton
Jamerson, Samuel
James, Blackburn
James, William
Kelso, Charles
Kimbrough, Bradley
Lacky, John
Laine, Samuel
Laster, Reuben
Litton, Ezram

Lowry, John
Luker, Joseph
Lusk, Samuel
McCray, Mc.
McGhee, Merryman
McGuire, Michael
McManis, Eli
McReynolds, David W.
McSpadden, Samuel
Malone, Jesse
Mansfield, Thomas
Marr, Benjamin
Marshall, Joseph
Matheny, James
Melton, Jesse
Mitchell, James
Mitchell, John
Morgan, Mark
Morrison, John
Moser, John
Newman, Joseph
Parker, Benjamin
Parsons, Joshua
Payne, Jacob W.
Pitman, Jesse
Price, Josiah
Price, William
Ragan, Nathaniel
Ramsey, John
Rider, Austin
Roach, Aaron
Roach, David
Rogers, John
Rollins, George
Rollins, William
Rush, John
Sliger, Thomas
Sloan, Archibald
Smalling, Nathaniel S.
Smalling, Robert M.
Smith, Joseph
Snider, Frederick
Snider, James
Springfield, Hugh
Starrett, David
Straw, Strain,
  or Strane, James
Taylor, Leroy
Taylor, Shadrac M.
Taylor, William
Telford, James
Tipton, John B.
Trotter, Philip

Twomey, William B.
Upton, William
Utter, William R.
Vernon, Thomas
Waugh, John
Wear, William
Webb, Martin
Whitson, Jesse
Wilburn, Isaac
Williams, Archibald
Williams, William
Wilson, John L.
Wilson, Joseph
Wilson, Robert
Wilson, Robert H.
Woods, Joel
Worthy, George, Jr.
Worthy, George, Sr.
Wright, Iredell D.
Yoakum, George
Young, Mathew M.

TENNESSEE JOURNAL

II-36, 22 Apr 1835: On 10th inst by Rev. John G. Likins, Mr. John
Spencer of McMinn Co. to Miss Martha A. Likins of Monroe Co.

HIWASSEE PATRIOT

II-19, 21 Jul 1840: We learn that Miss Mary Pettegrew, daughter
of the steward of the poor house in Monroe Co., was married to
Mr. Thos. McClellan, an inmate of that institution, by E.D. Malone,
Esq., on 11th inst...he being unable to turn or move without
assistance, from the effects of rheumatism of 20 years standing.
She procured assistance and had him removed to a neighbor's house
where she was united in holy bonds of wedlock to her gay Lothario.

II-25, 1 Sep 1840: On 18th inst by Rev. A. Grigsby, Mr John
Carmichael, Merchant of Blair's Ferry, to Miss Ann Jane, dau. of
James Johnston of Roane Co.

ATHENS POST

IV-171, 2 Jan 1852: In Madisonville on 31st inst by Rev. H.F.
Taylor, Mr. Samuel M. Henderson to Miss Sarah Moore all of that
place.

IV-179, 27 Feb 1852: On 19th inst by Rev. John Scruggs, Mr. George
W. Wilson of Monroe Co. to Miss Mary Glaze of McMinn Co. On 11th
inst, by Rev. John Tate, Mr. Chas. Canon of Roane Co. to Miss
Lodusky Caroline, daughter of Aley and Joseph Jones of Philadelphia,
Tenn.

IV-208, 17 Sep 1852: At mouth of Tellico, Monroe Co., on 6th inst
by Rev. J.L. Gay, J.W.J. Niles, Esq., Pres. of Bank of East Tenn.,
and Mrs. Margaret W. Humes.

V-212, 15 Oct 1852: On 12th Oct by Rev. John Tate, Joseph W.
Lemons, Esq., of Maryville to Miss Mary Ann Yoakum of Madisonville.

V-223, 31 Dec 1852: On 23 inst by Rev. J.W. Shelton, Mr. Chrystian
Brown to Miss Eliza Ann Maclin Lane, all of Monroe Co.

V-231, 25 Feb 1853: On 10th inst by Rev. H. Dugan, Mr. Samuel B.
Ellis of Jonesborough to Miss Elizabeth Ghormley of Monroe Co.
On 3d Feb at residence of Mrs. Ann Lotspeich by Daniel Heiskell,
Esq., Mr. Maxwell Alexander to Miss Loretta Rey, all of Monroe Co.

V-234, 18 Mar 1853: On 9th inst in Madisonville by Rev. Geo. A.
Caldwell, Rev. J. Lyons to Miss E.C. Dickson of Greeneville, Tenn.

VI-276, 6 Jan 1854: In Madisonville on 29th ult at residence of
Dr. Joseph Upton, by Rev. Robert Snead, Mr. Oliver C. Henderson
to Miss Margaret R. Stephenson, all of Monroe Co.

VI-282, 17 Feb 1854: On 31st ult by Rev. Wm. Harrison, Mr. Samuel
H. Richards to Miss Arta M. Baker, all of Madisonville.

VI-302, 7 Jul 1854: In Madisonville on 24th ult by Rev. Wm.
Harrison, Mr. Thomas H. Crookshank to Miss Lavinia J., daughter
of Thomas Boyd of Knox Co.

ATHENS POST

VII-325, 15 Dec 1854: On 4th inst by Rev. Daniel P. Hunt, James M. Charles of Polk Co. to Miss Caroline M. Boyd of Monroe Co.

VII-336, 2 Mar 1855: At residence of Dr. Foute in Greeneville on 13th ult by Rev. W.M. Steel, Rector of St. James Church, Col. Wm. Heiskell of Monroe Co. to Miss Julia J. Gahagan late of Marietta, Ga.

VII-337, 9 Mar 1855: On 4th inst by G. Milton Hicks, Esq., Mr. Clark W. Stone to Miss Dialtha Hicks all of Monroe Co.

VII-339, 23 Mar 1855: On 15th inst by Rev. W. Haymes, Mr. Joseph Peace of Madisonville to Miss Caroline Poindexter of Polk Co.

VII-342, 13 Apr 1855: On 29 Mar 1855 by Rev. James Sewell, S.A. Wallis of Monroe Co. to Miss Harriet Maxwell of McMinn Co.

VII-344, 27 Apr 1855: On 22d inst by Newton J. Spillman, Esq., Col. Caswell Albread, late of Overton Co. to Miss Esther North of Monroe Co.

VII-359, 10 Aug 1855: On 26 inst /sic/ by John B. Cole, Esq., Mr. Isom A. Airheart to Miss Sarah E. Mosier, all of Bat Creek, Monroe Co.

VII-363, 7 Sep 1855: On 2d inst by Rev. D. Fleming, Mr. J.C. Wasson of Meigs Co. to Miss M.M. Abernathy of Monroe Co.

VIII-367, 5 Oct 1855: On 25th ult in Monroe Co. by Rev. John Scruggs, Mr. James Hamilton to Mrs. Elizabeth Maxwell, both of McMinn Co.

VIII-368, 12 Oct 1855: On 4th inst by Geo. Milton Hicks, Esq., Mr. Taylor Sneed to Miss Ruth Hicks, all of Monroe Co.

VIII-378, 21 Dec 1855: On 13th inst by Rev. T.R. Bradshaw, Peter Bohannon, Esq., age 85, to Mrs. Ann Coffin, age 75, all of Monroe Co.

VIII-380, 4 Jan 1856: On 1st ult /sic/ by Rev. John Scruggs, Mr. S.P. Hale to Miss Elmira Cantrell, all of this county.

VIII-384, 1 Feb 1856: On 27th ult by G.M. Hicks, Esq., Mr. Samuel R.W. Snead to Miss Mary Ann Hicks, all of Monroe Co.

VIII-385, 8 Feb 1856: On 30th ult by Rev. B. Abernathy, Mr. Jesse O. Webb, formerly of Yancy Co., N.C., to Miss Huldy Harrington of Madisonville.

VIII-387, 22 Feb 1856: On 17th inst by Wm. Dyer, Esq., Mr. Joseph P. Williams to Miss Lizzie McBride, all of Monroe Co.

VIII-388, 29 Feb 1856: On 14th inst by Rev. John Boring, Mr. John F. Key to Miss M. Margaret Peace, all of Monroe Co.

VIII-389, 7 Mar 1856: On 28th ult by Rev. Thomas Brown, Mr. Wm. Cannon of Roane Co. to Miss Susan Bogart of Philadelphia, Tenn.

VIII-390, 14 Mar 1856: On 6th inst by G. Milton Hicks, Mr. George F. McKeehen to Miss Mary M. McLemore, all of Monroe Co.

ATHENS POST

VIII-391, 21 Mar 1856: On 24th Jan last by Wm. W. Dickey, Esq.,
Mr. Wm. F. Ferguson of Roane Co. to Miss Nancy E. Dickey of Monroe
Co. On 14th ult by same, Mr. Robert Hull of Roane Co. to Miss
Margaret M. Dickey of Monroe Co.

VIII-392, 28 Mar 1856: On 27th inst by James Baker, Esq., in
McMinn Co., Mr. William Rentfro of Bradley Co. to Miss Melvina Roy
of Monroe Co.

VIII-404, 20 Jun 1856: On 20th ult by Rev. Jos. Pealer, Mr. J.R.
Wyly to Miss Sarah E. Stephens, all of Monroe Co.

VIII-410, 1 Aug 1856: On Jul 29th by Rev. J.H. Bruner, Mr. Joseph
M.G. Southard of White Co., Tenn., to Miss S. Nancy F. Cunnyngham,
daughter of Rev. Jesse Cunnyngham of Midway, Monroe Co. On 27th
ult by G. Milton Hicks, Esq., Mr. W.R. Hicks of McMinn Co. to
Miss Minerva Jane Sneed of Monroe Co.

VIII-415, 5 Sep 1856: On 21st ult at Tellico Plains by M.F.
Johnson, Esq., Michael F. Harris of Vermont to Miss Rebecca
Perkins of Tellico Plains.

IX-418, 26 Sep 1856: On 17th inst by G. Milton Hicks, Esq.,
Mr. Alfred Goins to Miss Elizabeth Stone, all of Monroe Co.

IX-424, 7 Nov 1856: On 6th inst in McMinn Co., Mr. Andrew J.
Coltharp of Monroe Co. to Miss Harriet R. Lowry of McMinn Co., by
Rev. G.A. Caldwell. On 28th ult by W.W. Bayless, Esq., Mr. John
Minnis of Madisonville to Mrs. Sarah A. Everette of Morganton.

IX-436, 30 Jan 1857: On 21st inst by Rev. T.R. Bradshaw,
Dr. Frank Bogart of Philadelphia, Tenn., to Miss E.M. Gaines,
daughter of Maj. G.W. Gaines of Tellico Plains.

IX-441, 6 Mar 1857: On 1st inst by Rev. B. Abernathy, Mr. Russell
Givins to Miss Mary Harington, all of Monroe Co.
IX-444, 27 Mar 1857: On Feb 17th in Loudon, by Rev. A.H. Barkley,
Mr. L.J. Johnston of Monroe Co. to Miss Mary Jane Blair, daughter
of John Blair, Esq., of Loudon. On 18th ult at residence of
bride's father by Rev. A.H. Barkley, Mr. J.B. Wall of Knoxville
to Miss M.A. Russell of Monroe Co.

IX-447, 17 Apr 1857: On 13th inst by Rev. Robert Snead, Mr. Jas.
Wilson of McMinn Co. to Miss Sarah McReynolds of Monroe Co.

IX-464, 14 Aug 1857: On 8th inst by Rev. Jo. Peler, Mr. J.D.
Wyscarver to Miss Mary E. Lowry, daughter of William Lowry, Esq.,
all of Monroe Co.

IX-468, 11 Sep 1857: On 3rd inst by Rev. J.H. Bruner, Mr. Hugh
Goddard of McMinn Co. to Mrs. Mary Taylor of Monroe Co.

X-493, 5 Mar 1858: On Feb 25 at Hiwassee College by Pres. Bruner,
Wm. Gardner of Blount Co. to Miss Nancy Forshee, daughter of
Rev. Joseph Forshee, dec'd.

X-505, 28 May 1858: On 20 inst by J.R. Wyly, Esq., Wm. C. Roberts
to Miss Rebecca Jane Hammontree, all of Monroe Co.

ATHENS POST

X514, 30 Jul 1858: On 7th inst near Memphis at residence of
bride's father, by Rev. R.R. Evans, Mr. Walter F. Lenoir of Monroe
Co. to Miss Harriette E. Osborne, daughter of Mr. John Osborne.

XI-522, 24 Sep 1858: On 13th inst at Murphy, N.C., by Rev. John
W. Brady, Rev. W.B. Bailey of the Ga. Conference to Miss Sallie
E. Rudd of Madisonville.

XII-606, 4 May 1860: On 26 Apr at residence of Wm. Burns /Athens7
by Rev. G.W. Alexander, Mr. Henry Mayes of Sweetwater to
Mrs. Adaline Treadaway of Rome, Ga.

XV-748, 23 Jan 1863: At residence of bride's father on Pond
Creek, Monroe Co., by Rev. G.A. Caldwell, Mr. Gideon Blackburn
Caldwell to Miss Julia Ann Ramsey.

XV-768, 12 Jun 1863: On 27 May by Rev. Joseph Peeler, Capt. James
G. Blair to Miss Margaret E. Carmichael, all of Monroe Co.

ATHENS REPUBLICAN

I-28, 16 Jan 1868: On 12 Jan at residence of bride's father near
White Clift Springs, Monroe Co., by Rev. J. Albert Hyden, Maj. Wm.
Gambol of Polk Co. to Miss Maggie Denton.

III-8, 28 Aug 1869: On Aug 18 at residence of Samuel H. Richards,
by Rev. James Dyre, Col. John W. Thompson to Miss Mary Jane Baker,
all of Monroe Co.

IV-178, 20 Feb 1852: Tribute of respect by Hiwassee Section
No. 58, Cadets of Temperance, upon death of Brother Joseph L.
Bogle...one so young and lovely...copy to brothers of deceased.

IV-190, 14 May 1852: Miles Cunningham died at his residence in
Monroe County on 23d ult, aged 54 yrs. 3 mos. and 9 days; Presbyterian; died intestate.

IV-191, 21 May 1852: Hiwassee College, Died 23 Feb 1852, Jno. E.
Patton at his parents residence on /sic/ Sweetwater; Resolutions
of Eromathesian Society; some years since he left Hiwassee.

V-240, 29 Apr 1853: Tellico Iron Works, Skeleton found about 7
miles from this place; supposed to be remains of John J. Bulger, a
school teacher formerly seen around here.

VI-275, 30 Dec 1853: Tribute of respect by Eroslethean Society of
Hiwassee College to brother Robert W. Malone who died at the College Jul 14, 1853.

VI-278, 20 Jan 1854: Died at Sweetwater, of scarlet fever, Dorcas
Ann, youngest daughter of Daniel and Mary W. Heiskell, aged 3 yrs.
and 9 mos.

VI-298, 9 Jun 1854: Resolutions of Eroslethean Society, Hiwassee
College, upon death of W.S. Gaines who died at his father's residence in Monroe Co., Feb 29, 1854; copy to parents of deceased.

VI-306, 4 Aug 1854: James Chesnutt, a highly esteemed citizen of
Philadelphia, Monroe Co., died 31 Jul. Died at Philadelphia,
Monroe Co., on 29th inst, Mrs. S.A. Clark, wife of Jas. W. Clark,
and daughter of the late Robert Cannon of Roane Co., in her 24th
year.

VI-307, 11 Aug 1854: Tribute of respect by Masonic Lodge in
Madisonville, to Madison Clibourne, who died in the West where he
was seeking a home for his family; copy to wife and his family,
now smarting under the recent death of a husband and beloved
daughter.

VI-310, 1 Sep 1854: Tribute of respect for John Perigen, dec'd,
by Madisonville Sons of Temperance. Tribute of respect by same
for John Agnew, dec'd; copy to widow.

VI-312, 15 Sep 1854: Tribute of respect by Masonic Lodge at
Madisonville for James P. Minis, who died in middle age surrounded
by a loving companion and dutiful children, and for Dr. William
Glass, who died in vigor of youth, the only support of an already
bereaved mother. Tribute of respect by Madisonville Sons of Temperance for John Mowry, who died in his youth.

VII-313, 22 Sep 1854: Cholera at Madisonville, seven deaths:
Mrs. Sarah Bayless, aged about 100 years, together with a female
servant also very aged; Mrs. Celia A. Cuson; Mrs. Emily Stephens;
John Agnew; James Payne, aged 17; and James Peace, aged 10. Four
deaths in the county attributed to cholera: Peter, an aged man of
color; David Starritt; Dr. William Glass; and ____ Parigen. The
last death with cholera symptoms was A.K. Cheynie who was aged;
other diseases have caused deaths of James P. Minnis, a child of

Mr. Cuson's, a child of Mr. Payne's, and a servant girl of Mr.
Joseph Johnston, in town, and of Mrs. Louisa Bayless, in the
vicinity.

VII-319, 3 Nov 1854: Died at Hiwassee College on 29th inst of
scarlet fever, Thomas A.H. Long, son of Mrs. F. Long, aged 3 yrs.
2 mos. 29 days.

VII-320, 10 Nov 1854: Died in Monroe Co. on 18th Oct, Mrs.
Susannah Bain in her 63d year; Presbyterian; leaves husband and
eleven children.

VII-326, 22 Dec 1854: Died at Tellico Iron Works on 13th inst of
typhoid fever, Robert D. Miller, aged 22.

VII-330, 19 Jan 1855: Tribute of respect by Allegany Lodge No.
114, Masons, Blairsville, Ga., upon death of Robert W. Young of
Oak Bowery Lodge, Ellijay, Ga., and recently from Monroe Co.,
Tenn.; far away from a kind parent's home.

VII-348, 25 May 1855: Died in Monroe Co. at his residence on 7th
inst, Mr. Robert Hutcherson, aged 38, of pulmonary consumption;
Methodist; left wife and five children.

VII-363, 7 Sep 1855: Died in Monroe Co. on 25 inst /sic/ of flux,
Hugh Hamilton. Some three weeks before, three of his children
died of the same disease within three days of each other.

VIII-404, 20 Jun 1856: We regret to learn that B. McGhee, Esq.,
of Monroe Co., died at Chattanooga a few days since, from wounds
self-inflicted while laboring under a sudden attack of insanity.
He was a man of many good qualities and was generally esteemed.
Tribute of respect by Madisonville Sons of Temperance upon death
of John Roberson who died 4th inst; leaves wife and family.

VIII-409, 25 Jul 1856: Died at his residence in Monroe Co.,
Mr. Isaac Marshall, in his 24th year.

VIII-413, 22 Aug 1856: Died in Madisonville Aug 12th, Emily Jane,
daughter of Guilford and Jane Cannon, aged 1 yr 18 days.

VIII-414, 29 Aug 1856: Died at Madisonville Aug 25th, 1856,
Mary Humphries, only child of Col. Robert and Elizabeth Humphries,
aged 15 mos.

IX-419, 3 Oct 1856: Died at their residence in Monroe Co. on
24th Sep, infant son of Dr. W.W. and Fidelia A. Stephens, aged 2
mos. 5 days.

IX-428, 5 Dec 1856: Died at Philadelphia, Tenn., on 26 Nov, John
Mentger of Middleton, Ohio, aged 22 years.

IX-439, 20 Feb 1857: Died at her residence in Monroe Co., 15th
inst in her 53d year, Mrs. Nancy Leslie, wife of Thomas Leslie;
faithful daughter, wife, sister, and mother.

IX-448, 24 Apr 1857: Died on 9th inst in Sweetwater, Miss Nannie
E. Hill, aged 17 years.

IX-452, 22 May 1857: Died in Sweetwater on May 19th, Mrs. Sarah
Pickel, wife of John H. Pickel; born 25 Dec 1823.

IX-455, 12 Jun 1857: Died on 21st May in her 29th year, Nancy, wife of Cornelius W. Coffin of Madisonville and only daughter of Rev. Dr. McCorkle of Greeneville, Tenn.

X-493, 5 Mar 1858: Died at Hiwassee College, 23 Feb, Mrs. N.C. Clark, consort of E.P. Clark, formerly of Loudon.

X-513, 23 Jul 1858: Tribute of respect by Bar and Officers of Monroe Co. upon death of Maj. H.H. Stephens; died at his residence in Loudon, Roane Co., on 19th inst; native of Tenn.; studied law under the late Judge John O. Cannon.

XI-523, 1 Oct 1858: Died at Hiwassee College 29th Sep, Margaret Itasca, only daughter of Pres. Bruner.

XI-531, 26 Nov 1858: Obituary of Col. Jonathan Tipton, aged 82, for last thirty odd years a citizen of Monroe Co.; died at his residence on Tenn. River Monday the 8th inst. His father emigrated to this country when he was quite young from Shenandoah Co., Va. He served his State as Militia Officer, a Justice of the Peace, a member of the State Legislature for 21 sessions. Leaves large family of children.

XI-550, 8 Apr 1859: N.J. Spillman died suddenly at his residence at Mt. Vernon in Monroe Co. on 4th inst.

XIII-635, 23 Nov 1860: Died at Sweetwater on 5th inst, Mrs. Martha Jane Haines, 32; leaves husband and two little children.

XIII-663, 7 Jun 1861: Sampson (Simpson) Harrold, of Capt. Morelock's Co., Col. Vaughn's Regt., injured in train wreck near New Market, on way to seat of War; dies of injuries. Died on 31 May in Sweetwater Valley in 83d year, Presley Cleveland.

XIII-664, 14 Jun 1861: Tribute of respect by Tellico Lodge, Masons, upon death of Philip Stephens, who died at his residence in Monroe Co. on the /sic/ day of May 1861; leaves wife and children.

XIII-667, 5 Jul 1861: Died 25 Jun, David Cunningham, age near 12 years, in Monroe Co., son of Miles Cunningham, also dec'd.

XIV-691, 20 Dec 1861: Died on 5th inst at residence of his father, James A. Coffin, Esq., near Madisonville, Hugh M. Coffin age 21 on 7 Aug last.

XIV-695, 17 Jan 1862: Tribute of respect by Tellico Masonic Lodge, Madisonville, upon death of Wm. M. Brown, who died in the service of his country at Cumberland Gap, Dec 1861.

XIV-696, 24 Jan 1862: Died at her father's residence near Madisonville on 15 Jan, Miss Eliza L. Humphreys, in her 25th year; leaves aged parents and brothers and sisters.

XIV-712, 16 May 1862: Died on 8th May at her residence, Tellico Plains, Mrs. Jane Elizabeth McDermott.

XV-741, 5 Dec 1862: Died at her residence in Monroe Co. on 20th ult, in her 35th year, Mrs. Martha A. Donohoo, consort of Henry Donohoo, and only child of S.S. and Dollie Glenn.

XV-749, 30 Jan 1863: Died at Philadelphia, Tenn., on 25 Jan, G.T.
Beauregard Jones, aged 1 yr. 3 mos. 23 days, son of W.P. and
Manilla Jones.

XV-753, 27 Feb 1863: Died of diphtheria on 13 Feb, Newton J.
Spillman, 3 yrs. 8 mos., youngest son of late N.J. Spillman and
Mary A. Ross, Mt. Vernon, Tenn.

XV-756, 20 Mar 1863: Died on Fork Creek, Monroe Co., 14 Feb,
little Lizzie M. Roberts, 9 mos. 5 days, of scarlet fever, daughter of R.C. and Addie Roberts.

MISCELLANEOUS ITEMS IN ATHENS NEWSPAPERS

HIWASSEE PATRIOT

I-2, 29 Jan 1839: Trustees of Fork Creek Academy have employed
Rev. Thomas Kendall, from the North, as principal. B.M. Bayless,
M.D., Philadelphia, will attend to any cases of dental surgery.

I-11, 21 May 1839: William L. Atlee, Athens, advertises that
John Burris, an apprentice bound to him in Monroe Co. to learn
trade of coach making, now about aged 14, ran away about 18 mos.
ago.

I-18, 11 Jul 1839: Madisonville Circuit Court, James Cogburn VS
Polly Cogburn; Petition for divorce.

I-38, 28 Nov 1839: Reward: On Sat. 16th inst in Morganton,
Tenn., Patrick Thurman, about 17 or 18, murdered Aden G. Wimpy;
Thurman's father lives in Knox Co.; Thurman was arrested between
Madisonville and Tellico Plains, but escaped.

I-39, 5 Dec 1839: David Brown is no longer responsible for an
apprentice, Samuel James Moore, in Monroe Co.

II-12, 28 May 1840: Reward by Armstrong Morrow on Tellico River,
2 miles above mouth of river, for return of apprentice named
William Ivy, aged 13 or 14, bound to learn brick mason business.

ATHENS POST

V-221, 17 Dec 1852: Chancery Court at Madisonville, John
Stanfield, Adm. of James Taylor, dec'd, VS William and Thomas
Taylor, Susannah Andrews and husband Thomas Andrews, and others,
heirs; the four defendants named are nonresidents.

VII-332, 2 Feb 1855: Monroe Co. Circuit Court, Sale of land and
negroes of Richard Stephens, dec'd, in case Lewis Stephens, Exec.
VS G.J. Cunningham et al, heirs, at late residence of Nancy
Stephens, dec'd, on Island Creek, Monroe Co.

VII-333, 9 Feb 1855: Chancery Court at Madisonville, John
McClain, Adm. of Samuel Douthet, dec'd, VS Isaac T. Douthet,
Francis A., Samuel D., and Robert N. McClure et al, heirs. The
McClures are minors and nonresidents. Chancery Court at Madison-
ville, Ansel Gad, Exec. of Wm. Gad, dec'd, VS Tellithee Gad and
others, Legatees. Tellithee resides in Illinois.

ATHENS POST

VIII-394, 11 Apr 1856: Chancery Court at Madisonville, Barclay
McGhee VS Margaret Morgan, widow, and G.W. and R.M. Morgan and
others, heirs of Gideon Morgan, dec'd. Margaret now resides in
Arkansas.

IX-442, 13 Mar 1857: Josiah Rowan advertises for return of lost
Bounty Land Warrant.

IX-447, 17 Apr 1857: Chancery Court at Madisonville, Nancy
Marshall VS Henry Marshall and William H., Martha J., John W.,
and Mary C. Marshall, minor children of John W. Marshall, dec'd.
The four minors reside in Texas.

IX-448, 24 Apr 1857: Chancery Court at Madisonville, Rebecca
Wilson, Gdn. of George, Isaac, Sarah, and Mary Wilson minor
children of Isaac Wilson, dec'd, VS Uriah Wilson, Joseph, Samuel
Polly, and Elender Winkle, John and Malinda Bell, and others,
heirs of Charles Willson, dec'd. Defendants are nonresidents.

X-486, 15 Jan 1858: Notice by Tellico Lodge, Masons, Madisonville,
that they have expelled Thomas J. Young, a Physician, who has left
the country. Expelled for conduct not befitting to a Mason.
(Gives description of Dr. Young and warns other lodges from accept-
ing him.)

XIII-667, 5 Jul 1861: Monroe County now has three Companies in
Virginia, who were first in forming the First East Tenn. Regiment,
commanded by Col. Vaughn and Major Morgan. She now sends a Cavalry
Company commanded by Capt. John A. Rowan, 1st Lt. C.W. Lotspeich,
2nd Lt. William M. Brown, 3rd Lt. W.A. Upton, Jr., 1st Sgt.
Hightower. This Company bears name of McGhee Invincibles, in honor
of C.M. McGhee, Esq.

8 May 1863 /no front page of this issue was printed/: Divorce
petition at Madisonville, Edwin Hall VS Nancy Hall, of North
Carolina.

ATHENS COURIER

15 Jun 1844: John Mitchell, of Monroe Co., warns against trading
with his wife Louisa.

THE WATCHMAN

I-26, 9 Jul 1842: Chancery Court at Madisonville, James W.
Stephenson, Adm. of John R. Davis, dec'd, VS Lewis, Susan, and
Peter Davis, Polly Kennedy and husband Robert, Martha and Elizabeth
Smitherton and their husbands John and Joseph Smitherton, heirs.
All defendants except Lewis and Susan Davis are nonresidents. In
Jul 1841, John R. Davis died leaving neither wife nor legitimate
child and owning land in Monroe and Hawkins counties, which
descended to respondents.

ATHENS REPUBLICAN

III-13, 2 Oct 1869: We learn that J.W. Kelsoe of Monroe Co. was
thrown from his horse last week a few miles above Sweetwater and
has since died.

PETITIONS TO TENNESSEE LEGISLATURE

The Tennessee State Archives, Nashville, has many original petitions which were made to the Legislature. These petitions have
recently been indexed as to the style and date of petition.

There are many petitions from citizens of Monroe County and from
citizens of the Hiwassee District, with long list of signatures.
Below are abstracts of a few of these petitions from Monroe County.

1825, John Carson petitions for divorce from wife Cynthia, formerly
Cynthia Spillman.

19 Nov 1827, Margaret Smith petitions for divorce from John Smith;
she was widow with children when they married, Feb 1827.

1827, Petition of Peter Brakebill, Revolutionary Soldier.

1833, Petition of Mary Quillan; she represents that Zachariah
Luster had, previously to land sales in 1820, made an improvement
on land; land was bought and Luster was turned out of possession
and never received anything for improvements; said Luster and wife
died in a few weeks of each other in 1822 leaving four orphans,
then very young, the oldest not yet being sixteen years old;
Petitioner, a widow and the aunt of said children, took the
children and has supported them ever since.

Undated, but in the 1841 petitions, Petition of the congregation
of Germans who cannot understand the English language and who have
settled on Bat Creek, who are destitute of a minister who can
preach in their own language, and pray for land for a minister;
signed by John Mowry, Abraham Buck, David Mowry, Adam Mowry, Henry
Kyle, Jacob Kyle, John Gardner, Peter Michael, Peter Moser, John
Moser, Daniel Buck, Jacob Buck, Michael Gardner, Jacob Sheets,
Jacob Cook, Henry Sheets. There are also thirty women who belong
to this church.

The following items are found in Entry Books A, B, and C, in the
office of the Register of Deeds, Athens, McMinn County, Tennessee.

McMinn and Monroe Counties were both formed from the Hiwassee District, which was ceded to the United States by the Cherokee Indians
by Treaties of 1817 and 1819. The land thus ceded, for the most
part, was entered by general enterer, by occupant enterer, or
"agreeably to law". After the final payment for the land was made,
the Grant was then issued to the enterer or to his assignee. Many
of the entries were assigned several times before the actual Grant
was issued.

BOOK A

(1) About 1827, Rachel Lillard, A. and Nancy Coleman, James,
Margaret, and Augustain Lillard assign their rights to Entry made
by William Lillard in 1825 to William Lillard, Jr.

(3) 1 Aug 1825, John W. Roach Entry as Occupant Enterer. 6 Feb
1838, Lucinday Webb assigns her interest, as heir of John Webb
Roach, to Martin Webb. 14 Jan 1845, William Webb relinquishes his
right as son of John Webb Roach, and Martin Webb assigns his interest as heir of John Webb Roach.

(26) Copy of Circuit Court Decree, 9 May 1853. Samuel J. Rowan
and John Scruggs, Adms. of William Carter, dec'd, VS Elizabeth Neil
and husband William Neil, Robert Carter, Fleming B. Carter, Jane C.
Rowan, and John A. Debrill by his Gdn. ad litem Wm. A. Spencer.
Land is sold subject to dower of widow Elizabeth who has married
William Neil. Complainant Samuel J. Rowan and the Defendants are
heirs of William Carter, dec'd.

(100) 8 Feb 1825, John Carmichael purchased Island No. 18 above the
mouth of Hiwassee in Tennessee River; 8 Sep 1829, Carmichael assigns Entry to John Harrison of Roane Co. who reassigns; 22 Apr
1832, Entry assigned to William Blair; 20 Sep 1849, John Blair and
Vincent Blair, Execs. of William Blair, dec'd, reassign to John
Carmichael; 22 Sep 1849, Grant issued to heirs of John Carmichael.

(121) 9 Sep 1830, Robert Haly makes oath in Hardeman Co., Tenn.,
that he is owner of a Certificate of Entry for land in Monroe Co.
assigned to him by John C. Haly and that the Certificate is lost.

(128) 30 Mar 1827, Wm. Gay enters as occupant enterer land in
Monroe Co.; 25 Aug 1835, Elizabeth, Isabel W., James C., John W.
Gay, and William Gay, Jr., Adm. of William Gay, dec'd, assign to
David Spradlin; 24 Jan 1834, A. Conger assigns his right to David
Spradlin.

(159) 7 Mar 1850, Alfred R., Enos H., James L., Elizabeth C.,
Richard I., and Mary C. White, heirs of John White, dec'd, enter
land in Monroe Co.

(164) 5 Nov 1825, Benjamin Howard enters land in Monroe Co.;
15 Mar 1828, Benjamin Howard assigns to Nanse Howard; 18 Sep 1843,
Nansey Howard assigns to C.M. Howard to hold or sell directly
after her death, but he is to have nothing to do with the land
until after that time; 31 Aug 1849, Grant issued to C.M. Howard.

(191) 13 Nov 1834, Elizabeth Gladden assigns to Robert Eakens an Entry to land in Monroe Co., which was entered by Michael Ghormley and by him transferred to Robert Eakens, reserving a life support to her.

(270) 30 Nov 1820, John Duggan makes Entry for land in Monroe Co. and 19 Sep 1827 assigns it to his son John Duggan, Jr.; 22 Oct 1830, John Duggan, Exec. of John Duggan, Sr., makes payment; 14 Feb 1831, James P. Duggan assigns to John Duggan his part left to him by his father, John Duggan, Sr.

(281) 1821, Daniel Dugan is assigned Entry; 10 July 1822, Daniel Duggan assigns part of land to Jane Duggan; 27 Oct 1826, Daniel Duggan assigns part of land, including wagonroad, to Daniel Duggan, Jr.

(300) 26 Nov 1831, Circuit Court, Monroe Co., John Headrick VS John McGhee, Mahala Blair, John O. Cannon, Adms. of William S. Blair, the Heirs of William S. Blair, and Henry Headrick. Sale of land in Monroe Co.

(332) 14 Aug 1825, Absalom Harrill, Adm. of Harle Harrill, dec'd, assigns Entry to land in Monroe Co. which was assigned to Harle Harrill by William McCray.

(395) 17 Nov 1840, Charles Kelsoe assigns Entry for land in Monroe Co. to his daughter Teressa M. Carmichael and to her two eldest daughters Frances Adline Price and Laura Almira Price. /This entry is marked through with large crosses./ Grant issued to Charles Kelsoe.

(400) 4 Sep 1826, Thomas Adams enters land in Monroe Co.; 6 Nov 1830, Martha Adams the wife of Thomas Adams, dec'd, assigns to James Adams, signed by Martha Adams, James Adams, Zachariah Melone, Lazarus Davis, Elyas Adams, David Cross.

(420) 20 Mar 1833, Lucrecy (Lucretisha) Nicholson and William Nicholson, Adms. of James Nicholson, dec'd, all of Monroe Co., release their entry of land.

(425) 29 Sep 1824, Survey of four acres "in name of James Hier, Robert M. Reynolds, & William Bidwell, Trustees of a religious denomination of people called Methodist & their successors including their Meeting House known by the name of Roper's Meeting House in Monroe Co."; on Fork Creek.

(429) 1828, Mary Bell assigns her occupant Entry in Monroe Co., for love, one half to son-in-law Robert Hutson and daughter Margaret Hutson and one half to daughter and son, viz Jane Bell and Samuel R. Bell.

(433) 23 Dec 1826, Hugh W. Cathcart enters as occupant enterer, land in Monroe Co.; 12 Dec 1827, assigns to Susannah Cathcart; /no date/ Mary Ann Tharp and Margaret Jane Tharp assign to James Thompson; Next entry: Mary Ann Thompson and Margaret Jane Thompson assign.

(437) 9 Jan 1829, Hu Smith assigns entry in Monroe Co. to Josiah Johnston, Exec. of Francis Johnston, dec'd; 21 Apr 1838, Josiah Johnston assigns to Joseph and George Johnston, heirs of Francis Johnston, dec'd.

(443) 24 Mar 1828, Gideon Carson assigns his entry in Monroe Co., except ten acres where Margaret Drew now lives.

(462) 23 Jul 1825, Thomas Eldridge assigns entry in Monroe Co. to Larkin Webb; 6 Feb 1838, Lucinday Webb assigns her interest as one of heirs to Martin Webb.

(483) 28 Jul 1824, Joshua Smith and Joseph Woods enter land in Monroe Co. as occupant enterers; 30 Sep 1833, "We the widow and heirs of Joshua Smith dec'd" assign to Russell Smith, signed, Nancy, Jn. H., and Wm. J. Smith, G.W. Hutchison, Polly and Mahala Smith.

(494) 5 Dec 1825, Ann Hackney enters land in Monroe Co.; 9 Mar 1829, Edward Westmoreland and John Hackney, Sr., Legatees of Ann Hackney, dec'd, assign the land.

(495) 1819, Act of General Assembly at Murfreesboro: a Life Estate Reservation of 640 acres for Caty Harlin laid down in Monroe Co.; Grant issued 25 Oct 1830.

BOOK B

(83) 23 Nov 1820, Rebecca Copland purchases land. 2 Jan 1823, "We Rebecca Copland now Rebecca Duggan and John Duggan, Sr." assign entry to William Copland.

BOOK C

(93) 3 Feb 1846, John Daughtery and wife Isabell appear before Isaac C. Rowden, J.P. of Hamilton Co. and saith that they are assignees of an Entry in Monroe Co. on Cane Creek, entered 3 Sep 1827, that money has been paid, but certificate of entry is lost. The above affidavit is then assigned by the Daughertys to Larkin Carden.

(101) 8 Feb 1821, Entry in Monroe Co. is assigned to John N. Smith; 22 Sep 1827, sale by Sheriff; title divested out of Ashley W. Smith and other heirs of John N. Smith, dec'd.

(131) 1 Jan 1863, Articles of Agreement and Lease between Tellico Mfg. Co. and Henry B. Latrobe late of Baltimore, Md.; lease of whole of real estate known as Tellico Iron Works.

MONROE COUNTY OCCUPANT ENTERERS

The list of names below includes only those occupant enterers who are not listed in "Inhabitants before 1830" on pages 160-176 of this Volume II.

This list may be misleading for the following reasons:

(1) The earliest entries, made in 1820, give a description of the land as to Township, Range, Section, et cetera, but no County name is given as in the later entries. While the position of the land can usually be determined from the map of the Hiwassee District, this task would be impossible as far as this Volume II is concerned.

(2) The Entry Books are apparently copies and Entry Book C is a typewritten copy made in 1898, with many noticeable errors.

(3) There are several instances of a person being listed as an occupant enterer of more than one county.

Therefore, these names are offered, with many misgivings, for what they may be worth to the researcher.

1824

Ball, Lewis
Bond, Stephen
Brown, Joseph
Brown, William
  and Jacob
Burns, William
Cleveland, Presley
Coleman, Spencer
Greenlea, Lewis
Griffith, Jane
  and Elizabeth
Gross, William
Headrick, Henry
Johnston, Lewis
Lillard, William
McClure, Samuel
McCray, Thomas
Mayes, James
Michael, Barney
Morrow, Armstrong
Plumlee, Daniel
Prater, Benjamin
Ragsdale, Edward
Sloan, Archibald
Stow, Abel
Taff, William
Tankersly, Richard
Tucker, James, Jr.
Welker, Henry

1824

Whitson, Charles
Wolf, John

1825

Ballew, William
Beeson, Richard
Blades, Edward
Blair, Samuel
Browning, Nathaniel C.
Brymer, William
Cleage, David
Coil, Henry
Coker, William
Cook, William H.
Eblin, John
Estill, Benjamin
Everette, Orville
Gad, William
Girdner, Michael
Glenn, Squire S.
Henderson, James
Honey (Honea), Abner
Hope, Thomas
Ivy, Burrel
Jemmison, John R.
Johnston, James
Johnston, John H.

MONROE COUNTY OCCUPANT ENTERERS

1825

Kelly, John D.
Kerr, Jessee
Kile, Henry
McCall, John
McGonigle, Floyd
McGuire, Josiah
Manes, Seth
Matlock, Charles
Maxwell, Archibald
Melton, Elisha
Mowry, John
Pitman, William
Ray, John
Redman, William
Reeves, Joseph
Renshaw, Moses
Roach, John W.
Samples, William
Sanders, James G.
Sitsler, William R.
Smith, Nathaniel
Smith, Robert
Taylor, Benjamin
Thompson, John
Twomey, William
Underwood, Benjamin
Utter, William R.
Wassom, Jacob
Wear, James, Sr.
Wilkinson, Thomas
Woody, James
Wyly, James

1826

Bell, Mary
Brakebill, Peter
Burns, George
Cathcart, Hugh W.
Chadwick, Jacob
Dehart, Nathan
Dyer, Benjamin
Evans, Robert
Glaze, Henry
Gowan, Obediah
Gray, John W.
Gregory, Clemuel
Griffin, James
Harris, Moses
Howard, Benjamin
Howard, George
Kennedy, James

1826

Likins, John
Loveless, George
McAllister, James B.
McGuire, Michael
McNabb, David
Melone, Zachariah
Miller, Rutha
Morgan, Henry P.
Moses, Samuel
Ogle, John
Pruett, Calvin
Reagan, William S.
Rush, James
Sliger, Jacob
Smith, William H.
Stamper, Asa
Tetter, William R.
Thompson, Daniel
Tindle, William
Vinzant, Delilah

1827

Borden, Augustus
Burris, H. Martin
Cain, William
Carden, Leonard
Chaimbers, James
Clayton, Austin
Conger, Abijah
Edington, Thomas
Ezell, James
Fulks, George
Gay, William
Gunter, Daniel
Hackney, Jane M.
Hamilton, James
Hamilton, Joseph
Harmon, Nathan
Harmon, Trenton
Harris, John
Hooper, Enos
Hooper, John
Justus, John R.
Knox, Joseph I.
Maroon, Samuel
Matheny, James
Miller, Cullinas
Miller, Samuel
Mills, Burnett
Pain, Landy
Phillips, Josiah

MONROE COUNTY OCCUPANT ENTERERS

<u>1827</u>

Phillips, Polly
Ragsdale, Hubbard
Ruth, Hezekiah
Smith, Jacob
Swanson, William
Thomas, Jonathan
White, David and
  Hezekiah Ruth
White, Joseph
Williams, Hannah
Wright, Willis

INDEX
MONROE COUNTY, TENNESSEE
RECORDS 1820-1870
Volume II

Note: Surnames with various spellings are grouped together in form most commonly used.

Names on pages 160-176 and 190-192 are not included in this index as they are in alphabetical order.

McDANIEL, cont'd-52, George
52, Jack 69, Jackson 44,
Linda 69,Lucinda 44,
Marion 136, Martha E.
70, Mary A. 70, Nancy 6,
Rebecca J. 16, Rebecca
Jane 136, Richard 152,
Sarah E.G.H. 70, Thomas
152, Thomas E. 70

McDERMOTT, Alexander 131,
Augustine 131, Inez 131,
Jane 2,130,137, Jane
Elizabeth 183, John 131,
Julia 131, Louisa 131,
Penelope 155, W.P.H.
130,131,141, William
2, William P.H. 112,
122,130,155

McDONALD, Abbott G. 67,
Albert G. 68, Charles
29,35,40,67,68, Ellen
68, Gates 68, George
67,68, George H. 68,
James 117, Josephine
67, Martha A. 67, Mar-
tha J. 68, Mary 67,
Mary A. 68, Sarah 117,
Sarah E. 68, Thomas 67,
Thomas A. 68, William
68

McDOWELL, Samuel 93

McEARLY, Sarah 108

McELDRY, Edward 82

McELRATH, Hugh McD. 106,
123

McENOLLY, Elizabeth 14,
James 14

McGAUGHEY, John 150

McGHEE, Alexander 2,7,
Anne E. 58,107,134,141,
B. 12,58,107,182, Bar-
clay 7,8,58,72,107,129,
134,141,185, Betsey J.
46, Bettie 72,134,139,
C.M. 72,107,185, Charles
8, Charles M. 8,58,98,
134, Elizabeth M. 7,
58,107,129, Jane 47,
John 2,7, 46-48,58,
72,94,107,121,124,128
134,141,188, Lavinia
58,134,141, Lavinia M.
107, Magill 72, Margaret
W. 2,58,107,134, Mary
Jones 7, Mary K. 7,
107,129,134, Mary K.
Henly 12,107, Matthew
W. 2,78,91, Thomas L. 7

McGHEE INVINCIBLES 185

McGILL, See MAGILL

McGINLEY, William D. 96

McGINTY, Hiram 51

McGOWAN, Margaret 63,
Thomas 63

McGUIRE, D.J. 41, Delilah
J. 41, Eli 113, Henry
122, James 113, Jere-
miah 57,113, Josiah 12,

McGUIRE, cont'd-26,57,113,
Matison 113, Michael
113,114, Nicholas 113,
Nicholas M. 41, Sarah
57,113, Stephen 113,
T. 148, Thomas 26,
William 148

McINTOSH 82

McKEEHAN, George F. 178,
Job 97, William H. 58

McKELVEY, James 140

McKENZIE, D.A. 19, Donald
A. 19,151, E.J. 151,
John L. 151, John R.
19,151, Kenneth 6,
Margaret P. 63, Mark 6,
Mary A. 19,151, Nancy
C. 151, Samuel A. 79,
W.G. 151

McKINNEY, Andrew Thompson
8, David 8, Elizabeth
8, Jane 8, Josephine
8, Margaret 8, R.J. 23
Samuel 23

McLEABY, Jane 157, Robert
157

McLEARY, James 67

McLEMORE, A.D. 38, Andon
151, D. 34, John 8,
Mary M. 178, Wesley
156

McLENDON, Captain 150,
Margaret J. 37, Moses
17, Moses J. 37

McLIN, William 144,156

McMAHAN, A.J. 18, McClu
43, Mroclah C. 18

McMILLAN, Malizza Alabama
103, Narcissa Tenne-
ssee 103, Rutha 99,
S.B. 99

McMINN, Joseph 80

McMULLIN, Jason 19,22,30,
36,73, Sallie M. 73

McNABB, Archibald W. 44,
John 158, Louisa A.
44, Pinkney S. 44,
Sophira A. 44, Wily B.
45

McREYNOLDS, David W. 93,
Hugh 133, I.D. 9,
Isaac D. 133, James
134, Joseph 24,25,
Mary 13, Nancy 134,
Robert 13,28,48,133,
Sarah 179, Sarah L.
9, Woods 93

McROUNDALS 22

McSPADDEN, Catherine M.
67,74, George 67,74,
Green C. 89, Hannibal
33, Henry 22,116, Inos
74, James F. 6, John
C. 68, John T. 67,74,
Joseph 128, Joseph W.

McSPADDEN, cont'd-67,74,
Kings Berry 13, Lucinda
6,22,128, Margaret 6,
16, Mary 1,19,74, Mary
C. 67, Mary E. 74, Mary
I. 6, Mathew 6,128,
Nancy 13, S. 8, Sallie
19, Samuel 6,71, Samuel
A. 6,128, Samuel E. 44,
74, Thomas T. 73, Thomas
W. 67,74, W.L. 73,
William T. 73

McSWAIN, James 12, William
12

McTEER, J.C. 24, James 64,
Montgomery 5, Samuel 78

McVEIGH, John 158,159

M

MACKERY, Polly 1

MADDOX 115,116

MAGILL, A.N. 11, Easter E.
6, Franklin 19,67,
Harrett 14, Harriet W.
50, Hugh M. 6, I. 6,
J.F. 18,34,44,74, J.H.
11,26, James 11, Jane
112, Margaret 11, Ma-
tilda 11, N. 6,11,14-16
18, Nathaniel 1,2,13,
40,41,137, Roland 112,
Samuel 11, Samuel W.
26, Sarah 11, W.R. 14

MAHAN, M.C. 43

MALCOM, John 93

MALONE, E.D. 54,56,177,
Fereby B. 24, Joseph 61,
Louisa 54,59, Mary 16,
136, Robert W. 181,
Thomas 136, Zachariah
188

MARION, Owen 109

MARISSA, Ellen 124, John
124

MARQUAM, Alfred 144

MARR, MARRS, Angeline 5,
Gelina 131, Joseph 68,
William 131

MARSHALL, Charlotte E.M.
13,103, David J. 140,
Henry 33,37,83,125,
185, Henry S. 14, Isaac
182, Isaac C. 27,84,
James H. 13, John W.
128,185, John Wesley
128, Joseph 84, Joseph
E. 14,27, Martha J. 185,
Martha Jane 128, Mary
C. 185, Mary Caroline
128, Nancy 128,185,
Nancy A. 140, Orvill
27, R.G. 27, Rebecca
14,27,83, Robert G. 14,
Thomas 101,149, Willet
W. 84, William B. 27,
William H. 185, William
Henry 128, William N.
13,14,27,103

216

TAYLOR, cont'd-35,40,44,
56, Elika A. 125,142,
143, Elizabeth 120,
142, Garrett 2, Gar-
rett R. 7,21, H.F. 155,
177, Isaac 7,19,21,
64, James 7,19,21,27,
109,120,129,139,184,
James P. 44, James W.
3,7,85, Jesse 129,
John 89,120, John Dou-
thet 7, Keziah 2,7,
21,32,36,44,70, Leo-
nidas 2,11, Leroy 2,
7,21,32,36,44, M.C.
44, Margaret Isabelle
19, Martha P. 6, Mary
89,179, Mary Anne 7,
139, Mary Jane 157,
Maryanall 12, Milly
85, Paulina 13,54,129,
Peggy 98, Phoebe 120,
Pleasant B. 120, Robert
157, Thomas 89,129,
184, Thomas D. 142,
Thomas J. 96, William
7,120,129,184, William
H. 58

TEDFORD, Louisa G. 3

TEFFETALLER, Amy 110,
Anna 110, John 110

TELASKAKI &(

TELLICO Iron Works 181,
182,189, Mfg. Co. 113,
128,189

TEMPLE, Evaline 140, Mary
E. 140, N.J. 117

TEMPLETON, Allie 146,
Bettie 146,148, Billie
146, Bird 146,148,
Hubert 146, Jerome
146,148, Loula 146,
Madie 146, Mahala 148,
William 148

TENDLE, Henry 89, Isaac 89,

TENNESSEE CITIES AND PLACE
NAMES: Athens 21,47,
48,107,122,123,151,
157,180,181,184,187,
Ballplay 45, Belltown
22, Benton 147, Big
Spring 52, Bristol
150,151, Cannon's
Store 45, Chattanooga
40,156,182, Chota 154,
Citico 2, Citico Old
Town 78, Cleveland 42,
Conasauga 155, Coyatee
45, Daggins Ferry 153,
Elizabethon 147, Eve
Mills 76, Four Mile
Branch 148,156, Fayet-
teville 146, Goshen
154, Greeneville 152,
177,178,183, Hopewell
Springs, 157, Jones-
boro 153,177, Kings-
ton 47,93, Knoxville
7,24,43,45,47,114,146-
148,152,153,179, Lou-
don 45,47,138,179,183,
Madisonville 1,8,19,
21,24,28,45,47,48,84,
85,108,117,121,122,
144,146-149,151-154,

TENNESSEE CITIES, cont'd-
156,177-185, Maryville
46,121,177, Memphis
180, Midway 179, Mil-
ler's Cove 45, Morgan-
ton 79,179,184, Mossy
Creek 148, Mouse Creek
26,29, Mt. Vernon 184,
Murfreesboro 189,
Nashville 146,186, New
Market 183, New Phila-
delphia 46, Philadel-
phia 9,28,45-48,76,105,
112,128,129,177-179,
181,182,184, Rockville
46, Sweetwater 23,44,
45,151,153,180-183,186,
Taylorsville 153, Taze-
well 142, Tellico 7,46,
80, Tellico Plains 21,
155,179,183,184, Vonore
146, White Cliff Springs
180

TENNESSEE COUNTIES: Anderson 89, Bedford 80,
Bledsoe 89,93,107,132,
Blount 2,6,7,16,19,45,
47,66,79,80,84,89,93,
102,106,113,120,121,
123,125-129,138,140,
151-153,155,179, Brad-
ley 59,93,94,96,97,100,
104,120,125,126,140,
143,148,152,153,155,
179, Campbell 84,93,
Carter 156, Claiborne
111,145, Cocke 12,27,
78,79, Davidson 84,
100,140, Grainger 142,
102,104,106, Hamilton
7,9,15,18,42,89,93,100,
120,147,189, Hardeman
187, Hawkins 124,185,
Humphreys 80,106, Jeff-
erson 84,93,96,101,
Jones 121-123, Knox,
3,13,24,70,72,82-84,
89,93,101,106,108,130,
144,153,177,184, Lou-
don 148, McMinn 16,26,
29,78,80,81,86,88,89,
93,96,98,100,101,104,
106,107,122-124,135,
142,152,153,177-179,
187, Marion 89, Meigs
139,144,178, Monroe -
not indexed, Montgomery
89, Overton 89,178,
Polk 96,97,100,101,106,
107,178,180, Rhea 5,22,
93,100, Roane 3,21,46,
78,79,83,89,93,100,101,
106,117,138,139,154,
177-179,181,187, Scott
106, Sevier 45,79,80,
102, Sumner 106, Wash-
ington 81,93,100,146,
154,155,158, White 84,
179

TENNESSEE CREEKS: Abraham's
127, Baker's 16, Bat
39,45,178,186, Big 81,
Cane 189, Citico 83,
Fork 15,46,81,184,188,
Island 24,90,184, Not-
chey 7,102,154, Pond
180, Spring 123

TENNESSEE DISTRICTS: Hi-
wassee 78,103,105,186,

TENNESSEE DISTRICTS: cont'd
187,189, Ocoee 125

TENNESSEE FERRIES: Blair's
46,177, Niles 65,
Wright's 46

TENNESSEE, General Assembly
of: 122,189, Hospital
for Insane 142, Legis-
lature of: 122,183

TENNESSEE NEWSPAPERS:
Athens Courier 185,
Athens Post 155,177-181
184,185, Athens Repub-
lican 180, Hiwassee
Patriot 47,177,184,
Kingston Gazeteer 47,
Knoxville Enquirer 47,
Knoxville Register 45,
Loudon Free Press 45,
Philadelphia Pilot 76,
Tennessee Journal 177,
Watchman 185

TENNESSEE RIVERS: Big
Pigeon 78, Hiwassee 88,
187, Tellico 81,154,
177,184, Tennessee 46,
78,81,183,187

TENNESSEE, Starr's Reser-
vation 126, State
Archives 186, Supreme
Court of: 125,132,133,
142, Treasurer of: 78,
University of: 148,
Colunteers 21,61,147,
152

TERRITORY SOUTH OF RIVER
OHIO: 154

TERRY, James M. 115, Joab
131, Joab H. 26, John
67, Louisa 44, Louisi-
ana 67, M.M. 20

TEXAS, Bonham 153, Corsi-
cana 146, Fannin County
153, Fort Worth 157,
Waxahachie 146

THACKER, James L. 28,
Valentine 28

THARP, See THORP

THOMAS, Elizabeth 97, James
153, John 13,52, Jona-
than 19,64,140, Joseph
97, Mary 111, Nic 152,
Samuel 111, Stephen 106

THOMPSON, Captain 147,
Elizabeth 56, Elizabeth
H. 120, George 121,
James 81,127,188, Jesse
120, John W. 57,180,
Margaret Jane 188,
Mary Ann 188, Samuel 9,
Sarah 121

THORNBURG, J.M. 116,117,
Martha A. 116, Regi-
ment 148

THORP, J.R. 145, J.T. 145,
Jacob 90, Margaret Jane
188, Mary Ann 188

THURMAN, Patrick 184

www.ingramcontent.com/pod-product-compliance
Lightning Source LLC
Chambersburg PA
CBHW021139030426

R18078200001B/R180782PG42334CBX00001B/1